€97.69

THE ORIGINS OF AGRICULTURE IN EUROPE

THE ORIGINS OF AGRICULTURE IN EUROPE

I. J. Thorpe

London and New York

First published 1996
by Routledge
11 New Fetter Lane, London EC4P 4EE

Simultaneously published in the USA and Canada
by Routledge
29 West 35th Street, New York, NY 10001

Typeset in Garamond by
Keystroke, Jacaranda Lodge, Wolverhampton
Printed and bound in Great Britain by
Biddles Ltd, Guildford, Surrey

British Library Cataloguing in Publication Data
A catalogue record for this book is available from the British Library

Library of Congress Cataloging in Publication Data
Thorpe, I. J.
The origins of agriculture in Europe/I. J. Thorpe.
p. cm.
ISBN 0–415–08009–6
1. Agriculture, Prehistoric—Europe. 2. Mesolithic period—
Europe. 3. Neolithic period—Europe. 4. Europe—Antiquities.
I. Title.
GN803.T57 1996
630′.936–dc20
96-7574
CIP

ISBN 0–415–08009–6

CONTENTS

FIGURES

To Richard Bradley and Barbara Bender for inspiring
my interest in this subject

PREFACE

A steadily growing body of information exists for the latest Mesolithic and earliest Neolithic of northwest Europe. This is the result of the continuing interest in the transition to agriculture in the region, and the impact that differing interpretations of this 'event' have on our understanding of the Neolithic in general. A variety of alternative positions have been adopted relating to this material – an essential continuity with pre-farming populations, or radical population change; the Neolithic as a result of necessity or choice; a swift development of a fully fledged agricultural economy, or horticulture within a landscape little changed from the Mesolithic; monuments as a later addition, or as an integral element of the Neolithic. Although continuing excavations (a number of these undertaken as a part of projects specifically examining the transition; e.g. the Bally Lough Project [Green and Zvelebil 1990] in Ireland and the Saltbæk Vig Project in Denmark [Gebauer and Price 1990]) have had a significant impact on the information available, there has so far been little attempt to set this within a wider framework, especially one of comparative analysis.

One element fuelling a vigorous debate is unquestionably the impact of radiocarbon dating. Some twenty years ago broad brush dating schemes based on a small sample of dates smoothed out variation, allowing for the possibility of a steady rate of agricultural advance across the whole of Europe (e.g. Ammerman and Cavalli-Sforza 1973). It is now widely argued, however, that a distinct hiatus, lasting several hundred years, occurred in the spread of agriculture after leaving the loess belt and before it reached the fringes of northwest Europe.

Although this gap is generally agreed to exist, interpretations of it are theoretically inadequate or only sketchily outlined, and explanations for the renewed spread of a farming economy across Europe are at present piecemeal and highly unconvincing. One major problem in interpretation is that the two main areas of northwest Europe concerned – Britain and southern Scandinavia – have tended to be studied in isolation, a separation made more complete by the development of divergent national traditions of archaeological research.

This study attempts to redress the balance by examining the transition to agriculture through the comparison of sequences of social and economic developments in both Britain and southern Scandinavia. These two regions share common influences from earlier European Neolithic societies, along with a number of monument types such as causewayed enclosures, long barrows and megalithic tombs. These monuments are, however, used in rather different ways in the two areas, reflecting the different social settings in which they are found.

The enquiry will begin with general theories of the transition to agriculture, focusing on their application to the Near East as the source of European agriculture. The spread of farming across Europe will then be addressed, in order to assess the nature of the common European agricultural background, looking at both the initial transmission to southeast Europe and its subsequent movement into the loess of central Europe. The breaks in the onward spread of an agricultural economy as it reaches the Baltic and Atlantic fringes will be examined from the perspective of gatherer-hunter societies and economies.

More detailed coverage of the two study areas – southern Scandinavia and Britain – is presented in order to examine fully the various general and specific reasons given for the transition to agriculture in these two instances. The Earlier Neolithic in the two areas is then followed down to c. 3000 BC (all dates given in the text are calibrated dates BC) and the quite different trajectories of development outlined. These are then set against the Mesolithic background, and the different experience of agricultural transition, to see how far these factors may be seen to shape subsequent events.

ACKNOWLEDGEMENTS

This present volume grew out of a Ph.D. thesis (Thorpe 1989) undertaken at University College London with the aid of a Major State Studentship from the Department of Education and Science and financial support from the Thomas Witherden Batt Fund of University College.

I am indebted to many colleagues both in Britain and abroad for providing information on and discussion of various issues: Niels Andersen, Sven Thorkil Andersen, Søren Andersen, John Barrett, Jens-Henrick Bech, Barbara Bender, Aubrey Burl, Bob Chapman, Dave Coombs, Peter Didsbury, Tim Earle, John Frankish, Robin Holgate, Roger Jacobi, Peter James, Helle Juel Jensen, Brian Jones, Robin Kenward, Ian Kinnes, Nikos Kokkinos, Kristian Kristiansen, Torsten Madsen, Terry Manby, Roger Mercer, Anna Louise Haack Olsen, Mark Patton, Colin Richards, Mike Rowlands, Steve Shennan, Andrew Sherratt, John Steinberg, Don Spratt, Julian Thomas, Jørgen Westphal and Alasdair Whittle.

The staff and students at many institutions are to be thanked for their suggestions and comments on many of the ideas contained in this work, most particularly those at University College London, King Alfred's College Winchester and the Institute of Prehistory at Moesgård.

I also wish to thank Phil Marter for his excellent illustrations.

1

APPROACHES TO THE TRANSITION TO FARMING

GENERAL THEORIES

Four main competing theoretical schools of thought will be discussed. Although fitting the most influential reviews of the subject into just four categories must inevitably involve some simplification of differences between them, this does not seem to represent too unfair a procedure. The four categories adopted are:

1 Agriculture is inherently superior to gathering-hunting, therefore its adoption was automatic if the ecological setting was favourable, and if the Mesolithic population was 'culturally ready'. Those gatherer-hunter groups who were not on the starting blocks were simply swept aside. The most important recent version of this approach is the 'wave of advance' model, which proposes that there was a steady spread of farming (and farmers) across Europe. As others have pointed out, this strongly implies that existing gatherer-hunter (Mesolithic) populations were passive, reacting to events rather than bringing them about.

2 An imbalance came about between population and resources, either general or local, which forced a shift to an agricultural economy. Most formulations of this approach propose that this was caused by an increase in population, rather than by a decline in available resources. The former again presupposes a rather passive gatherer-hunter society, while the latter assumes an inability to adapt to changed conditions in the long run. In some formulations both population pressure and resource shortage (sudden or seasonal) are believed to combine together to force the adoption of farming.

3 Economic domestication was preceded by social and symbolic domestication: controlling the wild through enculturing it began with housing and was only later extended to plants and animals. This relatively recent approach has as yet only been applied to the Near East in any systematic manner.

4 Social competition among Mesolithic groups using surplus production led to the adoption of farming in order to secure the higher level of output necessary to support the holding of periodic feasts. This approach gives the greatest emphasis to knowledgeable actors making positive choices which impact on their society. This is again a recent approach to the problem, and one which has yet to be set against the available data in any sustained way.

1

The original interpretation of the transition to agriculture was that farming was an unquestionably superior mode of production. Darwin (1875: 326–7) suggested that the determining factor for the beginning of agriculture was knowledge. Once the knowledge that a seed planted in the ground would grow into a plant existed then food production would certainly follow. This theory arose from Darwin's own unquestioned assumption that agriculture had self-evident advantages over a gathering-hunting lifestyle and so would be taken up without hesitation once the ability existed.

In 1952 the geographer Sauer concluded that agriculture must have arisen among fishing communities. He reasoned (1952; 1969) that communities with access to fish became virtually sedentary, as they had no need to search out alternative food resources with such a dependable supply to hand. This sedentary lifestyle, without the risk of food shortages, allowed them the opportunity to experiment with plant cultivation. This might begin with the cultivation of poison-producing plants (for use in fishing), but would then be followed by food plants. Once discovered, food plant cultivation naturally took over from fishing as the economic basis of existence.

Braidwood, by contrast, set agricultural origins firmly inland. After many years of excavation in Iraq, he concluded (Braidwood and Willey 1962: 132–46) that food production was the product of a long process of ever-increasing cultural differentiation and specialisation. He believed that agriculture would inevitably accompany greater familiarity with plant and animal resources gained through long years of slowly acquired knowledge from the end of the last Ice Age. Once a sufficient level of knowledge had been reached, the transition to an agricultural economy would naturally take place, as people realised their new-found ability to manipulate the environment to their own ends.

Although this school of thought has found few adherents in recent years, it can certainly be argued that something of this viewpoint underlies the 'wave of advance' model promoted by Ammerman and Cavalli-Sforza (1971; 1973; 1984) as an explanation of the transition to agriculture across Europe. Zvelebil and Zvelebil (1988), for instance, appear to feel that the 'wave of advance' model represents Mesolithic populations as static entities unable to adapt to changing circumstances. The views of Ammerman and Cavalli-Sforza will be discussed in Chapter 2, in a survey of the general spread of agriculture across southeast and central Europe.

The earliest instance of an approach which stressed resource imbalance or 'stress' as a mechanism pushing communities into becoming agriculturalists comes from the writings of Childe (1928; 1934). His 'Oasis Theory', or 'Propinquity Theory', of agricultural origins postulated that the end of the last Ice Age some 10,000 years ago led to greatly increased dessication of large areas. This created a pattern of aggregation of all animals (including humans) in those river valleys where water was still available. This increased degree of propinquity between different species led to new relationships between them. In these highly favoured environments, where all varieties of plant food would grow, stubble from harvested crops would be a significant food source for grazing animals. The interests of people and animals therefore coincided, and agriculture was born.

The best known of the theories placing emphasis on population increase as the source of the imbalance between resources and human numbers is that of Cohen (1977; 1989; Cohen and Armelagos 1984). He argues that the only factor which can possibly account for the irreversible and nearly uniform development of agriculture on a global scale is a growth in population levels beyond that which gathering-hunting could support. While agriculture did not necessarily improve the overall diet or make it more reliable, it did provide a higher calorific output per unit of time invested and space set aside than gathering-hunting could do. He suggested that the degree of imbalance between population and resources had not reached crisis point by the time food production was developed, so starvation was not imminent, but that the problem had become clearly visible. At first attempts were made to intensify resource use through such measures as focusing on common game species, but as population growth continued its inevitable upward trend such efforts proved inadequate. In the end the only remaining solution was the development of a food-producing economy.

A more sophisticated population pressure model, with an explicit social dimension, has been developed by Binford (1968). He suggested that food production will begin in circumstances when changes in the demographic structure of a region force two groups to overlap the territories they exploit. The previous equilibrium is disturbed, and the population density of the region is increased to a point above its natural carrying capacity. Strong incentives therefore exist for groups to intensify production through agriculture. The particular circumstances Binford envisaged, in which two groups would begin to compete, were if a more sedentary society, probably based on aquatic resources, began to expand into the territory of a more nomadic group.

Ironically, Binford has himself (1983: 195–211) moved away from this quite specific model towards a more generalised approach in which population pressure acts as a 'trigger'. Unlike Cohen, he does not believe in a gradual and inexorable growth in population, but instead argues that a particular system of adaptation to the natural environment may persist for long periods, offering a high degree of stability. Changes will occur when the system is unable to cope with changed conditions in the environment. Binford stresses the role of population growth leading to 'packing', in which there was no longer room to move freely around the landscape. Sedentism becomes the only real option and smaller animal species are exploited, especially aquatic ones, as they occupy less space, along with wild plants. With continuing population growth, demand soon reaches the point where the more intensive production methods of agriculture become a necessity.

A slightly different approach has been taken by Redding (1988), who proposes that food production arose as a search for greater resource security. He argues that farming first developed in areas where fluctuations in available food resources were unpredictable, frequent and severe, and where there was also population growth. His model places a greater emphasis on supply than demand by comparison with Binford's work.

Harris (1990) has taken up the suggestion of resource shortage due to an increasing population, but suggested a rather different timescale. He argues that when gatherer-hunter populations become less mobile and adopt a sedentary lifestyle, the controls on female fertility which are essential in a mobile society will be relaxed. The consequent population growth leads to resource shortage, this becoming apparent first in the critical 'hungry' season during the year. Four possible responses existed: to move; to split the group into smaller units; to attempt to curb the population; or to intensify production.

MacNeish has independently developed a rather similar model, in which he produces a series of *necessary* and *sufficient* conditions for the emergence of bands of incipient agriculturalists (1992: 23–31). His *necessary* conditions are: (1) an ecologically highly diverse environment; (2) the existence of potentially domesticable plants in one or more ecozones; (3) the exploitation of a variety of resources which cannot all be reached from a single base; (4) a natural seasonal cycle, with a harsh season when few resources are available; (5) a gradual rise in population. His *sufficient* conditions are: (1) a change in the environment which reduces available resources and, in particular, makes the harsh season worse; (2) an increase in the degree of sedentism leading to further population pressure; (3) an increase in the structuring of food procurement, with a wider range of resources exploited and the use of storage; (4) a change in the ecosystem and/or in the genetic makeup of some of the seeds being collected, reducing the energy expended in gathering each seed. Once this scene is set, MacNeish argues that base camps will turn into year-round villages with an increasing population which then renders increased food production a necessity, hence agriculture.

The role of symbolic domestication has been developed by Hodder (1990: 11–13) following earlier suggestions by Cauvin (1978; 1989). Cauvin had noted the importance of cattle cults among the earliest farming communities, and suggested that wild cattle were an ideal symbolic expression of internal psychological and social problems. The domestication of wild cattle and the external wild world more generally could therefore be seen as an attempt to domesticate and control internal and wider social problems.

Hodder has expanded on this theme to link the control of social difficulties to the control of people. The process of domestication – controlling the wild – would therefore be both a metaphor for, and a mechanism of, social control. In this view of agriculture as a social–symbolic process, nature (the wild) is transformed into culture (the domesticated) through the medium of human action. Animals, plants, clay, death and perhaps physical reproduction are all natural phenomena which are encultured to bring them under the control of a cultural and social system. He argues (1990: 292–3) that relations of dominance existed within social groups during the Upper Palaeolithic, displayed through production, exchange and feasting. With the end of the Ice Age resources changed, and strategies of production had to change as well to maintain relations of dominance. One newly possible method was greater sedentism based on a wider variety of resources. This allowed groups to increase in size in order to produce more and to participate further in competition.

A more explicitly political interpretation of the transition to agriculture has been presented by Hayden (1990; 1993: 192–265). Like Hodder, he is influenced by Bender's calls (1978; 1989) for a social perspective on the transition. He believes that the importance of social competition among complex and economically specialised gatherer-hunters has been underrated. Specifically, he suggests that social competition and feasting as aspects of economic rivalry among groups were the driving forces behind the adoption of agriculture.

Hayden proposes the existence of 'accumulators' within groups of ecologically secure and specialised gatherer-hunters. These 'accumulators' are individuals who attempt to maximise power and prestige through the accumulation of foodstuffs, goods and services and the subsequent disposal of them as gifts. The earliest domesticates would be items appropriate to feasts – which are used as a medium for the disposal of wealth and the accumulation of prestige. The adoption of agriculture in this approach is a quite small-scale affair, as domesticated foodstuffs would be consumed only at feasts rather than as a dietary staple and therefore need not necessarily result in a wholesale change in production (Hayden 1993: 225–7).

Before moving on to consider the specific models put forward by these writers, and others working within the same frameworks, to explain the specific case of the transition to agriculture in the Near East it is appropriate to consider their overall character. Any model must have its underlying assumptions, and in the case of the four schools of thought considered above these have important implications for the approach taken to the archaeological evidence. The main division is between those which regard gatherer-hunter groups as free agents, with a potential choice to develop agriculture or to leave it aside, and of those approaches which either treat agriculture as a self-evidently superior mode of production or as the necessary response to a situation in which there is an imbalance between resources and population there is little choice given to gatherer-hunter groups. They frequently appear as passive spectators, looking on as their destiny is determined by external events beyond their control, able only to react and not to shape their future to any significant degree. In those models which stress social factors, either symbolic domestication or social competition, the gatherer-hunter groups act with a greater degree of purpose.

In recent times it is significant that the theoretical divisions over the question of agricultural origins are largely mirrored by the nationality of the participants. Models which favour 'stress' as a factor are largely adopted by archaeologists from the United States of America and social models by those outside the USA. This in turn reflects the strong tendency towards either evolutionist or adaptationist thinking (e.g. Binford 1983: 203) among the USA archaeological community. In Europe the influence of the New Archaeology has unquestionably fallen away during the 1980s, leading to a renewed interest in social and religious aspects of archaeological research.

THE NEAR EAST

The chronology of food production in the Near East is reasonably well established following the application of radiocarbon dating to the problem. In the tenth millennium BC there are a number of Natufian (or Khiamian) and related sites in Palestine and Syria with evidence for the collection or harvesting of wild cereals, e.g. at 'Ain Mallaha, Hayonim Cave, Mureybet and Tell Abu Hureyra. This takes the form of the remains of wild seeds (the subject of exhaustive examination at Tell Abu Hureyra concerning both their identification and date [Hillman *et al.* 1989]), pounding tools such as mortars and pestles and some grinding stones and querns (Bar-Yosef and Belfer-Cohen 1989; Moore 1991). Elsewhere, Bar-Yosef and Belfer-Cohen (1992) have cautioned that pounding tools could of course have been used for processing a wide variety of foodstuffs, including acorns, nuts and dry legumes as well as cereals, and might even have been used to break down burnt limestone or ochre.

Analysis by P. Smith (1989; 1991) of skeletal remains from the terminal Natufian site at Nahel Oren has thrown some light on the importance of cereals in the diet. The pattern of dental disease at Nahel Oren differs from other Natufian sites, and instead resembles that found in the Pre-Pottery Neolithic. There is a relatively high level of periodontal disease and dental caries, pointing to a high carbohydrate diet, presumably derived from eating cereals. In addition, the Nahel Oren skeletons have a rather different facial structure to that of earlier Natufians. The changes appear to show a reduction in chewing forces, presumably derived from a different diet, or new methods of food preparation.

One other artefact type commonly found on these sites is the flint 'sickle' with usewear gloss, generally interpreted as a harvesting tool (see Figure 1.1). Unger-Hamilton (1989; 1991) has compared the microwear traces on modern copies with those found on Natufian examples. The presence of striations on these flint blades is, she has argued, an indication of the cereals being harvested from areas with loose soil. Such disturbance of the soil would suggest that wild cereals were being grown on tilled land. So wild cereals were, according to Unger-Hamilton, actually a farmed crop, although they did not yet show genetic changes towards domestication.

Unger-Hamilton's conclusions have been taken up widely (e.g. Harris 1990; Rosenberg 1990), but have subsequently been subjected to severe criticism by Anderson (1991), another microwear analyst. Anderson's experience is that striations on sickles occur when cereals are harvested close to the ground (so nearer the soil) rather than up by the head. Anderson further suggests that tilling the ground would not in fact have improved wild cereal yields, as they suffer if covered with soil. Unger-Hamilton's suggestion of wild cereals being given a helping hand therefore seems to be unjustified on the present evidence.

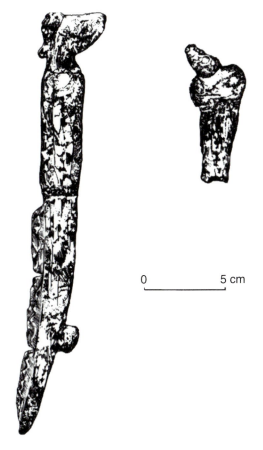

0   5 cm

Figure 1.1 Natufian flint sickles – left, reconstructed example from Kebara; right, haft from El Wad (after Henry 1989)

We are on more secure ground with the dating of the earliest definitely domesticated cereals. In the ninth millennium BC emmer wheat and barley seeds are found in quite substantial numbers at Pre-Pottery Neolithic sites in Syria and Palestine (Miller 1992; Zohary and Hopf 1993: 43, 62–3). The use of radio-carbon accelerator dating to check a number of claims for very early cultivation (Harris 1986; Legge 1986) has proved invaluable in producing a solid database out of a welter of steadily earlier supposed dates for domestication. The importance of the current consensus on dating the earliest cultivated crop remains is underlined by the suggestion of Hillman and Davies (1990) that the transition from wild to domesticated cereals may have been extremely rapid. Experimental study of wild einkorn wheat showed that one of the defining characteristics of cereal domestication – the change from a brittle to a non-brittle rachis – could well have become dominant in a mere 20–30 years, and certainly within 200 years.

7

They suggest that there is no reason to believe that emmer wheat or barley would have taken any longer to undergo this change in form.

There is, unfortunately, far less agreement concerning the evidence for the earliest domestication of food animals. While wolves appear to have been tamed (so becoming dogs) in the Natufian around 10,000 BC (Davis 1987: 137–48), cattle and sheep/goat were domesticated much later. Early claims of domesticated sheep/goat from Iran were based on the age profile of the assemblage rather than physical changes, and recent evaluations of the evidence are rather more sceptical (e.g. Davis 1987: 150). Current opinion is that sheep and goats were probably domesticated around 7500 BC (Legge and Rowley-Conwy 1986; Davis 1987: 150). Likewise, some suggestions of precocious cattle domestication based on the small size of some bones are now seen as using too small a sample to draw such conclusions. In a recent review of the material Grigson (1989a) concludes that the earliest secure evidence of cattle domestication comes from Fikirtepe in eastern Turkey around 6000 BC.

Given the present state of uncertainty it seems premature to claim that herding economies predate agricultural ones (Hole 1989), or that they began in the eastern part of the Near East (Hole 1989), or that sheep may have been domesticated there and goats in the western Near East (Davis 1987: 150). What is clearly required is a methodological advance which will enable a greater degree of certainty concerning the identification of domesticated animals.

Having set the scene for the emergence of farming in the Near East we can return to advocates of the different theoretical positions outlined at the beginning of the chapter and their specific formulations for the transition in this case.

The 'agriculture as naturally superior' approach can hardly be said to have laid down a detailed framework of explanation of individual case studies. It did not, after all, really need it. The main implications of Sauer's model (1952; 1969) are, however, that sedentism was a necessary prerequisite, and that the most sedentary groups would primarily be those relying on fish. His favoured areas of primary domestication were Southeast Asia, West Africa and Brazil, but we can still assess the implications if his model is applied to the Near East.

The primary condition for Sauer's theory is undoubtedly sedentism. The question of whether or not Natufian and equivalent populations were sedentary has been much debated in recent years from a variety of perspectives. The well-built houses with stone walls, the construction of storage pits, the creation of cemeteries, the thick occupation layers, the high density of artefacts and the sheer size of some Natufian sites are often taken together as pointing strongly towards permanency of occupation (e.g. Henry 1989: 39).

The evidence of both plant and animal exploitation has been brought to bear on the question. Intensive study of the plant remains from Tell Abu Hureyra in Syria (Hillman et al. 1989) has led to the conclusion that the 157 wild species exploited would have been available from April to January (or possibly even March). Even if only the twenty or so most heavily used species are considered the seasonal range is little reduced. In any case, as Hillman and his colleagues argue, the situation would have been little or no better elsewhere, so there was no great incentive to move.

The animal bone evidence from Tell Abu Hureyra has also been subjected to intensive analysis. Legge and Rowley-Conwy (1987) have examined the gazelle remains which form 80 per cent of the bone assemblage. They suggest that the presence of newborn, yearling and adult gazelles shows that they were killed in early summer during an annual gazelle migration to the north. They did not, however, take this to demonstrate that the site as a whole was only seasonally occupied.

Campana and Crabtree (1990) have examined the faunal data from Salibiya I in the lower Jordan Valley, concluding that this strongly suggests that the Natufians practised communal hunting of gazelle. While proposing that the social organisation engendered by communal hunting brought about a society pre-conditioned to an agricultural economy and one with a degree of social hierarchy, they do not believe that this would necessitate sedentism. Using ethnographic examples, they argue that a pattern of seasonal population aggregation and dispersal is equally likely.

Davis (1987: 79) has undertaken an analysis of the gazelle remains from Natufian contexts in general, which reveals an increase in young gazelle being caught through time, while examination of young gazelle teeth from Hayonim Cave and Terrace has shown that they fall mainly in the 8–12 month range. From this, Davis (1987: 79) and Lieberman (1991) conclude that the bone evidence supports the idea of a year-round occupation.

The small animal bones found in owl pellets at 'Ain Mallaha have also been put forward as evidence, with the species contained representing six months from April to November, while the migratory birds from the same site could have been caught for ten months of the year (Belfer-Cohen 1991).

Another approach using small animal bones has been to argue for the presence on Natufian sites of human commensals: species such as the house mouse, the rat and the house sparrow which co-exist with people in permanent settlements (Tchernov 1991). In particular, the house mouse found in Natufian base camps appears to be different in form from the ordinary *Mus musculus* found in pre-Natufian deposits, suggesting long-term change. Although widely accepted as a significant indicator (e.g. Bar-Yosef and Belfer-Cohen 1989), Byrd has tried to downplay the evidence from Hayonim Cave by suggesting that the commensals reached the site inside the owls whose pellets were found in the cave, where they lived during periods of human absence (1989). Even if Byrd is correct in this view, it would only mean that the owls were hunting in some nearby location rich in commensals. It seems an implausible coincidence that these species should emerge without any connection to the greater residential permanency being claimed on other grounds for the Natufian.

Finally, some human skeletal evidence exists which seems to indicate sedentism. At Hayonim Cave the continued use of the same site by members of a single lineage is indicated by the presence in successive layers of the burials of individuals with a congenital absence of the third molar (Smith *et al.* 1984); this condition occurs among this particular group far more frequently than in the Natufian population as a whole.

Byrd (1989) has argued that there may be regional variation in the degree of sedentism, with coastal and forest areas which are better watered and perhaps richer in plant foods being more likely to see long stay occupations. In the steppe and desert areas, by contrast, he believes settlements to be of relatively short duration. In his opinion the different flint assemblages found on larger and smaller sites support this view. However, Belfer-Cohen (1991) has criticised Byrd's use of the lithic evidence, as it takes biased samples to be representative. Bar-Yosef and Belfer-Cohen (1989) themselves suggest that there was an expansion of Natufian groups into steppe and desert areas, and that in these newly occupied environments there was a seasonal pattern of movement from winter base camps in the lowlands to early spring or summer camps in the highlands. In any case, their model does not imply a complete absence of sedentary settlements among the Natufians, just that this was not the case in more marginal areas.

A certain amount of evidence, both direct and indirect, can also be brought to bear on Sauer's belief in fish as a major resource. Again the intensively examined site of Tell Abu Hureyra plays an important part, as soil sieving has revealed that despite it being situated on the Euphrates there was very little exploitation of fish as a food source. Similarly, sieving on Natufian sites in Palestine has produced few fish remains, a result confirmed by bone chemistry looking at trace elements and the amount of C^{13} present (Sillen and Lee-Thorp 1991; Bar-Yosef and Sillen 1993). The diet of Natufians and their contemporaries thus appears to be overwhelmingly terrestrial.

So we can say that there is as strong a case for at least some Natufian settlements being permanent year-round occupations as it is possible for archaeology to produce with present methods. Given that, it seems unreasonable to continue to demand further evidence and more fruitful to assess the significance of this development. Against Sauer, there is nothing in the development of sedentism in itself which must lead on to a fully agricultural economy, and there seems little support for his notion of fish-eating economically secure gatherer-hunters. Most archaeologists also begin from the standpoint that groups are in general unwilling to change and therefore require something to push or pull them in a new direction.

As we have already noted, the earliest model proposed along these lines was Childe's 'Oasis Theory' (1928; 1934). This clearly relied on there having been a climatic shift at the end of the Ice Age towards a drier climate. At the time he wrote there was no real means of checking this hypothesis, but important pollen analytical work has been undertaken subsequently. Later archaeologists believed for a long time that there had been no significant changes in the environment, but from the 1960s onwards pollen evidence for a climate shift has been accumulating. Unfortunately, internal consistency is lacking in the results, which have been obtained from the Ghab marshes in Syria and Huleh in the Jordan

Valley, some 300 km apart, so that two or three quite different models with different implications can be produced (Byrd 1989; Bar-Yosef and Belfer-Cohen 1992).

In Version One the northern Levant and the northern highlands of Iran and Turkey were cold and dry until around 10,000 BC when they became warmer and wetter, while the central and southern Levant were more varied, being cold and dry down to 12,000 BC, wetter until 10,000 BC, then drier and warmer down to 9000 BC. In Version Two the southern Levant became wetter and warmer after 13,500 BC, then drier during the Natufian from 11,000 (or a little earlier) to 9000 BC, especially in the Late Natufian, a pattern which could possibly be extended to the northern Levant. In Version Three the southern Levant was cold and dry down to about 13,000 BC, then wetter until 12,000 BC, followed by a return to dry conditions from 12,000 to 10,000 BC, then a wetter spell which lasted until 9000 BC or later. There are thus two main areas of disagreement: did the northern and southern Levant follow separate paths; and precisely when did the climate turn dry – during the Natufian, or before it?

In Henry's view (1989: 27–52) Version One created a pull–push situation for Natufian populations. The change to a wetter climate around 12,000 BC led to the expansion of Mediterranean forests onto higher ground, where cereal and nut crops flourished. This created a much longer season for cereals and nuts, as those growing down on the coast would ripen in April, while those up at 1400–1500 metres above sea level would not be ready until July. This made it advantageous to develop large permanent base camps on the slopes with good access to both low and high ground. When the climate deteriorated around 10,000 BC, becoming much drier, the Natufians could not cope. Social stress increased, as attempts were made to limit access to resources to a favoured few. Many sites were abandoned, and only by beginning to cultivate crops were those fortunate sites near to springs able to maintain their existence and so keep the community together. Henry's model thus depends on Natufian sedentary communities being created before the climate turned drier.

For Bar-Yosef and Belfer-Cohen (1989; 1992) the climatic crisis took place in the twelfth millennium BC. The cold and dry glacial climate had been succeeded by wetter conditions, but at this time there was a reversal to drier times, with falling rainfall leading to dwindling resources. This mainly affected steppe and desert environments, while the Mediterranean forest zone was relatively untouched. Population congregated in this Mediterranean core area, resulting in sedentary groups exploiting a wider range of resources, particularly game animals. As these species became over-killed resource shortages set in and intra-group conflict arose. To solve these new problems agriculture was developed. So here the emphasis is on a climatic shift to drier conditions bringing about the Natufian itself; sedentism is seen then as a point of no return.

The most recent evidence has come from a new pollen diagram from Huleh (Baruch and Bottema 1991; Wright 1993). The original core showed a fall in oak pollen after around 11,500 BC to a low point at roughly 8500 BC, suggesting a change from wet to dry conditions around 10,000 BC or earlier. The new diagram suggests that the oak woodland dominated from about 14,000–10,500 BC, declining to a low point by 9500 BC. The transition to the Natufian in the early twelfth millennium BC now appears to fall in the middle of a long period of highly favourable climate rather than at a significant shift to either wetter (following Hayden) or drier (following Bar-Yosef and Belfer-Cohen) conditions. This new diagram from Huleh does, however, leave open the possibility of a decline in rainfall playing at least a contributory part in the transition to farming. Baruch and Bottema (1991) raise the possibility that the Ghab marshes diagram may be wrongly dated, given that it has only a single radiocarbon date, so there may well be a re-evaluation in store for the northern Levant as well. Until a much larger sample of environmental evidence is available, however, it would seem wise to be extremely careful not to push the pollen analyses too hard, given the broad brush nature of the evidence they are able to provide at present.

The most influential alternative model of an imbalance between resources and population has been the population pressure theory of Cohen (1977; 1989; Cohen and Armelagos 1984). Cohen argues that population pressure was an ever-present and growing problem for gatherer-hunter societies. This would reveal itself archaeologically in a decline in health among later gatherer-hunter populations. There were two attempts to deal with this problem: first the 'Broad Spectrum Revolution' of the Natufian which expanded the resource base to include less favoured but more common foods such as plants, invertebrates and aquatic species; second, the domestication of plants and animals.

The first implication of Cohen's model is of course that there should be indications of a steadily growing population. On theoretical grounds (e.g. Hassan 1981) it has been suggested that the population was kept in check through high infant mortality, low adult life expectancy, or cultural controls such as sexual prohibitions or infanticide. Estimates of the population of Natufian sites do indeed show that they were larger than those of the earlier Kebaran culture, perhaps housing up to fifty individuals (Smith et al. 1984). However, this does not itself imply that the carrying capacity of the environment was being approached, and it certainly seems difficult to envisage population pressure in the Kebaran, with a relatively small number of sites housing less than twenty people each. Henry (1989: 23) argues that the evidence from caves (less subject to problems of site preservation) shows that the increase in population happened in the Natufian and not before.

The second major implication is that there should be a definite decline in average health as population pressure bit. Cohen himself (Cohen and Armelagos 1984) admits that the anatomical evidence is uncertain. Roosevelt, however, concludes from the same data (1984) that there is no real trend to increasing physical stress during the Mesolithic. The specific study by Smith et al. (1984) on Natufian material concludes, against Cohen, that it does not show deteriorating health status and compares well with Middle Palaeolithic skeletons.

The final element in Cohen's general model is the Broad Spectrum Revolution.

This concept has recently been subjected to a critical analysis by P. C. Edwards (1989), who compared the Natufian pattern of animal exploitation with that of supposed specialised Palaeolithic hunters. He found that there was actually very little difference in terms of the diversity of animals caught between these two supposedly distinct economic regimes. He concluded that not only sedentary groups practised broad-spectrum economies, including some communities in the Palaeolithic: the 'Broad Spectrum Revolution' is therefore a myth in Edwards's view.

More specific population pressure models such as Binford's (1983: 195–211) or McNeish's (1992: 320–1) also suffer from the problem of lack of evidence for either overpopulation or stress in the form of declining health, while Binford's earlier model (1968) also depended on sedentism being tied to the use of aquatic resources, which appears not to be the case in the Natufian (see above). Equally, theories involving the need to create more dependable resources because of seasonal shortages (e.g. Redding 1988; Harris 1990; McCorriston and Hole 1991), seem not to be supported by the available data. Indeed, McCorriston (1994) has subsequently argued that Natufian communities could have subsisted on acorns at lean times of the year; she compared them with the California Indians, who lived in groups of up to 360 people within densely populated territories. Such population agglomerations are well above those proposed for the Natufian, which suggests they were living comfortably within the carrying capacity of the land.

Returning to McCorriston and the acorns (1994), it is interesting that she concludes that acorns were a little used resource. This may be set alongside similar assessments for fish (Moore 1989; Sillen and Lee-Thorp 1991; Bar-Yosef and Sillen 1993), even though at Kebara Cave marine shells were found which had been imported from the coast (Bar-Yosef and Sillen 1993), showing that some marine resources were being exploited. Together, this suggests that there were major unused food resources which can hardly have been unknown to the Natufians, but which they chose not to exploit. That they did have a choice in the matter goes strongly against all theories of overpopulation or resource shortage which argue that the Natufians attempted to maximise already existing foodstuffs before being pushed into adopting agriculture.

The two 'social' models may be considered together, in that they stress very different aspects of Natufian society. Hodder (1990: 32–42) focuses on the house and related activities, including practical household duties, food preparation and burial. He links these various elements together through the concept of the *domus*. This arose as secondary symbolic connotations grew from these practical activities, leading to the house developing into a focus for symbolic elaboration and to the use of the house as a metaphor for social and economic strategies and power relations. Practical acts such as preparing and serving food, placing female figurines in the house and the burial of women and children in and around the house associated the house with more general concepts of nurturing. The provision of shelter and the storage of food associated the house with caring. The *domus* is therefore the concept and practice of nurturing and caring, while when defined negatively it excludes, controls and dominates the 'wild'.

Features which Hodder detects in the Natufian that he relates to the *domus* are the emphasis on the house (see Figure 1.2), including the elaboration of hearths, plastering of walls, burials in and near houses, including in storage pits; the importance of the household as a productive unit; the use of decoration in burial to tame death; and an element of increased social control seen in larger settlement units with similarly ordered living spaces. Social control was extended by the holding of feasts to gain prestige and the expansion of numbers to increase production, related back to the *domus* through funeral or house-painting feasts. Given that intra-group competition existed even before the Natufian, then changes in the relations of production would have occurred along with climatic shifts – specifically greater sedentism based on a wider variety of resources. A major concern of social groups would in these circumstances have been to 'domesticate' people within settlements. The adoption of more intensive methods of production, climaxing in agriculture, would have matched the desires of dominant groups within society in that the new relationships trapped people within relatively fixed economic and social structures on which they came to depend.

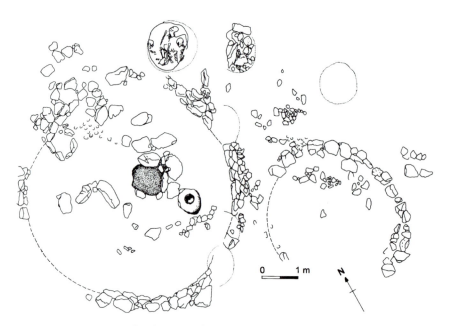

0   1 m

N

Figure 1.2 Natufian houses and associated burials in pits at 'Ain Mallaha
(after Hodder 1990)

14

This political element of the model is clearly rather underdeveloped and it is here that Hayden's interpretation may fit with Hodder's. Hayden (1990; 1993: 192–265) brings to the fore the emergence of socioeconomic inequalities and competition among complex and economically specialised gatherer-hunters. More specifically, Hayden sees economic rivalry within these groups as the driving force behind food production, with competition taking place through the medium of feasting. Hayden's 'accumulators' would attempt to maximise power and prestige through accumulating food, goods and services owed, in order to be able to give them away at a later date.

The specific implications of his model are that the initial move to domestication should occur in areas with abundant resources for gatherer-hunters; that the development of unequal status occurred with or before domestication; feasting remains and specialised buildings should again accompany or predate farming; the earliest domesticated species should be those which were particularly suitable for feasting, such as delicacies, intoxicants, foodstuffs that would fill dietary deficiencies, or rarities; resource shortages or overpopulation should not be visible. In the case of cereals Hayden wonders if Katz and Voigt (1986) may be right to speculate that cereals were first domesticated in order to produce beer for feasts. Finally, according to Hayden (1993: 225–7) the beginning of farming will be difficult to detect directly, as domesticated foodstuffs would be a special item eaten as part of feasts, rather than as a staple, and thus would not come to dominate the economy as a whole for a considerable time.

Hayden (1990) suggests that 'accumulators' can be seen in the Natufian through inequality in burial, houses and status goods (see Figure 1.3). He believes that the importation of goods from the Red Sea, the Mediterranean and Anatolia and their use as grave goods shows the existence of powerful individuals within Natufian society. He further argues that special communal structures, decorated mortars, polished stone cups and dishes demonstrate the importance of feasting.

The primary implications which the Hodder and Hayden hypotheses have in common are that Natufian society was complex and unequal, and that feasting was a key means of expressing that complexity and inequality. Looking at the issue of complexity first, there is general agreement on this issue at least. The most frequently cited criteria to judge this question would be settlement patterns, burials, exchange contacts and art, and in all these areas there is ample evidence for the Natufian.

First, Natufian settlements can be grouped into three size groups (Bar-Yosef and Belfer-Cohen 1989): small, from 15–100 m²; medium, from 400–500 m²; large, over 1000 m². There are settlements which can be classified as villages, such as 'Ain Mallaha. Here there were a series of some fifty houses (from three occupation phases) constructed on artificially levelled terraces, four to nine metres in diameter, with bench-like plastered walls, postholes and hearths, and associated storage pits. The levelling of the ground, the preparation of plaster and the transportation of stones, and the digging of pits all show a considerable

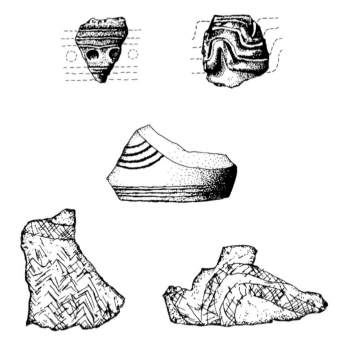

Figure 1.3 Natufian decorated items of stone (top) and ostrich shell (bottom)
(after Henry 1989)

investment of labour. At Hayonim Cave (Bar-Yosef 1991) one area contained a distinct layer of pounded lime, indicating the presence of a kiln, a suggestion supported by the charred stones surrounding the area; the lime was probably taken out for use in building on the Hayonim Terrace site.

The burial evidence has been much examined in recent years with the aim of uncovering regular patterns of depositional practice (e.g. Belfer-Cohen and Hovers 1992). One pattern which does emerge very clearly is that there is considerable variety, even in formal burials. Natufian burials are, however, concentrated at a relatively small number of the larger and probably permanently occupied sites (Belfer-Cohen and Hovers 1992). This concentration of activity does point to these sites having a greater symbolic significance than more temporary camps, and to the existence at these favoured locations of what may be termed cemeteries containing up to a hundred burials (Belfer-Cohen *et al.* 1991). Considerable variety of treatment of the skeleton has been noted (Belfer-Cohen and Hovers 1992): there are both single and multiple (up to seven individuals) burials, with the multiple burials sometimes showing a clear stratigraphic succession and on other occasions not; both sexes and all ages seem to be represented in both single and multiple burials. There are definite graves, but these are relatively rare, although this may be a result of later disturbance. Some tombs of limestone slabs exist, and other graves are covered with slabs, and there are rare examples of stones below bodies or in the grave fill, although at least some of the latter may result from stones tumbling in during the reopening of the grave. It is possible that some graves are actually reused storage pits. Some graves appear to have been marked by stone circles or by stones, sometimes with drilled cupmarks, as at Hayonim Cave and 'Ain Mallaha (Bar-Yosef 1991).

The reopening of graves could involve the abstraction of skulls, as at Hayonim Cave, a practice which became much more common with the earliest Neolithic (Bar-Yosef and Belfer-Cohen 1989). In the Neolithic this 'skull cult' is frequently interpreted as an element of an ancestor cult, denoting ownership and emotional ties to a place and so implying the existence of established territorial divisions; there seems no good reason not to apply this line of thinking to the Natufian (Belfer-Cohen 1991), and it would correlate well with the development of cemeteries.

One little acknowledged variation on Natufian burial practice is partial cremation, but this appears to be adopted at Kebara Cave. The excavations by Turville-Petre in 1931 recovered the charred remains of at least twenty-three individuals, which he interpreted as pre-Natufian in date. However, a recent radiocarbon accelerator date on the bones places them in the Early Natufian, around 11,500 BC (Bar-Yosef and Sillen 1993), so we must expand the catalogue of Natufian variety in burial practice once again.

The final aspect of burial practice is the use of grave goods (see Figure 1.4). These are rare (Belfer-Cohen and Hovers 1992), being present only in some 10 per cent of burials. The vast majority are ornaments, including head decorations, necklaces, bracelets and belts, primarily made up of shells and bone and tooth pendants and beads. The burials may well have been interred wearing these items. Other grave goods include occasional animal bones, and three examples of dogs being buried (with their owners?), some evidence for the use of ochre, and a single example of a female burial at Hayonim Cave with a long bone dagger, and a burial at el-Wad with a limestone human head and a turtle carapace. The overall record is certainly not spectacular.

As indicated by the el-Wad burial, there is a body of Natufian art (Noy 1991; Bar-Yosef and Belfer-Cohen 1992), which can certainly be argued to demonstrate social complexity. There are figurines, mostly of animals (probably young gazelles or deer) but a few of indistinct humans, carved out of bone or stone; at Hayonim Cave several limestone slabs incised with geometric patterns; and from Wadi Hammeh 27 in Jordan some more substantial limestone slabs with carved meanders. The figurine record at least changes at the very end of the Natufian or earliest Neolithic, when distinct females are being produced (Bar-Yosef and Belfer-Cohen 1989). It is interesting that Palestine and the Levant is an area which is singularly devoid of Palaeolithic art (Bahn 1991), so the Natufian does represent a genuine shift from earlier societies in this respect.

The final area which suggests Natufian social complexity is that of exchange contacts. Many different exotic materials were brought into Natufian sites, some from quite considerable distances (Bar-Yosef and Belfer-Cohen 1992). The

Figure 1.4 Shell and bone bead necklace from Natufian burial at Kebara

marine shells which were turned into ornaments were brought from the Mediterranean and some from the Red Sea, while the greenstone found at many sites was brought from Syria, Jordan or Sinai to be crafted into beads. At 'Ain Mallaha obsidian from central Anatolia and the freshwater shell *Aspathria* from the Nile are unique finds, but suggest even more distant links. These appear to be built on in the earliest Neolithic (Bar-Yosef and Belfer-Cohen 1989), with Anatolian obsidian being found at Jericho, Netiv Hagdud, Nahel Oren and Hatoula.

There does therefore appear to be considerable scope for the manipulation of access to different materials and resources to manifest itself in the archaeological record as evidence for social inequality. However, such evidence is singularly elusive. The burial record does not seem to show any very clear patterns: both adults and children are buried, with children making up some 23 per cent of the 370 burials examined by Belfer-Cohen *et al.* (1991). Of the adult skeletons which have been sexed some two-thirds are males, the proportion of males to females apparently falling through time. There are the examples of slab covered and marked graves, but these are relatively few in number and have not been examined as a separate group.

The only really clear pattern is that a mere 10 per cent of the burials were accompanied by grave goods (Belfer-Cohen and Hovers 1992); within this group adults (both males and females), adolescents and children are all represented. The grave goods themselves are also quite modest, dominated by ornaments. It may be significant, however, that these ornaments are often made from exotic shells, so there is a hint that access to exotica was restricted. This apears to be a phenomenon mainly of the Early Natufian (Bar-Yosef and Belfer-Cohen 1992), however, so arguments of increasing inequality based on grave goods would be insecure. The settlement record may provide some evidence of social inequality, as there are apparent differences in the size of buildings within settlements. At 'Ain Mallaha, for example, in the Early Natufian the houses range from 25 m² down to 8 m² (Valla 1991), although the significance of this variation is not yet clear.

Both Hodder and Hayden stress the importance of food preparation and feasting. The symbolic significance of food preparation may be acknowledged by the presence of limestone mortars in graves at Nahel Oren (Kaufman 1986). Food processing equipment also occurs with burials at 'Ain Mallaha, Hayonim Cave and Hayonim Terrace (Boyd 1992). The evidence for the holding of feasts is minimal as yet. While there can be no doubt that the existence of storage facilities on Natufian sites certainly made it possible to build up a sufficient stock of foodstuffs to hold feasts there are no archaeologically attested examples, either in houses as Hodder would propose, or in special structures as Hayden would suggest. Perhaps further analysis of deposition patterns may reveal intense and concentrated episodes of consumption of animal remains – it is, however, highly unlikely that feasting involving only plant foods could be detected.

We may now turn to the areas where Hodder and Hayden emphasise different aspects of the social fabric. Hodder lays great stress on the importance of the house and household, suggesting that the house itself would be highly elaborated and the household the unit of production and social competition. Hodder (1990: 33) points to 'Ain Mallaha, where one Early Natufian house had a paved stone floor with plaster walls painted red. Each of the houses had a stone-built hearth, usually centrally placed, with a stone pavement surrounding it in some cases. In one instance a large mortar was placed on the hearth. Storage pits occur both inside and outside houses. Some of these features, such as plaster walls, continue into the Neolithic (Watkins 1992). This material does clearly show that there was a considerable emphasis on the house, and that some productive activities took place there, but it seems inadequate to argue that the household was therefore the primary unit of social competition and that feasting was tied to the house.

Hodder also believes that there was a strong link between the house and burial (1990: 33), with burial occurring in settlements and in the house and storage pits, while scattered human bones are recovered from occupation debris. So death was controlled culturally and thus domesticated. This would of course be a clear prefiguring of Neolithic practice, when the dead are buried below house floors (Bar-Yosef and Kislev 1989; Hodder 1990: 34–5). However, in their general survey of Natufian burial Belfer-Cohen and Hovers (1992) state that in general human remains were deposited apart from or adjacent to settlements, in order to separate the dead from the living; they interpret the scattered human bones found in occupation levels as earlier burials disturbed by shifting settlements. This appears to be the case at Nahel Oren, for example, where there is a cemetery with associated settlement (Boyd 1992). At Hayonim Cave it seems as though the earlier graves are related to the settlement, while there is a later separation between the living or working areas and the cemetery, which occupies the inner part of the cave (Bar-Yosef 1991). Boyd (1992) suggests that the late Hayonim Cave cemetery was used by those living on Hayonim Terrace, sometimes reopening old graves in an act of memory. Against this, Valla (1991) has argued that at 'Ain Mallaha the burials do not succeed the houses after they have gone out of use but belong with the occupation. The situation is thus anything but clear, but there is certainly not a universally close tie between burial and houses. The association may be stronger in the Early Natufian, which could perhaps lead to a modification of the Hodder model to one in which the domestication represented by bringing the uncontrolled and wild in the form of death into the house through burial was more important in the initial phase of sedentism.

The concept of transforming the natural into the cultural is obviously closely connected with domestication, and Boyd (1992) has pointed to the burials with food preparation equipment in this light. He suggests that these burials show the significance of transformation in the Early Natufian; as with the question of burials in houses, these transformative burials perhaps demonstrate the significance of symbolic domestication in this first phase of sedentism.

One apparently weak part of Hodder's specific model is his climatic explanation. He suggests that unspecified environmental changes led to the development of a broad spectrum economy. He himself (1990: 293) recognises that this may be described as environmentally determinist, not to say vague, by critics, but argues that climatic changes were nonetheless important. This may be true, but it does not mean that social change has to be driven by the climate. Current models of climate change would place any deterioration in the climate well within the Natufian, so pre-existing factors would be more likely to be the determining ones. If Hodder is following a Broad Spectrum Revolution model for the emergence of the Natufian, then he should be aware that its very existence is in considerable doubt (P. C. Edwards 1989).

In Hayden's model imported rarities (potential 'prestige goods') could play an important part, as these are items which might have been subjected to a degree of control over their exchange and subsequent movement within Natufian communities. They undoubtedly existed, although apparently in rather small numbers with the exception of shells from the Mediterranean. These do seem to have had a certain significance, given their frequent use as grave goods. Apart from the burial evidence it is difficult, however, to detect any real signs of differential access to exotica. Little information is available concerning the context of their discovery during excavation, so it is not possible to see if any clustering in or near particular structures can be determined. Given the small numbers of objects involved, this could in any case only again be feasible for imported shells.

One quite specific correlate of Hayden's theory is that although significant in terms of feasting, cereals should not be used as a staple element of diet in the Natufian or even in the Early Neolithic. Here there are two pieces of evidence which do not really fit. The first is P. Smith's anatomical and dental survey (1989; 1991) of the material from Nahel Oren, which seems to show that there was a heavy use of cereals in the latest Natufian. Some entirely contradictory evidence comes from the bone chemistry work of Sillen and Lee-Thorp (1991). Their analyses point to a decline in cereal consumption through the Natufian. At the moment the two cannot be reconciled, although it is important to remember that Smith's work does relate only to a single site. If one takes Hayden's model to imply that there should be a competitive spiral of consumption, then one would expect that to intensify with time. Clearly, more attempts should be made to develop a clearer picture of the actual pattern of food consumption during the Natufian.

CONCLUSION

The climatic models are unsatisfactory on both theoretical and practical grounds. The use of climatic shifts as a prime mover in human social change bypasses human control over events, presenting societies as passively reacting to the changing environment. In the specific case of the Near East the climatic evidence does not seem to fit with the models proposed. The social competition models have restored a much needed social dimension to the debate. Although Hodder's emphasis on the wider context of domestication is an important development in our understanding of the Natufian and agricultural origins, his reliance in the final instance on an environmental explanation does undermine the model. Hayden's suggestion of the central importance of political competition within Natufian society appears to offer a feasible motive for the social upheaval that the transition to a farming economy must have involved in terms of a social desire to keep increasing food production. So the social competition model is a fruitful way of thinking about the origin of agriculture in the Near East, but can it be applied to the European Mesolithic–Neolithic transition?

2

THE SPREAD OF AGRICULTURE ACROSS EUROPE

The dominant view of the initial transition to agriculture within Europe is undoubtedly that the agricultural staples involved (both plants and animals) must have come from outside, presumably from the Near East via Anatolia. Despite various claims that sheep could have survived in the West Mediterranean (e.g. Geddes 1981) as remnants of earlier populations, it now seems most likely that they were reintroduced. It is agreed that the wild ancestors of oats, einkorn and barley (but probably not emmer wheat) were once found in southeast Europe (Dennell 1983: 159–61; Barker 1985: 71), but again it is generally thought to be more likely that the idea of their cultivation came from outside. With cattle and pigs, however, the situation is rather different, as they were present across the whole of Europe and their local domestication is therefore at least possible in more regions.

The introduction of agricultural resources from the Near East through Anatolia to Europe is thus widely agreed. The real debate is concerned with how this was achieved (Barker 1985: 71). Can the presence of colonists be documented? If so, did they arrive as a result of planned maritime ventures to open up new lands? Or, once they had arrived, was there only a small-scale movement of colonists, these farming groups continuing to spread little by little until they had occupied most of continental Europe by 4000 BC? Was this 'wave of advance' related to the spread of the Indo-European language group? Or was the adoption of a farming economy the outcome of transformations within Mesolithic communities, with new items being taken up from outside to meet new needs or desires? Need there have been a single uniform procedure, or were local and contingent factors more important?

THE AEGEAN

From 10,000 BC the Mesolithic inhabitants of Franchthi Cave in southern Greece exploited a very wide range of wild plants (Hansen and Renfrew 1978; Hansen 1991) including lentils, peas, almond and pistachio nuts, pears, bitter vetch and oat and barley cereals, as well as catching both large and small game, especially red deer. This occupation was at the time of the post-glacial rise in sea levels, and it may be that the increased emphasis on plant foods was an attempt to replace the contribution previously made by other game animals, such as ass and goat. All these various plants would have grown wild on local valley slopes and riversides. In the eighth millennium BC (the Upper Mesolithic) obsidian was being brought from the island of Melos some 130 km away in the Aegean, slightly later in the sequence being followed by finds of tunny which were of sufficient size to argue that they were the result of offshore fishing (Renfrew and Aspinall 1990). Throughout the Mesolithic at Franchthi Cave inhumation burials took place (as well as occasional cremations), which were frequently disturbed by subsequent activity (Cullen 1995).

Around 7000 BC there was apparently quite a dramatic change in the life of the inhabitants of Franchthi Cave, as emmer wheat and barley, and sheep and goats arrived, along with polished stone axes and plain pottery; large seeded (thus potentially domesticated) lentil and bitter vetch appeared, as wild oats, barley and peas disappeared (Hansen and Renfrew 1978). (There are, however, doubts as to how simultaneous these changes actually were [Whittle 1985: 53]). The settlement expanded in size, spilling out of the cave. However, the flint and bone industries carried on much as before, while foraging continued to provide a substantial part of the diet (Jacobsen 1976). We therefore seem to see at Franchthi a thriving community, apparently under no stress (Angel 1984), with a sufficient surplus of time and energy to travel to Melos in search of stone or to produce material for exchange with those who had. A rapid transformation then occurred in both the economy and cultural symbols. This all points to a native community, with the capacity for developing contacts with Anatolian agriculturalists, taking measures into its own hands and bringing about its own domestication.

However, it is the case that Franchthi stands out not just for the quality of its evidence, but also for its sheer rarity as a Greek Mesolithic site. Although it is of course highly likely that sites have disappeared as a result of changes in both sea levels and landforms, this could not account for the almost complete absence of Mesolithic archaeology from Greece. Only four Greek Mesolithic sites are accepted by Demoule and Perlès (1993) in their review, and they note the absence of Mesolithic material from cave sites and below Thessalian Neolithic settlements. This lack of a native component has been seized upon by advocates of colonisation to show that a relatively empty, and therefore uncontested, landscape was available to Anatolian settlers. Together with this they can point to the undoubted strength of the similarities between the Anatolian and Greek Neolithic (Nandris 1970; Demoule and Perlès 1993). These are both economic (the use of wheat and barley, sheep and goats, pigs and cattle), and cultural (the presence of timber-framed buildings, polished stone tools, pottery and terracotta figurines).

Against this colonisation model it must be noted that the evidence for cattle domestication in Anatolia predating that in the Aegean is by no means secure. Smaller, therefore probably domesticated, cattle appear at sites such as Argissa in Thessaly and Knossos on Crete before 6500 BC, earlier than in Anatolia (Grigson 1989a). The case for continuity in flint working techniques at both Franchthi Cave and Sidari on Corfu is also widely accepted (e.g. Demoule and Perlès 1993).

Organised colonisation is thought to be detectable in the appearance of Neolithic communities on both Crete and Cyprus around 7000 BC (Broodbank and Strasser 1991). There is virtually no sign of pre-existing Mesolithic populations on the islands (Cherry 1990), so it is difficult to argue for any great degree of continuity in these cases. However, this argument from absence could also be applied to the earliest Neolithic on Crete, which is also limited to a handful of sites, by contrast to Cyprus, where over twenty are now known (Cherry 1990). This would suggest that any colonisation was extremely small-scale in nature, although if deliberate it must have involved a minimum number of around a hundred colonists (Broodbank and Strasser 1991). This general absence of settlements must lead to a suspicion that there are many more sites which have been destroyed or which await discovery. From the demographic perspective it is simply not feasible that the inhabitants of Franchthi Cave could have been a self-sustaining community, thus strongly implying the existence of other, as yet unknown, groups nearby.

The question of colonisation should also be assessed from the perspective of the claimed colonists themselves. The need for them to move into Europe has usually been assumed to derive from population pressure within Anatolia pressing them to open up new habitats. However, as Dennell pointed out some years ago (1983: 156), the model of surplus Anatolian population is hardly supported by the evidence of settlement patterns. Early Neolithic sites in western Turkey are unquestionably rare, although further discoveries have of course been made since Dennell wrote. There are, for example, now sites in Turkish Thrace with strong similarities to those of central Anatolia (Davis 1992), so Greece was not too far away. It is clear that without a definite motive for large-scale colonisation the model is undoubtedly weakened. This may, though, turn out to be a problem in our understanding of early agricultural societies rather than in the reality of colonisation itself. Social factors of internal conflict and competition could lie behind colonisation in the Neolithic as well as much later.

The degree of actual colonisation thus remains an open question. Although it is possible that the indigenist stance of Barker (1985: 71) or Dennell (1983: 152–68) is correct, it is surely more likely that the reality was more mixed and confused (Whittle 1985: 65), a situation in which both colonists, in fairly small numbers, and pre-existing inhabitants, in fairly small numbers, gradually coalesced.

One recent model taking a new approach is that of Runnels and Van Andel (1988): they suggest that in the post-glacial all the major regions of both Europe and the Near East were inhabited, but that resources such as food plants and animals and minerals were unevenly distributed across the landscape. Regions would thus have engaged in trade with each other in order to gain access to resources they did not possess and so developed specialised production and storage facilities enabling them to produce at a level above their subsistence needs in order to have a surplus available for exchange. Crops and animals would then have been acquired from Anatolia via trade networks and from new Anatolian agricultural colonists. These domesticates would have been exchanged for raw materials or craft items.

Tangri (1989) has presented a thorough critique of the Runnels and Van Andel theory, from a modified indigenist approach. He notes that the required exchange items were in some cases already present in Greece, that the evidence for Anatolian colonists is hardly overwhelming and that although Runnels and Van Andel document the existence of exchange networks in both the Near East and in Europe, at no point do these overlap. In his reply defending his model Runnels (1989) goes a long way towards making it redundant. He reiterates his belief in Greek contacts with Anatolia, pointing to the evidence of genetic similarity (Ammerman and Cavalli-Sforza 1984) and to the appearance of the same domestic plants and animals in the two areas. He argues for a combination of a steady movement of farmers (in Thessaly) with indigenous experimentation (at Franchthi Cave), but from his arguments it is difficult to see the need for anything other than a population influx, which would account for both the arrival of new domesticates and the genetic similarities. The single case of Franchthi Cave hardly seems much of a basis for a broad division of Greece into two areas, although Runnels may indeed be right in his guess.

THE BALKANS

We are fortunate in possessing rather better data from the Balkans, at least from the Iron Gates region of the Danube Valley, on the Serbian–Romanian border. From about 9500 BC onwards there appear to have been at least seasonally sedentary communities, living in rock shelters and on islands, sustained in part by the riches of the River Danube (Whittle 1985: 21–2). The subsistence economy included hunting red deer, ibex, chamois and pigs in the limestone hills which rise from the floodplain, along with trapping small game, fishing and collecting shellfish.

Dating from the seventh–sixth millennium BC, Lepenski Vir (Srejović 1972) is a well-known and highly complex site of potentially sedentary gatherer-hunters. The twenty-five well preserved buildings were constructed on terraces cut into the sloping river bank. They are trapezoidal in plan, varying greatly in size from 5 m^2 to 30 m^2, and show a considerable degree of regularity in proportions and internal layout. All had the wider entrance end facing the river (see Figure 2.1). The floors are of hard limestone plaster coloured red or white, with postholes, which would have supported the roof, edging the floor. Inside, the hearths are large rectangular pits lined with stone blocks placed roughly at the centre. The hearth quite clearly had enormous significance as a focus of

Figure 2.1 Typical Lepenski Vir house (after Srejović 1972)

activity. In some of the houses there are inhumations of adults (child burial is rare, except for newborns) near the hearth, all associated with stag antlers, and in almost every building there was a large rounded block of limestone placed near the hearth which had been carved into a hybrid fish/human image or into an 'altar'. Srejović suggests that these sculptures commemorate men's heads (1972: 120), although the only clear association is with a child skull (Srejović 1972: 119), or more generalised ancestors (1989). Also taken to refer to death are the V-shaped stone settings around the hearth, which in one case has its place taken by a human jaw (Hodder 1990: 25). Death and the house are further linked by the deposition of stag antlers, otherwise found as grave goods, behind the hearth, while the importance of fish is also stressed by 'offerings' behind the hearth and near 'altars'.

In some early phases there was a larger central house which had more cult objects, altars and sculptures than other buildings. Srejović (1972: 135–8) has interpreted this as the dwelling of a community leader chosen by household heads. The village as whole certainly has a 'planned' feel, which would have contrasted with the wild world outside.

Not surprisingly, Hodder has made considerable use of the Lepenski Vir material (1990: 21–31) in the light of his concept of the *domus*. He suggests that a series of oppositions may be manifest in the layout of, and activities in, the houses. The eastern (facing sunrise) entrance may be opposed to the western dark back part, where most of the dead and the sculptures are. One could therefore argue that death was set against life, the hearth and food preparation. The 'wild', in the form of stag antlers and fish offerings, goes with death. In conclusion, Hodder (1990: 27) proposes a provisional structuralist scheme of oppositions:

back	west	dark	death	wild	male
front	east	light	life	domestic	female

Hodder himself (1990: 28) recognises that this scheme would gloss over important patterns in the evidence. Most significantly, the fish/human sculptures appear to be carved precisely in order to blur the boundary between the two groups. Presumably, this acts as a form of symbolic domestication, just as the dead were domesticated by bringing them into the domestic sphere. Chapman (1992) has criticised the overall scheme of binary opposition as tending to marginalise the hearth (neither front nor back), which might well have been conceptually central. Chapman prefers to stress fertility rather than death as a basic symbolic concern.

Fish bones were, not surprisingly, very common finds during the excavations: the wel and the barbel, standard types in the Danube gorge, were an important element in the diet. The animal bone assemblage in the early phases consists of red deer, aurochs and wild boar, the only domesticated animal being the dog, but about 5500 BC domestic cattle, pigs sheep and goats were all introduced.

Chapman (1992) has argued that the site would have been flooded by the Danube once if not twice a year, and that this may have lain behind the choice of stone construction for their houses. These would survive the scouring flood-waters to be reborn when their inhabitants returned as the waters receded, a tie strengthened by the burial of ancestors within the houses and, if the boulder sculptures do represent ancestors, by cult observance as well.

Lepenski Vir is not alone, and other Iron Gates sites have a similar story to tell. Hearths, huts and burials all point to reduced mobility or seasonal sedentism beside a river with ample resources. Carved boulders decorated with abstract and naturalistic motifs are found at several other sites (Boroneanţ 1989). Graphite reached Vlasac, 4 km from Lepenski Vir, through exchange relations with communities outside the Gorge (Chapman 1992). At Padina, 10 km upstream from Lepenski Vir, an almost identical pattern can be seen in the faunal record, with a gathering-hunting economy giving way eventually to an agricultural lifestyle (Clason 1980). At Icoana (Bolomey 1973) the animal bone assemblage can be divided into three groups: occasional hunting of animals for their fur and of chamois and cattle; frequent hunting of red and roe deer; and selective culling of pigs, especially juveniles under a year old. Both the pig and deer bones suggest permanent occupation. Icoana and Vlasac have also produced coprolites with large grass or cereal pollen, suggesting that wild cereals were available in the area (Voytek and Tringham 1989). Perforated antler tools here and elsewhere have been interpreted as digging sticks or hoes, suggesting improvement of the ground to raise wild plant productivity or actual cultivation (Chapman 1989). Finally, Vlasac also has a substantial burial record (Chapman 1992).

The case for an indigenous development of agriculture has been put strongly by Barker (1985: 97–8), who concludes that a local origin of farming, together with the adoption of new resources such as emmer and bread wheat, seems more likely than that the inhabitants of the Danube gorge were simply swept away. His argument is strengthened by the evidence for anatomical continuity presented by Y'Edynak (1978), which would at least suggest that there wasn't total population replacement.

However, as Barker himself implicitly acknowledges (1985: 97), the Iron Gates sites are somewhat anomalous, as they existed within a short distance of fully Neolithic communities after 6000 or even 6500 BC. At Schela Cladovei, only some 30 km downstream of Icoana, a fairly typical Mesolithic site with a series of burials, some with red ochre and grave goods, is superseded by a layer with Neolithic Cris material (Whittle 1985: 33). A similar sequence can perhaps be seen at Ostrovul Banului, even closer to Icoana (Boroneanţ 1990). Chapman notes (1992) that at Padina it seems as though the 'Neolithic' Stratum B, with Cris pottery, was only nominally agricultural, for the percentage of domestic animal bones was minuscule, and he interprets both the ceramics and the animal remains as imports.

Lepenski Vir stands in clear contrast to this, for although the site had been in receipt of large quantities of imports from outside the Gorge, such as raw materials for stone tool production and shells, for some considerable time, this pattern shifted in later phases of the site (Chapman 1989). The number of sherds at Lepenski Vir is tiny by comparison to the amounts from both Padina and Schela Cladovei, while these same sites received joints of beef, mutton and pork, but Lepenski Vir did not (Clason 1980).

The Iron Gates sites seem to be the exception that proves the rule, in that they cannot be used to argue for a general continuity from Mesolithic to Neolithic in the Balkans, as Barker would propose. There is little evidence of thriving Mesolithic communities outside the Danube Gorge, in the area which first developed an agricultural economy. However, there is every reason to see the Iron Gates case as that of particular Mesolithic communities consciously deciding whether or not to become agriculturalists. This decision took longer for the more isolated and culturally stronger (to judge by the overt symbolic activity which does not include references to agricultural activities) groups such as that at Lepenski Vir. There does appear to be an extremely good case for a lengthy delay having occurred between the presence of a Neolithic economy in the wider Balkan region, then penetrating the Danube Gorge area, and eventually being taken up by groups in the Iron Gates. This lengthy process involved communities which were in contact, living within walking distance.

CENTRAL EUROPE AND THE ORIGIN OF THE LBK

The *Linienbandkeramik* (LBK) appears around 5400 BC and represents the next major agricultural transition. It is characterised by settlements of substantial longhouses, except in its eastern extension, mainly located on fertile soils (usually windblown silt – loess) close to water. This farming economy appears with what seems to be great rapidity, which has often been taken to demonstrate a swift process of agricultural colonisation (e.g. Vencl 1986). However, the recent application of accelerator radiocarbon dates using seed and bone samples, rather than the less reliable charcoal, has shown that the spread of the LBK may have been a rather slower process than often envisaged (Whittle 1990a). On the origins of the LBK there are two main schools of thought (Whittle 1985: 79–80): one suggests that the LBK represents a development within the late Starčevo-Körös culture of the Balkans, and that it spread with the continued movement of agriculturalists both north and west; the second proposes that it was created by indigenous groups lying just beyond the Starčevo-Körös area on the Great Hungarian plain. The majority view is that the colonisation model is preferable, but that there are important features of the LBK, such as the long-house and decorated pottery, which have no clear background in the Körös culture. However, so little work has been done on the indigenous groups of the Great Hungarian plain that this is little more than an appeal to the unknown.

Whatever its origins, there have been few archaeologists arguing that the Mesolithic population of central Europe as far north as the fringes of the north European plain and as far west as the Paris Basin played much part in the agricultural transition of the region, apart from some evidence for continuity in stone tool production (Clark 1980: 78). Indeed, traces of the Mesolithic themselves are very thin, so no clear picture of the nature of the indigenous communities involved has yet been built up (Whittle 1985: 74–6). A hint of potential complexity is given by the two nests of skulls (nearly thirty skulls in total) found in pits at the cave of Ofnet in Bavaria. Recent accelerator radio-carbon dates on skulls from both nests show that the two deposits both date to around 6500 BC (Hedges *et al.* 1989); these possible massacre victims are thus Late Mesolithic in date. A similar date has also recently been obtained from two skeletons found in multiple inhumations in pits at Gross Fredenwalde in eastern Germany (Hedges *et al.* 1995). In general, though, the Late Mesolithic record of central Europe is simply too insubstantial when set against the abundant evidence from the LBK to suggest that local inhabitants played more than a relatively minor role in the establishment of farming (Vencl 1986).

Bogucki (1988: 105–8) has suggested that there may well have been quite intensive contacts between Mesolithic and Neolithic groups, following Gregg's (1988) model of forager–farmer interaction. Gregg suggests a degree of cooperative exchange, with labour, building materials, firewood and gathered forest foodstuffs being contributed by the gatherer-hunters and dairy products and surplus meat by the agriculturalists. Bogucki (1988: 108) argues that these close ties are reflected in the speed with which the native population was absorbed into the agricultural community. This view can be criticised on a number of levels: at that of supporting material, Bogucki himself (1988: 108) recognises the lack of archaeological evidence for such exchanges; from an economic standpoint, Midgley (1992: 397) has pointed out that the kind of seasonal shortages proposed by Bogucki (1988: 110–11) would scarcely leave the community in a position to enter into exchange relationships; more significantly, the model presents Mesolithic and LBK communities as simple aggregates of economic behaviour, with no consideration of the social consequences of such exchanges. Would the two communities have wanted to take part in such interactions, given the degree of competition and hostility which may well have existed between them? What effect would this have on power relations within the two societies? What were the supposed motives of the Mesolithic side of the equation? These and further social issues would require examination in a full account of this proposal, but given the current paucity of the gatherer-hunter archaeological record for central Europe this is not yet feasible, as continued concentration on the agriculturalist point of view will not produce a more rounded approach.

The colonist point of view has recently been forcefully restated by Bogucki and Grygiel (1993), who put forward a series of distinctions between the LBK and Mesolithic communities in central Europe: that there are no potential ceramic industries to the north and northwest, except possibly on the fringes of the LBK area, so a developed pottery industry sprang up with no local roots; that there are some marked differences in the stone tool assemblages, with Mesolithic groups generally producing microliths and the LBK blades; that on the loess the earliest farming communities mostly occupy areas with little sign of a Mesolithic presence; finally, that the large solid longhouses of the LBK are completely different to the small oval or semicircular Mesolithic structures. This seems to represent a much more substantial break in economic and cultural continuity than is apparent in Greece or the Balkans.

LBK – ECONOMY AND SOCIETY

It has clearly been established that the LBK economy was almost completely agricultural in nature, with little or no contribution from wild resources. The main crop plants were einkorn and emmer wheat, barley, peas and lentils (Willerding 1980), although given the relatively small size of many of the available samples this picture may prove to be oversimplified. Substantial animal bone assemblages are rarely preserved on the acid loess soils, so the evidence for animal exploitation is little better. The general picture is of 80–95 per cent of animal bones deriving from domesticated species, and these being dominated by cattle, with sheep/goat a second preference and pigs generally rare (Milisauskas and Kruk 1989). Glass (1991: 75) has argued that the rarity of pigs is due to their lack of non-meat products in contrast to cattle and sheep/goat which also provide milk.

The subsistence economy of the LBK was traditionally characterised as slash-and-burn agriculture, in which the soil was quickly exhausted and settlements moved on frequently, perhaps once every generation (e.g. Clark 1952: 95–6). This interpretation arose from the apparently insubstantial nature of LBK settlement traces by comparison with the tells of southeast Europe and the relatively large number of LBK sites (Childe 1929). Apparent gaps in the sequence at major sites such as Köln-Lindenthal in Germany and Bylany in Bohemia seemed to confirm the model. A rather more sophisticated version of slash-and-burn was proposed by Soudský (Soudský and Pavlů 1972), in which a regular pattern of site movement took place within a limited area, returning to a location after it had time to recover, with the cycle lasting some sixty years.

The reaction against this hypothesis has come from both the archaeological and theoretical standpoints (e.g. Rowley-Conwy 1981; Bogucki 1988: 79–92). Current opinion is that LBK sites were continually occupied for hundreds of years rather than only intermittently, judging from radiocarbon dating and the presence of substantial longhouses. The analogy previously made with tropical cultivators has been dismissed as inappropriate, given the contrast between the shallow tropical soils and the rich thick soils of central Europe. The ground has shifted considerably (Bogucki 1988: 81–2), to the point where the current orthodox view is that the agricultural regime of LBK settlements involved intensive horticulture in gardens situated close by or within the site. The weed remains recovered from LBK settlements (Willerding 1980) suggest that the fields cleared were small in size and bordered by hedges or the edge of the forest. These fields or gardens could have borne a crop for several years without a break to judge by the results of experimental agriculture on loess soils (Milisauskas 1986: 162).

Turning to animal husbandry, Bogucki has stressed the importance of dairy production in a number of publications (1984; 1988: 85–91). In particular, he has focused on the existence of what appear to be ceramic sieves for straining cheese at many LBK sites. From this he has argued that milk rather than meat was the primary product of LBK cattle herds and that the existence of large numbers of cattle demanded a degree of mobility among these early farming communities due to their needs for forage and fodder (1988: 91). He sees sheep as of relatively little significance, only outnumbering cattle on a few sites in eastern Germany (Bogucki and Grygiel 1993). However, the idea of an LBK cattle economy exploiting the forest grazing of the North European Plain has been questioned by a number of authors (e.g. Whittle 1987; Milisauskas and Kruk 1989; Midgley 1992: 25) because of the relatively high numbers of sheep/goat at various sites, even where they are not in the majority, and because they envisage a fixed-plot agricultural regime which would not allow the degree of mobility demanded by large cattle herds. Although the use of ceramic sieves is certainly suggestive, the evidence from the animal bones themselves is as yet inadequate to pursue the issue much further, although a highly specialised economy seems inherently improbable.

Assessing the wider economy, it appears that both a degree of specialisation and exchange networks developed during the LBK. Evidence of specialised production can be traced at a number of LBK settlements (Keeley and Cahen 1989; Hodder 1990: 103–5), in the form of querns, ceramics, flintwork and stone axes. Exchange practices were significant, with items such as shells and lithics moving over long distances (Whittle 1985: 91–2). *Spondylus* shell bracelets are found throughout the area of the LBK, probably emanating from Aegean or Adriatic sources. The amounts involved are usually small, but can be extremely large even at the furthest extent of the LBK. Axes of hard, fine-grained, rock such as amphibolites and basalts travelled distances of some 200–300 km from their sources. Obsidian from northern Hungary reached southern Poland, while the chocolate-coloured flint from the Holy Cross Mountains moved in the opposite direction. The much wider distribution of barley impressions on pottery than as crop remains on LBK settlement has led to suggestions that pottery was also being exchanged (Dennell 1992). This high degree of exchange contacts may also have led to the quite remarkable homogeneity of early LBK pottery across the area from Holland to Hungary (Halstead 1989).

Halstead (1989) has provided an informative contrast between exchange practices and hospitality in southeast and central Europe. He notes that the location of cooking facilities in open areas between houses in Thessaly may indicate a tradition of sharing cooked food between neighbours, while the dominance of fine painted pottery points to the importance of consuming food and drink in the context of feasting. In central Europe fine painted pottery and communal cooking facilities are absent, which Halstead sees as an indication of food sharing and local hospitality being less important there. Instead, he argues that their place was taken by much wider networks of contact revealed by the movement of shells and stonework. Halstead puts this evidence in a highly ecological context of minimising the risk of food shortages, although he does not envisage a continental assistance network, merely one on a less local scale than in southeast Europe. Halstead's observations need not actually imply any food sharing between widely separated groups, and indeed could be seen in an entirely different light: the southeast European tradition of communal eating could be interpreted as evidence of competition between households, while the wider ties of the LBK may show the existence of competition between larger social groups, perhaps under the leadership of particular households. That local competition did not disappear is suggested by LBK pottery, which is still finely decorated if not painted and thought to be used in the preparation and serving of food (Hodder 1990: 108).

One significant context in which exchanged items appear in the archaeological record is as grave goods. LBK cemeteries dominate the burial record, although a number of 'settlement burials' are known which occur in or near houses or other elements of settlements (Veit 1993). The cemeteries are situated up to 500 m away from the settlements (Bogucki and Grygiel 1993). The layout and burial rites of the cemeteries are standardised and generally uniform within if not between cemeteries (Whittle 1988b: 153–64). There was generally a preferred orientation within each cemetery, and at some sites the graves are in rows, suggesting the use of grave markers. Both inhumations and cremations are known, but inhumations predominate. Children are generally underrepresented. There are also apparent token burials and cenotaphs, although some of the latter may reflect burial in variable soil conditions. There are between twenty and a hundred burials in a cemetery (Hodder 1990: 109).

The backfilling of the grave seems to have taken place as a single act, although it is noticeable that the main body of grave goods often lies slightly higher than the body itself. Grave goods are often placed near the head or waist. All major cemeteries have burials without grave goods, these amounting to between a quarter and a half of all burials (Whittle 1988b: 160). The grave goods represented were decorated or undecorated pots, probably containing food offerings, adzes, arrowheads and other flintwork, antler axes, copper objects, shell or stone bead necklaces or belts and bracelets of *spondylus* shell, and haematite (Veit 1993). There are some differences between male and female grave goods – adzes and arrowheads generally occurring with men and ornaments, querns and small tools such as awls with women (Hodder 1990: 109), but these are by no means absolute divisions, and in the frequent absence of sufficient bone surviving for an anatomical definition of the sex of the individual such arguments can soon become circular (Whittle 1988b: 161).

As Whittle notes (1988b: 164), it is difficult to decide what significance the variety in grave goods may have had in terms of status or wealth, as there are several cross-cutting possible indicators. At Niedermerz in the Rhineland (Dohrn-Ihmig 1983) eight categories of grave goods have been identified: 36 of 102 burials lacked grave goods, twenty-eight burials possessed a single category, and only a few all or most items; but a number of burials were accompanied by only one or two categories but had those in large quantities; alternatively, one could emphasise the thirty-one burials with adzes, which were the item imported from the furthest distance to the site. The pattern is clearly not simple, and it seems likely that a complex interplay of household origin, gender, age and perhaps manner of death is responsible for the final pattern of burial and grave goods.

For a fuller picture we must also consider the evidence from settlement burials (Veit 1993). Few of these are in separate graves, being found mostly in existing pits, and some in association with house walls or construction pits alongside longhouses. There are no known cremations among them. Children outnumber adults, although not sufficiently to balance their relative shortage in cemeteries, and few infants are found. Rather more females than males are found, although the imbalance is not great. Less than half the settlement burials were accompanied by grave goods, which may relate to the high number of children and females, but the nature of the grave goods was the same as in cemeteries. A separate category is the house burials, of which all twenty-three examples are of children. Veit concludes that the settlement burials are of those who were deemed of insufficiently high social status to enter the cemetery either because of an early death or because of the manner of their death. This seems likely to be part of the answer, given the difference in the presence of children and the smaller number of grave goods. It suggests, however, that access to grave goods by the burial party was in itself not sufficient to ensure burial in a cemetery, while both the settlement burials and the rows of graves in cemeteries point to the continuing significance of the household. Exotic items may well have been channelled through competing households and the links to the outside which they symbolised may well have been just as significant as the actual items themselves. Such exchange relations may themselves have been founded on surplus agricultural and other production organised through the household as a unit of supply, and both the public face of the household and its private being may have been expressed through different funerary rituals.

Available evidence indicates quite clearly that the focus of early LBK society was the longhouse (see Figure 2.2). These were 6–8 m in length and up to 45 m long, with complex post arrangements pointing to divisions of the internal space (Hodder 1990: 103–8). The longhouse was the centre of household activities, such as grain storage, and the production of flintwork, ground stone tools and antler axes. Longhouses seem to have been painted, and some were associated with foundation deposits in the walls and with child burials, while the use of fine decorated pottery on settlements is closely tied to the longhouses. The entrance may be elaborated, with the creation of a linear grading of space as one moves further into the interior of the building (Hodder 1990: 137). It is no wonder that Hodder can here identify the *domus*, his idea of a concept and practice of nurturing and caring which is tied to the household as social unit.

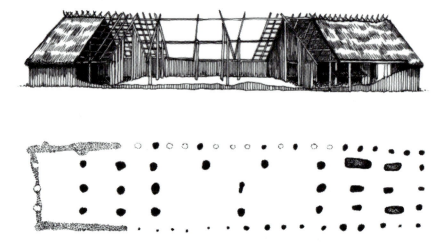

Figure 2.2 Plan and reconstruction of LBK longhouse at Geleen, Holland

The question of how many longhouses on these long-lived LBK sites may have been occupied at any one time is a vexed one, given the lack of stratigraphic controls (Whittle 1985: 82–3). Figures given for particular settlements vary between eight and twenty, but these generally rely on the application of particular assumptions about the life of the timbers in the longhouse walls. The often-quoted figure of fifteen years before replacement became necessary certainly seems to be an underestimate of their use-life (Whittle 1985: 82).

Distinctions between longhouses, and thus presumably households, are as yet little established, as the identification of different household activity areas has only recently been a priority of LBK settlement excavations (Bogucki and Grygiel 1993). This may well be because the traditional model of LBK social organisation has been of an egalitarian community, so differences between households would not be expected to exist. Traditionally, the issue of social ranking has been limited to comment on the varying size of longhouses, which can indeed be quite significant on individual sites. The larger longhouses do show differences from smaller examples, as at Langweiler 8, where Lüning (1982) noted that the longer buildings had more pits, more related finds (although this may simply be a product of greater pit volume), more decorated pottery and more weeds and wheat chaff, suggesting that primary processing of grain took place in them. Variation in subsistence related material may relate to functional differences between structures, although the decorated pottery is more difficult to explain in such terms, and discussion has generally stalled there. In his excavations at Olszanica in Poland, Milisauskas (1986) has, however, identified a degree of clustering of exotic obsidian and of fine imported pottery around certain quite small longhouses which he argues (1978: 88) reflects the control of exchange practices by certain families or individuals, while he suggests that a particularly substantial longhouse associated with large numbers of polished axes could be interpreted as a men's house, or the dwelling of a community leader. A simple analysis of the size of different buildings may thus be of relatively little significance, especially if some represent communal structures for use by a group larger than the household. The local level of social competition therefore lies largely beyond analysis at present, in the absence of further detailed contextual studies.

Social relations on a larger scale can be seen with the creation of substantial enclosures later in the LBK. There is considerable variety in Early Neolithic enclosures as a whole (Bogucki and Grygiel 1993), except that most of the early examples have several entrances even though these are not positioned to any clear pattern, and they tend to be quite small (Bradley 1993: 74). There is much debate concerning the function of the enclosures (Keeley and Cahen 1989), with three alternative theories for their use being proposed: as cattle 'kraals', as ritual sites, or as defended sites.

The cattle kraal theory has been revived by Bogucki (Bogucki and Grygiel 1993), based on his interpretation of the importance of cattle in the LBK economy. The evidence is slight, however, given that it is limited to certain

German enclosures lacking complex earthworks and being situated on the edge of the floodplain in locations which do not appear to be very defensible. That is not of course to deny that stock control may have been important at times, just that it need not necessarily involve the construction of permanent enclosures. Where the earthworks are both more substantial and seem to enclose buildings the standard view has been that these are defended settlements (e.g. Bogucki and Grygiel 1993). There are, however, some real difficulties with this as a general interpretation (see p. 39).

A less considered theory is that of enclosures as demarcating spaces set aside for ritual activities. This possibility has generally been raised concerning earthworks which do not enclose houses and have a non-defensive character (e.g. Lüning and Stehli 1989), but has yet to receive much genuine consideration (although see Whittle 1988a). Instead it often represents an interpretation entertained only if no other seems plausible (e.g. Bogucki and Grygiel 1993). However, it is clear that many causewayed enclosures in Scandinavia and Britain were the scene of intense ritual activities (see Chapter 7), and post-LBK enclosures in central Europe also have a definite ritual character. Midgley *et al.* (1993), reporting on excavations at the Rondel at Bylany in Bohemia, note the absence of settlement traces inside Rondels and suggest that the palisades are not defensive in intention but serve to constrict the entrance and so symbolically, and perhaps practically, restrict access to the interior. Special deposits are few in number, but perhaps include grinding stones.

Suggestions that enclosures may have been constructed on the site of founding settlements and may have played a significant role in the movement of raw materials (Bradley 1993: 74–5) bring us back to the question of competition between households and between communities. The construction of an enclosure to mark the primacy of one settlement over others must have been a source of considerable tension and competing claims over the prestige that this would confer on those in direct line of descent from the ancestral farmers. A degree of control over access to the enclosure would inevitably heighten such tensions and represent a significant source of power. That such conflicts were not, however, played out exclusively in the ritual sphere is demonstrated by the evidence from Talheim in Germany (Wahl and König 1987), where a mass grave of some thirty-five men, women and children, many apparently killed by blows to the head with a shoe-last adze, has been discovered. The precise significance of this unique discovery is as yet not established, but it certainly points to the possibility that competition and conflict within LBK society may not always have been constrained and channelled by ritual rivalries.

ON THE PERIPHERY

While the native inhabitants of central Europe are generally seen as contributing relatively little to the origin and development of the LBK, there is a very lively debate concerning the periphery of the LBK and the role played there by local gatherer-hunter populations. In Poland, Holland, western Germany, Belgium, Luxembourg and northern France there are indications of both continuity in some elements of material culture and the creation of new items which are significantly different from the main strand of LBK development. In Poland the site of Deby 29 in the lowlands has produced both Mesolithic flintwork and the remains of domestic animals; this has been interpreted as a conflation of two separate occupations, but Domanska (1991) has argued that there is only a single phase of activity and that the material therefore shows one stage in a lengthy process of Neolithisation.

In Holland and western Germany there is evidence for contact on both sides of the agriculturalist/gatherer-hunter divide. Gronenborn (1990) has pointed to the occurrence in early LBK sites in western Germany of substantial quantities of flint from the Rijckholt region of the Maas (Meuse) Valley some 200 km to the west. Kalis and Zimmerman (1988) have suggested that this material was acquired by Neolithic groups sending out expeditions, but Gronenborn finds this highly unlikely and prefers a model in which the flint was distributed by the local Mesolithic population. Following this interpretation, at least part of the very important LBK exchange of exotics would therefore have been in outside hands. Further support for the proposed contact model is seen in the finds of ceramics at Mesolithic sites along the western border of the LBK area, which Gronenborn (1990) believes reflects the existence of economic exchanges between the two areas over a period of roughly 250 years before the agricultural frontier moved further west.

Concerning this actual transition to farming itself, Arts (1989) has assessed the two prevailing models for the Lower Maas (Meuse) area: these are either that the Neolithic flint industry derives from that of the Younger Oldesloe, which contains both picks and axes, or that the Limburg pottery of the area reflects the acculturation of the existing Mesolithic population. He finds neither interpretation convincing, as he cannot see continuity from the Mesolithic to Neolithic in lithic industries, and instead revives the previous hypothesis of direct colonisation by intrusive migrant LBK groups. Louwe Kooijmans (1993) and Bogucki and Grygiel (1993) focus instead on the Limburg pottery (see Figure 2.3): this is different to normal LBK pottery in terms of its fabric, having heavy tempering with organic material and a tan or brown colour, while the decoration is elaborate. Bogucki and Grygiel conclude that the Limburg pottery itself is sufficiently distinct from the LBK ceramic tradition to represent a local contribution. Louwe Kooijmans has examined the context of Limburg material, found on those LBK sites which occupy a 20–30 km wide band off the loess, on sandy soils, as a low percentage admixture with LBK pottery in pit fills, and along with LBK flintwork. There is also a pure Limburg assemblage at Kesseleyk. LBK adzes and arrowheads are found more widely than this, scattered across the whole Meuse Valley.

Louwe Kooijmans argues, following Wansleeben and Verhart (1990), that these late LBK sites off the loess have a more ephemeral character than those in

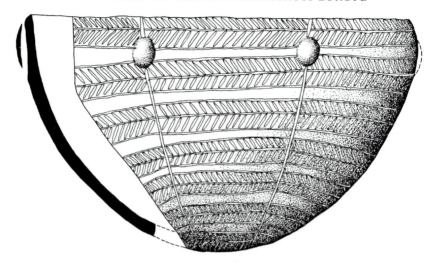

Figure 2.3 Limburg pottery vessel from Aubechies, Hainaut region, Belgium
(after Bogucki 1988)

the main LBK area, and may represent the remains of transhumant cattle camps, which would represent a change in the economy. Perhaps this would also reflect a more substantial existing population and influence on subsequent events than on the loess, as Louwe Kooijmans sees the producers of Limburg pottery as separate from the LBK, a group possibly with a semi-agrarian economy of native origin. Bogucki (1988: 109) suggests that interaction between Limburg-using groups and agriculturalists may have taken the form of exchange of animals or possibly labour for domesticated foodstuffs. Keeley, however, finds little archaeological evidence of such exchanges (1992).

In Belgium, Keeley (1992) notes the existence of bone-tempered pottery on sites (Weelde, Oleye and Melsele) of the local Rhine–Meuse–Schelde Mesolithic group which again is different to that of the LBK, but is found only some 30–40 km from areas of major LBK settlement. Keeley concludes that RMS groups ignored the LBK ceramic tradition nearby in favour of that from Late Mesolithic groups in Holland. Also associated with this ceramic material, at Weelde and at Melsele, are finds of what appear to be bones of domesticated cattle and pigs. Interestingly, the domestic cattle remains do not match those of the small LBK cattle, but are from a larger strain, suggesting a more recent domestication event. In general, Keeley can see little sign of significant interaction between what appear to be two separate groups.

Very similar developments seem to take place to the south and southeast, where the main ceramic type is La Hoguette ware, found primarily in the Rhine, Main and Neckar Valleys of western Germany, the Moselle Valley of Luxembourg and Lorraine, and to the west in northern France. This has deep and conical forms of vessel, tempering of bone and some sand and fine gravel, a red-brown colour and decoration consisting of parallel lines of stab and drag or raised bands or ridges running around the pot. A pure La Hoguette assemblage has been recovered at Sweikhuizen in Holland. As with the Limburg style, La Hoguette pottery is thought by Bogucki and Grygiel (1993) to show a local contribution to ceramic development, although they do acknowledge that it also has decorative links to Mediterranean Impressed Cardial Ware. Louwe Kooijmans (1993) has developed a similar model of a La Hoguette producing semi-agrarian acculturated native population to that proposed to explain Limburg ceramics.

A model of active conflict between farmer and gatherer-hunter groups in Belgium has recently been presented by Keeley and Cahen (Keeley and Cahen 1989; Keeley 1992). They argue that a series of LBK sites in the Hesbaye region of eastern Belgium were fortified enclosures, rather than cattle 'kraals' constructed to protect livestock from predators. They have earthworks backed by palisades and complex gateway arrangements. Unlike Whittle (1988a), Keeley and Cahen do not see these enclosures as evidence of increasing competition and conflict within LBK groups, but as a sign of violent struggles with the native Mesolithic population. They note that the boundary of the distribution of LBK does not here accord with the edge of the favoured loess soil, but with a river, and beyond this were local gatherer-hunter communities of the Rhine–Meuse–Schelde group. Together with the lack of evidence for peaceful interaction (Keeley 1992) they see this distribution as demonstrating a threat from Mesolithic societies towards farming groups. Keeley goes on to suggest that the overall distribution of LBK enclosures clusters at the edge of the LBK settlement zone and that their theory of warfare between incoming agriculturalists and indigenous gatherer-hunters could be extended to the LBK as a whole. This explanation would certainly argue for the existence of a temporary halt to the LBK advance in the face of sustained hostility from native populations, and could thus fit in with the emerging evidence for such a stop–go spread of farming.

However, as Bradley (1993: 79) has pointed out, the LBK enclosures as a whole do not make very convincing defensive settlements, given that even the most defensible still have several entrances, and that although some sites do contain houses which have been burnt down, this sometimes appears to have occurred before the construction of the earthworks. This latter point need not be too significant a problem, as it could be argued that a successful attack on the settlement led to the decision to construct a defensive circuit. It is still the case, however, that these LBK enclosures do not approach the defensiveness of some of the causewayed enclosures of Britain, with an almost continuous circuit of ditch, bank and rampart, and again unlike the later British sites, the LBK enclosures have no clear signs of attack followed by the death of the inhabitants or the slighting of the earthworks (see Chapter 7). None of this need mean that we should assume that relations between agriculturalists and gatherer-hunters never turned to violence, for a level of tension must have existed even when exchanges benefiting both sides were taking place.

The overall picture of the LBK fringe is that there was a definite halt to the agricultural expansion and strong evidence of a more significant native contribution. The degree of local variability in pottery styles and the economic regime increases significantly off the edge of the loess – it is surely no coincidence that it is in precisely these areas that the Mesolithic background can be much more clearly discerned. On a much larger scale than in the Iron Gates region of the Danube, we can see indications here of a process of conscious decision-making on the part of indigenous Mesolithic communities which eventually resulted in the onward transmission of a modified agricultural economy.

THE 'WAVE OF ADVANCE' AND PROTO-INDO-EUROPEANS

We may now have sufficient material at hand to assess two major attempts to model the spread of agriculture: the 'wave of advance' (Ammerman and Cavalli-Sforza 1971; 1973; 1984), and the LBK Indo-Europeans (Renfrew 1987). They may be taken together, in that the second model leans heavily on the first, although the first need not imply the second.

The 'wave of advance' is an attempt to model the spread of a population of agricultural colonists from the Near East across Europe. This should, however, be distinguished from suggestions of a process of deliberate and planned colonisation, such as that which has been argued for Crete. Ammerman and Cavalli-Sforza (1973) produced a mathematical model of local migration out from an area of population increase in a wave pattern which radiates outward at a constant rate. This 'demic diffusion', in a wave of advance, would involve slow, continuous expansion, with movements usually being over short distances.

Factors seen as driving this steady onward movement of farmers are temporary soil exhaustion or overcrowding with the growing up of a new generation (Ammerman and Cavalli-Sforza 1984: 134). Such movement as this would create would therefore be at a very local level, calculated by Ammerman and Cavalli-Sforza as being in the order of 1 km a year (1984: 134). However, they no longer believe this to be a constant rate, but rather an average, as they see variations produced by the use of boats in the Mediterranean, or by favourable conditions in the area of the LBK but slower in mountain regions such as the Alps. While admitting that cultural diffusion, agriculture spreading without farmers moving, may have been a factor they conclude that the available evidence provides a convincing fit for the wave of advance model (1984: 135). One factor present in the later analyses which was not in the earlier versions of the model is the mapping of blood groups in Europe. They suggest that the genetic affinities these reveal are an important support for the model (1984: 99–100).

Renfrew (1987: 147) has backed the wave of advance model, as it fits very neatly with his own theory of a movement by the speakers of Indo-European across Europe together with a Neolithic economy. He has rejected traditional suggestions of a Late Neolithic Corded Ware origin for the speakers of Indo-European (1987: 35–41) on the grounds that it need not represent a population influx. Searching for a major upheaval which might reflect the spread of Indo-European languages, he ends up with the Neolithic as the only possible candidate. Renfrew (1987: 266) proposes an eastern Anatolian homeland for Indo-European speakers, with farming groups spreading from here, initially to Greece, and then to points west and north, carrying their language with them. Renfrew (1987: 267) does allow for the likelihood of a indigenous Mesolithic contribution to the adoption of agriculture, particularly in the west Mediterranean, so that the spread of farming was not necessarily steady. He argues that there were pockets of resistance, in which the process of domestication was largely under the control of existing communities, and that these are represented by areas of survival of non-Indo-European languages, some of which lasted long enough to be recorded (e.g. Iberian and Etruscan) and others which are still extant today (e.g. Basque).

Both models have been severely criticised from different standpoints by a variety of other archaeologists. The most vocal objections to the 'Wave of Advance' model have not surprisingly come from those who favour a substantial Mesolithic contribution to the agricultural transition. At the general level, Dennell (1985) has questioned the ability of farmers to displace gatherer-hunters. He argues that early agricultural communities would have been extremely vulnerable to competition from the existing population: their fixed settlements could easily be attacked and standing crops destroyed and livestock killed or taken. Dennell further believes that analogies with modern colonisations which may provide a subconscious model for the spread of the Neolithic are inappropriate, as the population levels of early farming groups were too low to have a significant impact on the forest which sustained Mesolithic societies.

Zvelebil and Zvelebil (1988) have also put forward a series of specific objections: first, that in many areas of western and northern Europe there is a strong degree of continuity in some aspects of material culture (such as lithics) and a retention of important symbols (for example bears, water birds and fish); second, that the changes in physical anthropological appearance could result from shifts in diet rather than the replacement of the native population by incoming farmers, and that the genetic patterns outlined by Ammerman and Cavalli-Sforza and others (Sokal *et al.* 1991) need not relate to the Neolithic; third, that the process of the adoption of agriculture is much more slow moving than the 'Wave of Advance' model would predict; fourth, that it underestimates the gatherer-hunter population. Ammerman (1989) defends his model against Zvelebil by pointing to the case of Italy, where there seems to be a sharp break with the introduction of the Neolithic and a lack of pre-existing Mesolithic sites.

It is surely significant, as Zvelebil notes (1989), that Ammerman and he chose their examples from completely different regions of Europe. While Ammerman stresses southeast and central Europe and the Mediterranean, Zvelebil draws most of his examples from the north and west. This certainly suggests that while some movement of agriculturalists from Anatolia westwards or northwards is widely accepted, there is far less agreement concerning the more peripheral areas (e.g. Zvelebil 1986). The overall 'Wave of Advance' model is undoubtedly damaged by the criticism it has received. The nature of much of the evidence is far less clear than Ammerman and Cavalli-Sforza evidently believe, with only an arguable connection to the spread of agriculture. The findings of physical anthropologists are particularly susceptible to different interpretations, as suggestions of a change in the dominant physical type can be happily accommodated within either a traditional model of population replacement (e.g. Vencl 1986) or one of dietary and lifestyle changes. This latter process has been documented for twentieth-century Japan, with a shift to a much more bracycephalic population taking only some forty years (Kouchi 1986). Equally, as various commentators including Renfrew (1987: 158) have noted, the genetic distribution patterns used as supporting evidence by Ammerman and Cavalli-Sforza could have much more recent origins than the Neolithic (Zvelebil 1986; Donahue 1992). The only possible resolution of this question will be through the analysis of surviving genetic material from Neolithic specimens in order to rule out later population movements.

The most significant criticism of the 'Wave of Advance' model is that the apparent smooth forward movement of an agricultural economy across Europe is simply an illusion brought about by the imprecision of the available chronology, which allows the data to be formed into such a steady state progression. As Dennell (1992) has most recently pointed out, the greater the degree of chronological resolution obtained, the more it seems as though the spread of agriculture was a series of leaps forward separated by lengthy periods of standstill. In many areas of the Mediterranean there appear to be relatively small pockets of agriculturalists whose farming lifestyle spread only very slowly into surrounding areas. Elsewhere, such as the Iron Gates region, there are good grounds for suggesting that groups of gatherer-hunters maintained a non-agricultural economy long after coming into contact with communities using domesticated crops and animals.

The most vehement criticisms of Renfrew's vision of Proto-Indo-European-speaking agricultural colonists have come from the community of archaeologists actively considering Indo-European language spread. Mallory (1989) has extensively reviewed Renfrew's thesis and found it unconvincing. His primary objection is to the proposed Neolithic Anatolian homeland: first, it is clear that the earliest written sources (from the third millennium BC) document non-Indo-European populations occupying central and eastern Anatolia (Mallory 1989: 64, 178), making it difficult to see this as a centre from which agriculture spread. Instead, the evidence points to the relatively late arrival of Indo-European speakers in the region. Second, there are almost no Semitic loan words in Indo-European languages, suggesting a lack of contact which is difficult to imagine given the established Semitic presence in Anatolia (Mallory 1989: 150). Renfrew's Anatolian homeland has found little support, which fatally undermines the case for the spread of Proto-Indo-European languages occurring as early as the Mesolithic–Neolithic transition; to accept any other region as the homeland would strongly imply that the process had no real connection with the adoption of an agricultural economy.

The other great difficulty in Renfrew's theory is that such an early date for the spread of Proto-Indo-European produces considerable problems in dealing with those areas which did not adopt Indo-European languages, retaining non-Indo-European tongues such as Etruscan, Basque, Ligurian, Iberian, Tartessian and Pictish (Zvelebil and Zvelebil 1990). To explain their resistance to the trend, Renfrew (1987: 267) suggests that these territories were occupied by vigorous native populations of gatherer-hunters who held on to their identity for a considerable time before adopting a farming economy. However, while the Basque country of Spain may fit such a model, the same can hardly be said of Etruria, which had a substantial agricultural presence before 5000 BC. In general, there is no clear relationship between regions which were late in adopting agriculture and those where non-Indo-European languages survived sufficiently long to be recorded.

While a number of writers agree that LBK communities may have spoken Proto-Indo-European (e.g. Makkay 1987; Zvelebil and Zvelebil 1990), this need not mean that the remainder of Europe saw the transmission of the language in the Early Neolithic as well. Zvelebil and Zvelebil (1990) argue that the further spread west and north of Indo-European languages did not take place until the fourth millennium BC. A more radical alternative approach is the suggestion that no population movement need be proposed to explain the current distribution of Indo-European languages. Following Trubetskoy, it could be argued that contacts between neighbouring languages produced a series of changes in them which led eventually to them becoming Indo-European (e.g. Hodder 1990: 303–4; Robb 1993). This alternative mechanism has not yet been fully explored by archaeologists, but it may offer at least a partial solution, given that the most recent thorough survey of the evidence (Mallory 1989) comes to the conclusion that none of the suggested theories for the dating of the transmission of Proto-Indo-European are at all satisfactory.

3

THE ATLANTIC FRINGE

THE NEOLITHIC AFTER THE LBK

The LBK was succeeded by a variety of regional pottery traditions (Bogucki and Grygiel 1993). In eastern Germany and Poland it gave way first to *Stichband-keramik* (SBK) by 4700 BC, then around 4400 BC Rössen material appears across eastern France (replacing the Cerny group) and Germany and Lengyel material in Poland. These LBK successors continue until *c.* 4200–4100 when the *Trichterrandbecher* (Funnel-Necked Beaker) or TRB emerges across large areas of northern Europe and regional groups such as Michelsberg in the Rhineland and Chasséen in the Paris Basin.

What is the significance of these developments over the course of a millennium? Pottery changed from being highly decorated and regionally distinctive to being mostly plain. The plain pottery bowls were very similar across the whole area concerned, perhaps providing a common medium of expression, for at the same time the economy became more variable, with settlement dispersal and a greater use of wild resources (Thomas 1988a). Longhouses change in shape, becoming longer and clearly trapezoidal, with the entrance at the wider end and in some instances the creation of a separate entrance hall (Hodder 1990: 121). In some areas longhouses later disappear altogether, so that a number of late Rössen sites such as Berry-au-Bac in the Aisne Valley of France have small rectangular post-built houses (Bogucki and Grygiel 1993). Cemeteries near occupation sites continue to be the norm, while settlement burials are also quite common (Whittle 1985: 200). The most significant development in burial practice is undoubtedly the emergence of both earthen long barrows and megalithic tombs in the fifth millennium BC (see pp. 48–62). Enclosures are also constructed, again in some instances with substantial earthworks and surrounding settlements and in others of a more nominal character, although it appears that in general the significance of creating fixed boundaries between insiders and outsiders was increasing (Whittle 1988a).

A detailed consideration of the importance of these interlinked developments has been put forward by Hodder (1990: 119–40). He suggests that there was, through time, an increasing emphasis on the entrance of longhouses at the expense of rear and internal areas of the structure, while the walls became more solid. This served to stress the boundary between the inside and the outside of the longhouse. Compared to LBK longhouses he argues that later examples look outwards to the wider community, but also exclude it. The increase in the size of the buildings he attributes to larger households being formed, related to success in subsistence production, feast giving and marriage exchange (1990: 123). The longhouse itself would here be a statement in wood of the power of the household to organise labour and appropriate nature.

Hodder also suggests that the household was extended to cover the larger group by enclosing settlements (1990: 124–5). This meant the playing out of social competition on a larger stage and the drawing of social boundaries around the community as a whole. At later sites there is a tendency to deposit 'rubbish' further from the longhouse, until at sites such as Berry-au-Bac it is placed in a substantial ditch around the settlement as a whole. Other enclosures do not contain settlement debris; here their large size and multiple entrances suggest to Hodder that they were communal structures serving several groups. The multiple rings of enclosing ditches and palisade lines strongly emphasise the desire to separate the inside from the outside. As with the longhouses there is a sense of movement through socially significant space (Hodder 1990: 128); in both cases the 'deepest', most private, space was that furthest from the public entrance.

Hodder may perhaps overemphasise the common features, for the significant difference between the two situations lies in the apparent necessity for retracing movements in the case of the longhouses, whereas a series of different routes could be taken to and from the centre of the enclosure. The multiple rings of entrances through the various lines of enclosure also open up the possibility of different levels of access being allowed to different individuals or groups. The use of palisades may also have been significant in denying visual access to activities being carried out at the centre of the enclosure, something hinted at by Midgley *et al.* (1993). The possibility clearly existed with the creation of larger communal monuments for exclusion from access to become a powerful sanction and for controlling that access to be an important source of social standing.

We shall return later to the question of how far this shift to a wider outlook may have impacted on relations with contemporary groups of gatherer-hunters to the west and north. In some areas, such as western France, there were significant movements of the agricultural frontier in the fifth millennium BC, but in northern Europe this was not the case. To assess the meaning of these differences we need to return to the examination of non-agricultural communities.

THE NORTHERN FRINGE

The potential significance of the northern area of the Atlantic fringe is obvious from the chronology of the spread of agriculture. By 5300 BC there were LBK communities in the lowlands of northern Poland and northeast Germany some distance off the loess (Bogucki and Grygiel 1993), only 100 km from the Baltic coast. Yet a millennium later there were still thriving gatherer-hunter communities not only on the Baltic but also inland, with whom the farming groups to the south had regular contact, as seen by the movement of exchange items.

The first of these gatherer-hunter communities to be considered is the site of Hüde I am Dümmer in northern Germany on the shore of the large Dümmersee lake (Kampffmeyer 1983; Fansa and Kampffmeyer 1985). The earlier phase of activity at the site, dating from c. 5200–4600 BC, produced sherds of large pointed-base vessels along with a wild animal bone assemblage. The pottery shows strong similarities in decoration to Rössen material which would have been in use only a short distance away, but in technique it clearly resembles gatherer-hunter pottery traditions and only a relatively small percentage of the vessels were decorated. The uppermost level of the site has produced Funnel-Necked Beakers and a possible building. Wild animals are apparently predominant, but there is an increase in domestic fauna towards the top of the archaeological deposits. Although carbonised grain and cereal impressions on pottery were found, Kampffmeyer (1983) argued that there is no clear evidence for cereal cultivation at the settlement itself. The site appears to have been seasonal in use, with other related settlements perhaps to be found in the Dammer Berge hill region to the west of the Dümmer basin, which ceramic analyses point to as a possible source for the clays in the Hude I pottery (Kampffmeyer 1983).

It is difficult to take the analysis of the Dümmersee area much further given such a limited database. To the north and northeast of the Dümmer basin, on the North European Plain in northern Germany and Poland and up into Schleswig-Holstein are large numbers of Late Mesolithic sites of the Ellerbek group (Schwabedissen 1981). These show contacts with farming groups and with those foragers living around the Dümmersee to the south, and with gatherer-hunter groups – both to the southwest in Holland and with Ertebølle communities in Jutland and Zealand to the north. The evidence takes various forms including ceramics, bone and antler tools, the lithic industry and domesticated crops and animals.

The widespread nature of the Ellerbek group is emphasised by the discovery of related material in Poland (Midgley 1992: 11; Bogucki and Grygiel 1993) dating to the fifth millennium BC, although little detail is yet established concerning the economic standing and cultural connections of the sites involved. To the west, in Mecklenburg, Ellerbek material appeared around 4600 BC, where it is known as the Lietzow group (Midgley 1992: 11). On the island of Rügen in the Baltic off Mecklenburg SBK pottery and Lengyel-style bone ornaments show potentially long-lived contacts with agriculturalists to the south (M. Larsson 1988).

For a fuller evidential basis we have to turn to northern Germany and Schleswig-Holstein. The site of Rosenhof (Schwabedissen 1967) lies near the Baltic coast of Holstein by a former inlet; excavations have produced large numbers of pointed-base vessels similar to Ertebølle examples and antler T-axes similar to those of Lengyel agricultural groups in Poland (Bogucki 1988: 155), showing connections in both directions and with both economic regimes. Four major Ellerbek sites have been found inland around the edge of Satrup Moor, dating to *c.* 4900–4700 BC (Schwabedissen 1967). At two of these, Südensee-Damm and Pöttmoor, an early TRB level overlies the Ellerbek settlement, although there was not direct continuity of occupation, as the two are separated by a sterile layer which must have built up over several hundred years. Contacts with farmers are shown by the presence of Rössen-type shaft-hole axes.

There is a certain amount of evidence which has been used to argue that exchanges between Ellerbek gatherer-hunters and agriculturalist groups included the knowledge required to domesticate crops and animals, and that the Ellerbek economy was one of primitive farming. It has been suggested that cereal pollen extracted from soil profiles at the Satrup Moor sites (which may also show some clearance activity) and at Rosenhof predates the TRB phase of the sites and there-fore shows Ellerbek cereal cultivation (Schwabedissen 1967; 1972). However, this kind of indirect evidence is the source of considerable disagreement in both Scandinavia and the British Isles, and the possibility of the movement of pollen grains down through the soil profile from the overlying Neolithic layers is evidently a possibility here, while Zvelebil and Rowley-Conwy (1984) note the difficulties of identifying these pollen grains as cereals rather than grasses. A firmer piece of evidence is a cereal grain impression on a sherd from Rosenhof: however, given that in the same level there were imported Michelsberg vessels it may well be that some actual grain was brought to the site through exchange rather than being cultivated there.

There are a small number of animal bones and teeth which have been identified as coming from domestic cattle. Once again, Zvelebil and Rowley-Conwy (1984) have noted the problems of secure identifications, and also suggest that if the Ellerbek economy was semi-agricultural in nature there should be far more domestic animal bones than the handful found so far. Rowley-Conwy (1985) has interpreted these scattered finds as the result of acquisition through exchange or through the capture of escaped animals. In the latter case they might not even have been treated as domesticated by the Ellerbek groups concerned. While it has in the past been possible to doubt the association between the claimed domestic animal bones and the Ellerbek material this concern has been laid to rest by the direct dating of a domestic cattle bone from Rosenhof (Hedges *et al.* 1993) to *c.* 4850 BC. Whatever the interpretation of these individual finds they clearly confirm the obvious conclusion that agriculture and its products must have been well known to Ellerbek communities. Bokelmann (in Hedges *et al.* 1995) has concluded from the results of accelerator dating on sherds from Boberg (*c.* 4200–4100 BC) that Ellerbek groups of gatherer-hunters may have continued in existence in inland areas even after the first agricultural groups were established on the coast of Schleswig-Holstein. He suggests that the landscape was thus being used by two communities with a different way of life, at least for a short time. Given the imprecise nature of radiocarbon dates it is, however, just as reasonable to interpret the Boberg dates as showing that the transition to an agricultural economy was an extremely rapid event.

A hint of material which may have been moving in the opposite direction comes from the well at Kückhoven in Germany (Weiner 1994). In a layer dated to between 5089 and 5067 BC by dendrochronology, fragments from a bowstave were found (see Figure 3.1): in both the use of elm wood and its shape the Kückhoven bowstave closely resembles examples from Late Mesolithic Denmark, particularly that from the underwater site of Tybrind Vig (Andersen 1985). Weiner therefore concludes that this item may well have been made by local gatherer-hunters in northern Germany. Other possibilities include skins and furs.

One major interrelated topic of debate which needs to be set in this context is the origin of earthen long barrows, which appear during the TRB in the Kujavian lowlands of Poland (Midgley 1985: 215–16) and spread from there to Germany, Holland, Scandinavia and Britain. Discussion has centred around the issue of the relationship between earlier Neolithic longhouses and the long mound burial tradition. The use of LBK houses as the source of inspiration

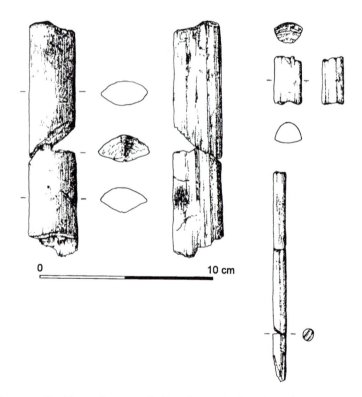

Figure 3.1 Kückhoven bowstave (left) and arrowshaft (right) (after Weiner 1994)

behind long mounds has been widely aired since the time of Piggott (1967), and given detailed treatment by Reed (1974) and Marshall (1981).

The most sustained recent examination of the theory has been by Hodder (1984; 1990: 145–56). In his original (1984) presentation he put forward several points of similarity between longhouses and long mounds (see Figures 3.2 and 3.3):

1 The construction involved the use of continuous bedding trenches and/or lines of posts.
2 They share a rectangular or trapezoidal shape.
3 The entrance is at the broader end in the case of trapezoidal structures.
4 The axes are generally aligned west–east or northwest–southeast.
5 The entrances often face southeast.
6 They have elaborated entrances.
7 They have internal divisions of space.
8 They are internally decorated.
9 They have ditches along the sides.

Hodder has himself (1990: 151) expressed doubts concerning the last two points, as later western longhouses show little sign of internal decoration and lack associated ditches. He would now add to the first seven points the tendency for longhouses and long mounds to occur in clusters (Bogucki 1987) and the suggestion that long mounds were on occasion deliberately sited over old settlements (Midgley 1985: 161). Some of the nine points Hodder now accepts could also be questioned, such as the shared feature of internal spatial divisions: it could be argued that this is likely to be a feature of any large structure with a communal use; also one may wonder if part of the reason for settlement traces being found under long mounds is that they have been preserved from destruction by the presence of the covering mound. Nevertheless, the observations do seem to represent a real pattern of resemblance which requires an explanation.

In his original formulation of the idea, Hodder (1984) argued that the underlying motive for the construction of long mounds as symbolic longhouses was to control women as reproducers. Women were thus celebrated as the source and focus of the lineage group in the context of the house of the ancestors, where the community was stressed and differences submerged in the common inheritance. Thus competing claims to resources, particularly land and livestock, could be restricted by devaluing the domestic in favour of the ritual sphere. In his more recent consideration of the subject, Hodder (1990) tactfully avoids discussion of his old model. Presumably, he finds it too specific an interpretation, given that there is very little evidence which one can point to of women being celebrated in the context of long mounds. For example, the earliest long mounds, those of Kujavia in Poland (Midgley 1985), show a preponderance of individual male burials with mace-heads: hardly a demonstration of the significance of female reproduction.

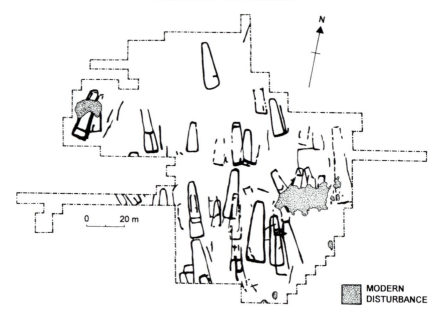

Figure 3.2 Longhouses at Breść Kujawski (after Bogucki 1988)

Hodder (1990: 153–4) has therefore now adopted a much more general approach to the problem, suggesting that, rather than direct copying, what was involved was a continuity in certain principles to be followed when major structures were built. These were monumentality and the linear ordering of space. Both the longhouse and the long mound involved a substantial effort of turning nature into culture, which would have involved the participation of several households, thus providing a new definition of the households which had joined together to define a new social group. The linear ordering of space represented at both kinds of site was particularly concerned with the entrance, and presumably distance from the entrance. The overall relationship between the two is that they both express Hodder's concept of the *domus* in a particular form of the domestication of the wild and of society.

Is this far more generalised model an improvement on the earlier highly specific one? As Hodder himself notes (1990: 154), the broadening of the link between longhouses and long mounds would mean that a connection could also be drawn between the circular mound passage graves of the Atlantic and longhouses because they are both monumental and both display a linear grading of internal space. He also concedes (1990: 152–3) that long mounds and megalithic burial are not a single unified phenomenon, but suggests that individual links need to be drawn in different areas (e.g. Midgley 1985: 215). Whittle (1988b: 165) accepts the general validity of the longhouse – long mound connection but considers it to be part of a more complex picture. He emphasises

50

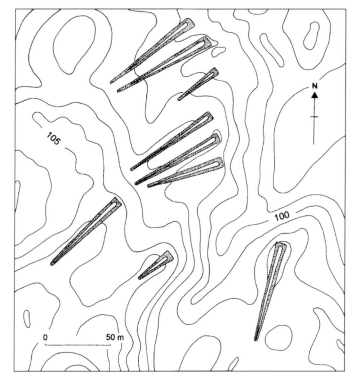

Figure 3.3 Group of long barrows at Sarnowo, Poland (after Midgley 1992); contours at metre intervals

the variety in early burial mound form and the presence of regions within the area of LBK settlement which did not see the development of monumental burial traditions until later, after a switch away from cemeteries to small mounds and settlement burials.

Turning Hodder's argument round, one could ask why enclosures are not part of this discussion. They too are monumental in character, and also show a definite grading of space, which Hodder refers to as linear. The shift in expression could then be towards a combination of the house and the enclosure in the form of a tomb. The difference seems to be that Hodder sees enclosures as communal monuments by definition, while long mounds relate to the individual household. However, he himself notes that the construction of long mounds was probably a communal undertaking, given the size of the task and the evidence for lines of stakes dividing the mound area into sections. One could also argue, as has been suggested above, that there is no reason to assume that the enclosures were equally open to all members of the community. The assumption of control over communal rituals in enclosures could well have its counterpart in the individual burials below early long mounds. The lasting significance of the long mounds seems to be as monuments which endured in the landscape, taking on perhaps an enhanced significance through time as settlement had become more dispersed and ephemeral. It may have become a permanent household of the ancestors, in some cases situated within a village of the dead, a fixed point in the cultural landscape of those living within its territory (Sherratt 1990).

Returning to consideration of the agricultural advance across Europe, the major question must be why there was this long halt in the onward transmission of an agricultural economy. For more than a thousand years the agricultural frontier barely moved. As Zvelebil and Dolukhanov (1991) point out, this can hardly have been for economic reasons: the frontier runs across a relatively uniform geographical area, and the soils as far north as southern Scandinavia are in many places light and fertile and thus eminently suitable for cultivation.

An explicitly social interpretation has been presented by Julian Thomas (1988a), who suggests that the TRB/Michelsberg/Chasséen represented a 'New' Neolithic in which social relationships, productive technology, monuments and prestige items were all linked together at an ideological level in a single conceptual package. He argues that the adoption of particular elements of the farming economy such as pottery, domesticated animals, or shaft-hole axes did not mean that gatherer-hunter groups became agriculturalists. He thus rejects the view (e.g. Zvelebil and Rowley-Conwy 1986) that the adoption of such elements placed communities on a slippery slope to becoming agriculturalists, one which allowed no turning back. Instead, the process of becoming Neolithic involved the transformation of social relations of production, thereby developing a Neolithic lifestyle. This 'New' Neolithic could therefore be adopted by indigenous gatherer-hunter communities where the 'Old' LBK Neolithic could not. A similar interpretation has been proposed by Hodder (1990: 182), who sees the changes in Neolithic societies in terms of a move away from the *domus* concept of nurturing based on the household towards a social and economic system in which dispersed settlement, exchange, defence and warfare were key elements. These he encompasses within the *agrios* concept of the wild outside the household.

By contrast, Zvelebil and Dolukhanov (1991) suggest that the reasons for the delay must lie in the nature of late Mesolithic society, with those communities consciously rejecting change (Whittle 1988b: 198). They argue that the gatherer-hunter groups of the North European Plain up to the Baltic were more populous, more permanently settled and more socially complex than those of central Europe encountered by LBK farming immigrants. They conclude that the TRB, which represented the first major shift in the agricultural frontier, must therefore represent a result of fusion between local Mesolithic and Neolithic groups, with gatherer-hunters forming the majority element in most places. The role of hunting remained important, with wild animals often representing over 50 per cent of the animal bones from sites (Bogucki 1987). While Thomas's and Hodder's emphasis on the social aspects of the transition to agriculture is important, their models do not fully account for the changes within the Neolithic and certainly cannot explain why gatherer-hunters should have chosen to adopt a Neolithic economy, even if it was now more similar to their own. Once ideas of farmer colonists are abandoned any interpretation must account for the motivation of both parties.

THE NORTHWEST FRINGE

The Rhine–Maas delta represents an unusual kind of estuarine environment on the North European Plain, one where there were, in addition to the standard lowland forest and riverine resources, also very extensive marshlands, tidal flats and peat bogs (Bogucki 1988: 159). The earliest signs of agricultural activity come from settlements in the peat zone on floating peat islands or along the banks of estuarine tidal creeks.

The Swifterbant dunes area by the later Ijssel valley in Holland has been the scene of intensive work during the last three decades, with well over fifty sites having been discovered (see Figure 3.4). The Swifterbant sites can be grouped into three main phases: around 5700 BC, 5150–5000 BC and *c.* 4300–4100 BC. There has been considerable debate concerning the ceramics found on a number of sites, with an apparent association between a radiocarbon dated hearth (*c.* 5100 BC) and pottery at Swifterbant site S23 leading Price (1981) to conclude that an aceramic phase around 5700 BC was succeeded by a ceramic phase *c.* 5100 BC. Others, however, have argued that the ceramics derive from the much later phase of activity after 4300 BC. The application of radiocarbon

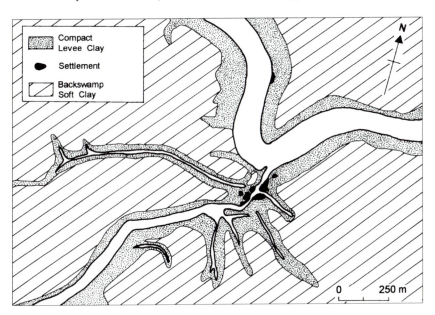

Figure 3.4 Location of Swifterbant sites (after Barker 1985)

accelerator technology has allowed an advance in our understanding of the pottery chronology, with the direct dating of encrusted material on sherds. At Bronnegar a vessel has recently been dated to *c.* 4700 BC using this method (Louwe Kooijmans 1993).

The later Swifterbant sites from *c.* 4300 BC onwards occupied an area alongside creeks running into larger channels, after a period of rising sea levels. At Swifterbant site S3 a broad range of animal bone remains were recovered. The main domestic species were cattle and pigs, along with dogs, while wild red deer, elk, aurochs, brown bear, otter, beaver, polecat and horse were found together with a wide range of birds (including cormorant, mute swan, crane and white-tailed eagle) and fish (both estuarine and seasonally estuarine species, such as salmon, sturgeon, gray mullet and the large catfish). Zeiler (1991) argues that the variety of domesticated cattle body parts shows that they were kept and slaughtered locally. Plant remains were also abundant, with wild apples, blackberries, hawthorn, rose hips, hazelnuts, cultivated naked barley and a little emmer wheat. The presence of cereal chaff and internodes as well as grain has led to suggestions that cereals were cultivated locally (van Zeist and Palfenier-Vegter 1981), although the nearest fields would have been at least a kilometre away.

The pottery of these later Swifterbant sites was still in the pointed-base S-profile tradition, while their flintwork also continued earlier traditions, although artefactual contacts with agriculturalists are seen with the presence of shaft-hole axes (Whittle 1985: 130). One other factor which tends to be over-looked by those primarily interested in the economic evidence is the burial record of these sites (Louwe Kooijmans 1987). At S3 human skeletal remains were found mixed with domestic 'rubbish', but at S2 and other sites there were definite small cemeteries. These contain an equal number of women and men and also children.

To the south of the Swifterbant dunes and creeks is the site of Bergschenhoek (Louwe Kooijmans 1976), dating to *c.* 4200 BC, located on a peat island among freshwater lakes and swamps. This has yielded a very wide range of fish, including eel, perch, carp, roach, bream, tench and the large catfish, which were caught in traps, the remains of which have been excavated. Birds were also heavily exploited, and mallard, tufted duck, bittern, swans, goosander and widgeon were all eaten. By contrast, the mammal element is limited to aquatic species such as seal and otter. No domesticated plants have been recovered either, with wild species including apples, hazelnuts and blackthorn being recovered from environmental samples.

Further inland is Hazendonk Site I (Louwe Kooijmans 1987), dating to *c.* 4200 BC, situated on a small river dune. Here domesticated cattle, pig and dog were present from the earliest phases. Clear links with the Michelsberg agricultural group are seen in the later Hazendonk pottery, which consists of plain bowls, following a phase in which the pottery and flintwork are similar to that from Swifterbant. Also found were large quantities of carbonised grain as well as chaff and internodes. Unlike Swifterbant S3, this has not been interpreted in terms of local grain cultivation, but instead the lack of surrounding dry land has led Bakels (personal communication cited by Bogucki 1988: 159) to conclude that the grain was brought to the site from the outside. Louwe Kooijmans (1987) has also applied this interpretation to Swifterbant. Zeiler (1991) has argued that for Swifterbant Site 3 to have seen the cultivation of cereals, most of the area of high ground occupied by the site would have had to be turned over to fields, so the grain must have been imported. He suggests that the exports could have been fish and also furs, as the cutmarks and signs of burning on beaver and otter bones from S3 show they were hunted for both meat and fur.

The variety in site types has been interpreted in economic terms as reflecting the difference between seasonal and permanent habitation. Louwe Kooijmans (1987) interprets Hazendonk and Bergschenhoek as seasonal camps because of their size and environmental setting. The Swifterbant sites, especially S3, stand out from this pattern by their larger size, thick occupation layer, clay hearths (periodically renewed) and posthole and stakehole arrangements. These factors all point to more permanent activity, although the lack of definite winter species does mean that they could have been annually reoccupied, as has been argued for the Iron Gorge sites on the Danube (see Chapter 2), rather than being year-round settlements. The development of cemeteries at the Swifterbant sites also points to a degree of social as well as economic attachment to those specific culturally laden places in the landscape.

These Rhine–Maas sites do appear to represent a transitional agricultural stage, with domestic animals and access to domesticated plants, with continuity from the local Mesolithic leading to the general conclusion that they represent the adoption by local gatherer-hunter groups of some elements of farming without this bringing about major changes in their economy or society (e.g. Bogucki 1988: 161). We should not, however, underestimate the importance of the links visible at the Swifterbant sites with gatherer-hunter practices to the north in the pottery, which is remarkably similar and possibly also the development of settlement burial, although this may have been a legacy of contact with agriculturalists along with the domesticates and the axes. In any case there is little sign of Thomas's (1988a) Neolithic lifestyle. Hazendonk phase 2 appears to represent a better claim for a special-purpose agriculturalist camp, as it is further inland and shares pottery types with farming communities.

Traditional interpretations have seen the introduction of the TRB into northern Holland (the western limit of the TRB) and Michelsberg into southern Holland as representing an immigration of newcomers, but Hogestun (1990) and Louwe Kooijmans (1993) have raised the idea that, as suggested for the north (see above), the long hiatus in the forward movement of an agricultural economy may finally have been ended by the transformation of Neolithic society into something more akin to that of gatherer-hunters. As Wansleeben and Verhart (1990) have noted, the loess is quite empty during the Michelsberg period and instead the overall settlement pattern is much more like that of the

Mesolithic, while the subsistence economy becomes far wider. This leads to the conclusion that here too there was an adjustment in Neolithic society to a less agricultural economy which was brought about by contacts with gatherer-hunter groups and the visible reluctance and lack of necessity for those communities to adopt a farming economy.

THE WESTERN FRINGE

The Mesolithic of Brittany has been the subject of much discussion, although there is in fact a distinct shortage of evidence by comparison with Holland, particularly from recent excavations. Normandy, to the east, is also implicated in discussions of the development of an agricultural economy on the Atlantic façade, but has even less in the way of pre-Neolithic archaeology.

The late gatherer-hunter sites of Brittany are coastal shell middens of the mid-sixth millennium BC, which show the exploitation of fish and shellfish, and the hunting of birds and game animals such as red and roe deer and pig (Bender 1985). They are particularly well known for the large number of burials located at Téviec (Péquart *et al.* 1937) and Hoèdic (Péquart and Péquart 1954): twenty-three were found at Téviec and fourteen at Hoèdic (see Figure 3.5). Men, women and children were all buried. They were interred in stone-lined cists, which in the most elaborate examples were then covered by further stones which had fires set on them, then animal jaw bones placed, finally being covered by small stone cairns. The graves sometimes contain multiple burials, of up to six individuals, with the earlier burials showing signs of rearrangement. The range of grave goods included engraved deer antler pieces, bone pins, flint blades, ochre and perforated shells. The shells were worn as bracelets, necklaces and diadems, mainly by those in the 14–30 age range (Taborin 1974). Males wore more bracelets than women, and are found with the *Trivia europea* species, while women are accompanied by *Littorina obtusata* shells. The apparent variation in grave goods has led Testart (1982: 135) to suggest the existence of a social hierarchy, but the burial evidence in itself is insufficient to support such claims. These midden sites show a degree of permanence of settlement; the accumulations of material may represent feasting debris, which would provide an element of social competition which could have led to the emergence of social differences (Thomas and Tilley 1994).

The occasional finds of domesticated sheep at Téviec and cattle at Hoèdic and Beg-an-Dorchenn (dating to the fifth millennium BC) have led to suggestions of a pastoral element in the economy (L'Helgouach 1971). These are, however, only a handful of teeth and bones and their attribution to domesticated species has at times been called into question (Zvelebil and Rowley-Conwy 1986).

The earliest Neolithic of western France has long been the subject of a vigorous debate between those who favour an eastern origin, deriving from inland France, and those who propose a southern origin in the Cardial Impressed Ware Neolithic complex of southern France. By 5000 BC the Rubané Recent variant of

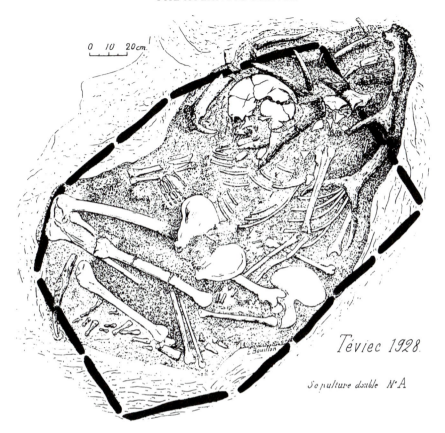

Figure 3.5 Double burial from Téviec with antlers (from Péquart *et al.* 1937)

the late LBK was present in the Paris Basin and Cardial Ware along the Atlantic coast, so influences at that date could have derived from either direction. Behind this debate lurks a division within French archaeology itself (Scarre 1992), between those based in Paris, who largely favour the eastern model, and locals, who tend to support the southern theory.

Are there perceptible farming influences on the Mesolithic coastal sites discussed above? The scattered finds of domestic sheep remains have been argued by Scarre (1992) to show southern contacts, as the earliest Neolithic in the Paris Basin is *c.* 5100 BC, and thus too late to be a source, and the southern French Cardial group concentrated on sheep rearing. However, given the occasional nature of the finds, and the lack of increase in domesticates through time, it may be that this shows only sporadic and relatively inconsequential contacts in any case.

Tied in with the question of the sources of influence on the earliest Neolithic of western France is the debate over the origin of megaliths and burial in chambered tombs. Megaliths emerge during the fifth millennium BC, although precisely when is much debated, and provide much of the material evidence for the first Neolithic of the area as well as virtually all the radiocarbon dates. We shall first attempt to trace the chronology and cultural associations of the primary Neolithic and the earliest monuments before turning to explanations of the development of megaliths on the Atlantic façade.

The earliest Neolithic of Brittany has traditionally been seen as the Carn group, defined by undecorated bowls and by early passage graves. This would represent a local response in the early fifth millennium BC to the introduction of the 'Neolithic package', as neither the pottery styles nor the associated monuments have parallels in final LBK or final Cardial. The Carn group appears to be linked to a larger Atlantic complex, including such groups as the Groupe du Cous of west central France, best known for the early passage grave at Bougon in Poitou (Scarre *et al.* 1993). However, there has been a recent shift in thinking which places the Castellic style as the earliest Neolithic pottery assemblage (e.g. Cassen 1993; Patton 1993: 37–45; Patton 1994). This is found below simple passage graves (e.g. La Table des Marchands) and below layers containing Carn pottery (e.g. at Sandun).

The connections of Castellic material seem to be with the Paris Basin, as Cassen suggests (1993), while Patton (1994) also links it with the Pinacle/Fouillages group of the Channel Islands. Patton (1994) supports this connection by citing the close similarities in form and decorative techniques between the three groups. Scarre (1992) has, however, raised doubts concerning the claimed links, on the basis of the evidence from Dissignac, where Cerny or Castellic pottery was found in an old land surface below a passage grave along with microliths and charcoal which provides three radiocarbon dates which range between 5100 and 4600 BC. These are earlier than Paris Basin Cerny, which starts after 4500 BC, so Scarre wondered if it might not be appropriate to look southwards. Patton (1994) quite reasonably counters Scarre's doubts by pointing to the dubious nature of the association between the radiocarbon dated charcoal and the pottery, which he also argues is difficult to classify. Patton's case is strengthened when one considers that the earliest date from the tomb itself is *c.* 3800 BC, allowing a considerable time-span after the last pre-tomb date in which the pottery could have been deposited. Certainly the strong similarities between the Castellic material and that to the north and east are difficult to gainsay.

The discovery of primary Neolithic material in megalithic tombs means that the spread of agriculture into western France has become identified with the debate over the source of these impressive monuments. The oldest theory of the origin of megaliths was that they represented the spread of religious cult by megalithic missionaries or the physical manifestation of the religious beliefs of Neolithic colonists (e.g. Daniel 1958). This was, however, ruled out by the impact of radiocarbon dating, especially calibrated dates, which showed the Atlantic megaliths to be considerably earlier in date than their supposed Mediterranean forebears (Renfrew 1973).

This rejection of a Mediterranean inspiration for megaliths led to suggestions of a local origin. The presence of burials at both Téviec and Hoèdic shows that ideas of communal burial already existed among the gatherer-hunters of Brittany long before the emergence of megalithic structures, and the notion of a purely local development has therefore been mooted (e.g. Case 1976). L'Helgouach (1976) has interpreted the microliths found below and in the passage grave at Dissignac in terms of a Mesolithic date for this particular monument, but as we have seen there are reasons to suspect that the microliths may belong to a rather earlier occupation horizon disturbed by the construction of the tomb. Such suggestions of a Mesolithic date for megaliths, with the implication that they were constructed by gatherer-hunters, have met with little approval, as there is a general agreement that monuments represent a different approach to conceiving of places (Bradley 1993: 17). By physically marking the landscape in such a dramatic fashion the way in which it could be experienced by people in the future was fundamentally altered. In the case of burial monuments they placed the ancestors visibly in the landscape with the result that they became an integral part of future social developments. Presencing the ancestors in this way could also be used by the living as a way of demonstrating their rights to the territory they controlled (Chapman 1981). However, it is possible that such a relationship is not exclusive to the Neolithic (see Chapter 4).

Renfrew (1976) developed a model for the local origin of megaliths with several interlinked elements: first, that the diffusionist approach was ruled out by the dating evidence; second, that the megalithic tombs acted as territorial markers for segmentary societies which would otherwise lack a focal point; third, that megaliths developed along the Atlantic fringe because of a unique set of circumstances involving the high productivity of the area, the ease of seaborne communication and the lack of land to the west to absorb a growing population; fourth, that the actual trigger for construction was the territorial pressure exerted by the expansion of agricultural groups; fifth, that the form of megalithic tombs arose from the burials at Téviec and Hoèdic.

Recent work has thrown fresh light on the problem in terms of new discoveries, new dating evidence and different approaches. One of the most dramatic developments of Breton prehistory in recent years has been the discovery that a number of passage graves contain reused stelae with a suite of very different carvings to those usually encountered in the tombs themselves. At Gavrinis (Le Roux 1985) the uncovering of the top side of the chamber capstone revealed that it was part of a substantial carved stone, which joined with the capstone from La Table des Marchands and possibly with another capstone from the mound of Er Grad near Le Grand Menhir Brisé, both at Locmariaquer (see Figure 3.6). The carvings on this 14-metre high stela and another possible original stela are of cattle, sheep/goat, axe-ploughs and axes. As Kinnes and Hibbs (1989) have noted, these are clearly evocative of food production through the stages of clearance, cultivation and pasturing; the 'crook' motif could either relate to sheep grazing or be a representation of a cereal crop, but in either interpretation would also relate

2 m

0

Figure 3.6 Reconstruction of decorated Breton stela reused as capstones for Gavrinis, La Table des Marchands and Er Grad chambered tombs (after Le Roux 1985)

to a celebration of the introduction of agriculture to the area. These stelae would perhaps take their place in a cultural landscape together with the long mounds, although these are not well dated and may be contemporary with the passage graves (Patton 1991), as symbols of the new importance of territorial rights. A similar line of thought has been followed by Bradley (1990: 48–9), although with slightly different identifications of the carved motifs.

An equally significant development of the last decade has directed attention to a recently rather neglected possibility that the megaliths and long mounds of western France derive from central Europe. At Passy-sur-Yonne in Burgundy a series of long mounds with central European material and burial customs (especially single burial), situated next to a settlement with Cerny pottery, have been excavated (Duhamal and Presteau 1987). This has been used as a bridge between central Europe and the coast, with the next link in the chain being formed by the site of Les Fouillages on Guernsey (Kinnes 1982), dating to around 4800–4600 BC. Hodder (1990: 234–5) thus employs his longhouse model of the origin of long mounds, which were transformed into round mounds when they reached Brittany. He downplays the contribution of Téviec and Hoèdic, arguing that they are not monumental, and lack any emphasis on the linear grading of space and thus also orientation. Sherratt (1990) has developed a similar model, in which he proposes that the earliest monumental burial in western France consisted of long mounds covering wooden structures or small stone boxes, while passage graves may reflect the local use of round houses. A whole Neolithic package including monumental burial thus spread west alongside the agricultural economy.

Scarre (1992) has led the fightback for the Atlantic model. First, he has argued that the recent dates from the Bougon passage grave on bone from the primary layers (Scarre *et al.* 1993), which show the monument to have been in use by *c.* 4700 BC, confirm the older dates on charcoal from Barnenez and Ile Guennoc in Brittany. The case made by Boujet and Cassen (1993) for a date after 4100 BC for passage graves, with simple graves in long or trapezoidal mounds starting rather earlier, around 4500 BC, which involved a rejection of the existing dates for passage graves and the presentation of an evolutionary framework for the development of megaliths, thus seems to be decisively undermined. The use of well-contexted short-life samples for erecting dating frameworks is always preferable to the creation of evolutionary schemes which inevitably require some drastic simplifications to provide a chronology.

Scarre (1992) goes on to argue that if these dates of *c.* 4700 BC for early passage graves are accepted then they would predate examples in Normandy or the Paris Basin, so the direction of influences would flow from west to east, rather than east to west, which would have to be the case if an agriculturalist origin of the monuments was to be maintained. Scarre reiterates the significance of the Breton Mesolithic burial, which are the best Mesolithic antecedents for megalithic burial practice in any part of Europe. He also makes the telling point that there are equally early megalithic tombs in Iberia, which lies well away from any central European longhouses. Against the central European theory he points to the lack of evidence for multiple inhumations in either LBK or Cerny contexts, so the eastern contribution would be limited to the development of the idea of a mound covering burials.

Also taking the line of a local origin, Bradley (1990: 48–9) has suggested that Renfrew's (1976) model of population pressure could be applied to Brittany without the need to postulate an incursion of farming colonists. A rise in sea level which culminated around 4800 BC led to the loss of many of the more productive areas of coastline around the Gulf of Morbihan, while the soils inland were relatively unproductive. A purely local pressure on local resources leading to territoriality could therefore be postulated. Scarre (1992) also disagrees with Renfrew, although he prefers a vague model of a developing Atlantic regional burial tradition, in which the Portuguese shell middens with multiple burials may have provided the basis for the stone cairn with multiple chambers, while Brittany gave the practice of multiple burial.

The most recent approach to the problem is that of Patton (1994), who has developed a model which divides Brittany into two areas: Finistère in the west, with early passage graves, and Le Morbihan and the Côte du Nord, together with the Channel Islands, in the east, with Castellic/Pinacle/Fouillages pottery.

Patton suggests that the eastern communities were more willing to emulate some Neolithic elements and so adopted Castellic pottery and long mounds, while those in Finistère produced Carn pottery, with no close connection to the Paris Basin, and passage graves, a new monument type. He puts forward two reasons why this would be so: first, that there may have been sufficient resources for both fishers and farmers around the Gulf of Morbihan (directly contradicting Bradley 1990) to make a living without conflict, while that was not the case in Finistère; second, that the Mesolithic communities of the Morbihan were more complex, living in larger and more permanent groups, with competitive social relations, one facet of which may have been access to Neolithic exchange goods.

This model certainly has its strengths in that there does seem to be a clear difference between the two areas of Brittany, particularly in terms of their oldest monuments, but the reasons put forward to explain the diverging fate of the two areas are not convincing. As Patton himself admits, there is little evidence for the nature of Mesolithic social organisation apart from Téviec and Hoèdic, so the distinction may be more apparent than real. Also, in the absence of good data on Neolithic settlement, the model of two communities exploiting separate areas of the environment in the Morbihan is difficult to assess, but does not seem immediately plausible; no real evidence exists for a continuing presence of fishers after the adoption of agriculture elsewhere in the area. Much further work is needed on the earliest Neolithic settlement to decide how far this was actually Neolithic other than in the use of pottery. Some indications of early agriculture do exist (e.g. Gebhardt 1993), but they are extremely scattered – a legacy of the concentration of effort on monuments rather than the subsistence economy. The possibility must exist that final Mesolithic communities akin to those of northern and northwestern Europe existed in western France as well, but have yet to be identified as long as all pottery use is ascribed to agriculturalists.

4

THE AGRICULTURAL
TRANSITION IN SOUTHERN
SCANDINAVIA

Many of the themes already discussed will be considered again here with reference to the introduction of a farming mode of production into southern Scandinavia (Denmark and the provinces of Scania and Blekinge in Sweden – northern Scandinavia has a quite separate history of development [Nygaard 1989]). Here, however, there is a substantially greater body of evidence for the Late Mesolithic, although there are clear regional biases in coverage. This far larger data-base is unquestionably a product of the much longer interest in the Mesolithic. In the 1840s a vigorous debate began among archaeologists concerning the mounds of shells found on the Danish coast (S. H. Andersen 1987a): had they had been formed by natural or cultural factors? The special committee set up to examine the question quickly concluded that they were products of human action, and they were termed 'kitchen middens'. The potential of these sites for an integrated study of economy and society led to the excavation of a major example at Ertebølle in northern Jutland, which produced the definition of the Ertebølle culture, characterised by transverse arrowheads, flake axes, thick-walled pots and a gathering-hunting subsistence base (Madsen *et al.* 1900).

The kitchen middens, or shell middens, are still the focus of considerable research today, with programmes of excavation, including re-excavating Ertebølle itself (Andersen and Johansen 1986), examining questions of diet, seasonality and resources, social organisation and continuity into the Neolithic. If anything, the concentration of resources on shell middens has increased in recent times, since the discovery that in a number of cases the middens have associated ceme-teries (Albrethsen and Brinch Petersen 1976). We should, however, bear in mind two important factors: first, that these are, of course, coastal sites, and that it is highly likely that they are not a good guide to activities being carried out inland, although there was presumably considerable contact between communities in the two locations. Second, the distribution of shell middens was not continuous around the southern Scandinavian coast (L. Larsson 1990a); the lower salt content and cooler waters of the Baltic hampered mollusc growth, so they are missing from the east-facing coasts, while they are absent from the Atlantic coast as a result of subsequent erosion. The evidence from shell middens should not, therefore, be stretched to encompass southern Scandinavia as a whole.

SETTLEMENT AND ECONOMY

Any analysis of Ertebølle settlement and economy must, however, begin with the evidence from shell middens, as this is clearly the primary source of information. The earliest middens belong to the Late Kongemose culture, or the Early Ertebølle, and date to *c.* 5600–5100 BC. These are small compared with later examples, and are only found in North and East Jutland, not in Zealand or Sweden (S. H. Andersen 1987a). They are little known, as they generally survive only when covered by later more substantial middens. The shell middens of the fifth millennium BC are substantial affairs, with Ertebølle occupying an area of *c.* 140 m long and 6–20 m wide, with a volume of around 1500 m^3 and the nearby site of Bjørnsholm occupying an even larger area at 325 m long and 10–50 m wide (S. H. Andersen 1991).

The duration of occupation of many shell middens is quite considerable, the well-known Tybrind Vig underwater site off Fyn lasting throughout the whole Ertebølle period, from 5400–4000 BC (S. H. Andersen 1985). Such long-lived occupation is by no means unique, and even the smaller sites may have been the scene of human settlement for hundreds of years. This length of occupation would suggest that over the timescale which has to be envisaged a considerable mound of shells could have been built up by even a small community. S. H. Andersen (1987a) has therefore suggested that a couple of family groups could have been responsible for forming the middens, although this may well be a minimal figure, and need not have been constant through time, even perhaps changing seasonally. Bailey (1978) has argued that a group of forty may have gathered each year at the Meilgård shell midden in eastern Jutland. Careful excavation has enabled the steps by which the middens were built up to be reconstructed, showing that at Ertebølle itself, for example, a series of accumulations of shells occurred, up to 50 cm thick and 2–7 m^2, associated with hearths and layers of ash (Andersen and Johansen 1986). These do seem to be quite minor episodes of activity, involving only a relatively limited group of people if they were of any significant duration, although it is quite possible that several occurred in rapid succession or that simultaneous episodes of deposition were taking place close by on the midden.

The hearths and ash layers are virtually the only sign of settlement activity (apart from occasional hollows used for flintworking, as at Ertebølle [Andersen and Johansen 1986]) yet recovered by archaeologists from the shell middens, suggesting to some that the inhabitants must have lived elsewhere but engaged in the majority of their economic activities on the surface of the midden. Andersen and Johansen (1986) have suggested that the house may have been situated by the midden only to be covered by it as the midden spread further through time. Against this, one must wonder why the inhabitants allowed the house to be engulfed in this way if it was of significance to them, and why they didn't then take the step of constructing another house slightly further away. One would imagine that such a sequence would produce a whole series of houses preserved by the midden build-up. Heavy erosion of the area inland from the middens as a consequence of ploughing may hold part of the answer, but any houses would have had to be situated sufficiently far from the midden to avoid being protected by it.

There are indications from recent excavations that more definite signs of settlement structures may yet emerge from the shell middens. At Åle, near Bjørnsholm in northern Jutland, an Early Ertebølle hut with a stone-lined hearth has been reported (Andersen and Johansen 1988), containing a substantial occupation layer with flintwork and animal bones. At Lollikhuse, situated on a dried-up arm of Roskilde Fjord on Zealand, three large hollows contained fire-places, a concentration of bone-working debris and a flintknapping area (Brinch Petersen 1987); one of these sunken areas, containing a fireplace and a pit, has subsequently proved to be surrounded by postholes (Brinch Petersen 1990a). A rather different angle on the question of settlement evidence comes from Tybrind Vig (S. H. Andersen 1985), where the remains of lines of substantial posts and a cobbled surface running out from the site into the water were interpreted as a dock for beaching boats (two of which have been recovered – S. H. Andersen 1986a). This indicates a degree of importance and possibly permanence for the site, but also shows that Ertebølle communities could construct more substantial structures as required.

Rowley-Conwy (1983) has argued strongly that the Ertebølle communities occupying the shell midden sites were sedentary. This view is based primarily on the wide range of resources available throughout most of the year, and the degree to which they overlap. Local land animals would have been hunted, plants gathered and sea fish caught in summer and autumn; in the autumn eels congregate before returning to the sea and harp seals may also have been available; in the winter, a lean time for land resources, migrating and breeding sea mammals could be hunted and migratory birds snared; the spring would have been the low point, and then oysters were to be had. He concluded that the larger middens, such as Ertebølle, Norslund and Bjørnsholm, were permanent settlements served by seasonal special-purpose hunting camps represented by smaller archaeological sites. Against this, P. O. Nielsen (1986) has argued that the occupation of a confined zone between open water and dense forest would limit settlement and lead to the build-up of rubbish at dumping areas within that zone. He concluded that the evidence for Ertebølle sedentism may have been exaggerated. While Nielsen's conclusion may be correct, his evidence is distinctly shaky: these limitations did not give rise to an almost continuous band of shell middens along the coast, as one would infer from Nielsen's thinking; instead, shell middens occupy particular areas within his favourable zone which do not seem to have advantages over other locations where they are lacking; finally, his characterisation of the inland as dense forest is too uniform a description (L. Larsson 1990a). In some areas, such as Jutland, the forest was naturally thinner, and there is also a certain amount of evidence for forest clearance within the Mesolithic (see pp. 75–76).

The difficulty of arriving at a secure verdict on the question of sedentism even at an intensively investigated site is shown by Ertebølle (Andersen and Johansen 1986). The presence of juvenile red deer and wild pig would point to activity in the spring/summer; the cockles in the midden were gathered from May to October; the garfish show summer fishing, while eels were caught in August; the finding of a single hazelnut points to early autumn; stag antlers still attached to the skull indicate winter hunting, as do animals trapped for their fur and several species of duck. So there are certainly indications of occupation during the summer, autumn and winter, but no guarantee that this would be from the beginning of summer to the end of winter, and no clear indication of spring-time settlement. A similar picture emerged from the analysis of the Tybrind Vig material (S. H. Andersen 1985).

Even if settlement at the shell middens was not continuous throughout the year, there is ample evidence for continuity of activity over a long time, with the same areas of particular middens being used for the same range of functions for much of the period over which the site was occupied. Andersen and Johansen (1986) concluded on the basis of the evidence from the recent excavations at Ertebølle that a stable settlement system must have existed, which would tend to point to the existence of a degree of territoriality in terms of claims over particular gathering grounds and the establishment of a strong sense of place through returning to the same encultured landscape time after time. The most likely possibility is of a seasonal movement inland (Newell *et al.* 1990: 43–4).

Settlements other than shell middens certainly existed in western and northern coastal areas, but have seen far less work. Survey work by S. H. Andersen (1989; 1991) along the Norsminde and Bjørnsholm fjords in Jutland has shown that shell middens form a minority of Late Mesolithic material concentrations, but he is still concentrating his efforts on the shell middens, as they provide the relatively alkaline conditions which allow animal bones to survive.

Outside the shell midden area, on the east coast of Zealand and Scania, Ertebølle sites are plentiful. The Vedbæk inlet in northeast Zealand was flooded by the sea around 6000 BC, creating a shallow inlet with several islands which were then occupied, along with peninsulas by the water. Over forty sites have been located from the Kongemose and Ertebølle periods, including Vænget Nord, a small island which was drowned by 5500 BC (Brinch Petersen 1989b). The excavation recovered simple hearths, larger cooking pits, a pit with a flint hoard of a core and thirty flakes which could be refitted, some fifteen postholes and over two hundred stakeholes. Usewear analysis suggested that one area of the site had been used for boneworking and another for hideworking and flint-working. Animal bones from the site were dominated by fish. Belonging to roughly the same period is the site at Gøngehusvej No. 7; this has produced an oval hut outlined by stakeholes with a simple central fireplace (Brinch Petersen 1990a); the site as a whole is thought to be a specialised herring-fishing site (Brinch Petersen 1990b). Preliminary reports also exist of a branch floor with bark covering, on which were a stone-lined fireplace, flintwork, fish-hooks, animal and fish bones, at the Early Ertebølle site of Møllegabet II off Ærø, to the south of Fyn (Johansen 1992 and 1993). Finally, an initial report has been made of a small hut consisting of a shallow pit outlined by postholes at Søholm 2 on Zealand dating to the Ertebølle culture (Johansen 1992).

The Ystad survey in Scania (Berglund and Larsson 1991) has revealed a substantial number of sites on headlands or on islands out in lagoons or on sandbanks at the mouth of the lagoons. These date mainly to the earlier part of the Ertebølle, and range in size from c. 200 m^2 to c. 1000 m^2; the position of the large sites suggests that they were situated to take advantage of good fishing grounds. One of the sites excavated as part of the Ystad Project was Bredasten (M. Larsson 1985–6), an apparently Early Ertebølle site (although the two radiocarbon dates date to c. 4100 BC), where a ring-ditch associated with postholes contained a hearth around which flintworking took place and a puppy burial in a pit.

Inland areas have seen few excavations by comparison with the coastal region, but there is evidence for occupation sites inland in all parts of southern Scandinavia (Madsen 1986). On Zealand, Præstelyngen seems to be a small Late Ertebølle summer camp occupied from March or April through to September, situated by a lake and not surprisingly producing large amounts of fish bones, mainly of pike (Noe-Nygaard 1987). More substantial sites do exist, however, although few have been examined (e.g. Brinch Petersen 1987). By far the most intensively studied is Ringkloster, situated by a large lake in eastern Jutland some 15 km from the shore (S. H. Andersen 1973–4 and 1986b). The settlement covers a substantial area, about 200 × 75 m, and dates to the later Ertebølle. Wild boar and pine marten are the main animals present, with birds and fish relatively little represented, suggesting mainly winter activities, although the piglets would point to springtime. Postholes make up several possible houses, some with large stone-lined fireplaces, which would imply a more permanent population (Madsen 1986). Contact with the coast is shown by finds of dolphin bones and oyster shells, the latter being used as scrapers.

One interpretation of these finds would be that seasonal movements did take place from the coast inland and back again; this idea would be supported for the Kongemose period by C^{13} measurements on two dogs from the site of Kongemose on Zealand itself, which showed that they had such a large intake of marine food that they must have lived for a large part of their lives on the coast, some 25 km away. By contrast, C^{13} measurements on dog bones from Præstelyngen demonstrate that they subsisted almost entirely on terrestrial foods, suggesting that they (and their owners) lived more or less permanently inland (Fischer 1993). The dolphin bones and oysters would then demonstrate exchange rather than seasonal movement (Madsen 1986).

The primary evidence for the subsistence economy also comes from shell middens, given that they provide the bulk of the finds of animal bones. A number of sites show a generalised strategy of hunting and catching, and perhaps also gathering, seen in the exploitation of land and sea mammals and fish (Rowley-Conwy 1983) as well as birds (Grigson 1989b). The Bjørnsholm midden in western Jutland had a very wide range of animals represented (S. H. Andersen 1991; Bratlund 1991). The main constituent of the midden was large oysters, which shrunk in size through time, along with cockles, mussels and periwinkles. The larger land animals were mainly wild boar and red and roe deer again, with a few aurochs bones, while smaller animals such as red fox, badger, wildcat, lynx, otter, wolf, pine marten and polecat may have been killed for their fur. Grey seal and porpoise were the main sea mammals killed. Birds were frequently hunted, especially ducks and swans. Finally, there were some 11,000 fish bones (S. H. Andersen 1991), of which 15 per cent were freshwater, 22 per cent marine and 63 per cent migratory. By far the most common species was eel (Enghoff 1991), which provided over half the bones (even this may underestimate their importance, as eel bones are very fatty and so do not preserve well). Enghoff suggests that the inhabitants of the site may have caught the eels at the mouth of the freshwater streams leading into the fjord using stationary fish traps.

Ertebølle lies nearby, and has a very similar economic base to Bjørnsholm (Andersen and Johansen 1986). The most common shellfish in the midden was oysters, then cockles and mussels. The main large game hunted was roe deer, red deer and wild boar, with some slight remains of elk and aurochs. Grey seals were hunted, and swans and ducks caught. The fish bones (Enghoff 1986) are dominated by freshwater species (67 per cent), such as roach, rudd, with a considerable number of eel as well (17 per cent), the remainder being marine fish including cod, saithe, garfish and a few flatfish.

The Norsminde shell midden in eastern Jutland (S. H. Andersen 1989) also had a very generalised economy. The midden was dominated by oysters (some 60–80 per cent), with smaller numbers of cockles, mussels and periwinkles. The larger land mammals hunted were primarily red deer, wild boar and roe deer, with a few bones of aurochs. Wild cat, beaver and wolf are thought to have been killed for their fur. Grey seal and large whales were hunted at sea. Swans and ducks were shot or trapped. The fish were dominated by flatfish (flounder, plaice, dab, turbot and brill), with gadids (cod or saithe) next in popularity, then eel and some herring (Enghoff 1989). All species are marine, some demanding very saline conditions, others frequenting brackish water; Enghoff believes that the fishing took place close to land.

The underwater midden site of Tybrind Vig off Fyn has also provided a clear picture of the subsistence economy (S. H. Andersen 1985). The most important shellfish was, as always, oysters, followed by mussels, clams and periwinkles. The primary species of large game hunted were red deer and wild pig, together with a few elk and aurochs. A high proportion of fur-bearing animals were killed, including pine marten, wild cat, red fox, otter, badger and polecat, especially after 4500 BC. The excellent conditions of preservation on this site allow a more definite answer to be given to the question of whether these fur-bearing species were actually hunted primarily for their pelts. Many of the mandibles and upper part of the skull showed cutmarks from skinning, while symmetrically placed depressed fractures on the rear of the skull were caused either by traps or by holding the animals down to be skinned. This detailed evidence makes it highly likely that trapping animals for their fur was an important part of the economy.

Turning to non-midden sites, at the various Skateholm settlements in and around a lagoon just in from the coast (Jonsson 1988; L. Larsson 1989a) an equally wide variety of land and sea mammals, birds and fish was exploited, not all for their value as food. Some eighty-five species have been identified all together. The forest animals killed included red and roe deer and wild boar, with an increase in wild boar over time, while red deer numbers remain stable and those of roe deer decrease. Pine marten, otter, wild cat and beaver were also trapped, presumably for their fur, along with very occasional brown bear. Grey seals were hunted at their breeding sites, for small pups were included in the kill, and sharks may possibly have been hunted, although their teeth are nearly all found as grave goods, so they may not have been hunted locally. A few duck were caught, along with representatives of many marine and coastal bird species, although their small numbers led Jonsson to conclude that, like the birds of prey found, they may have been prized for the feathers, which were turned into arrow flights. Finally, there seems to have been little effort expended on sea fishing, either from boats or with traps, as the main fish recovered were all species that would have been found in the lagoon, such as flatfish, cod, herring and perch. Lars Larsson (1989a) has suggested that an increase in saltwater fish and seals through time may relate to rising sea levels.

Although there are unquestionably some common patterns in this material, the variation in certain resources, particularly fish, stands out. There is a wide range of fishing strategies, from ignoring freshwater fish at Norsminde, and perhaps Vedbæk (Enghoff 1989), via specialising in eel, a migratory species, but also catching both freshwater and marine species at Bjørnsholm, through to freshwater dominance together with a substantial eel catch at Ertebølle, ending with largely ignoring marine resources at Skateholm. One more variation is seen at Møllegabet II (Grøn and Skaarup 1991), an Early Ertebølle underwater site off Ærø, to the south of Fyn. Here some 95 per cent of the fish bones were of cod, with a few dogfish, mackerel and flatfish and only a single eel bone. The lack of eel could be due to the fatty nature of the bones, but they have survived reasonably well elsewhere. These differences show that lack of knowledge was not a problem, nor does it seem likely that lack of resources would have been either. Instead it seems as though a degree of economic specialisation may have occurred in fishing, while the hunting of large game was relatively standard throughout southern Scandinavia. How significant might this have been? Jonsson (1988) argues that at Skateholm fish were probably the most important source of protein, so this specialisation may have led to exchanges between communities for part of their subsistence diet.

There are two rather different views which could be taken of the role of shellfish in the Ertebølle economy. Rowley-Conwy (1984) has strongly argued that oysters had the status of a seasonal food, eaten during the spring when few other resources were available. Since they were inferior in nutritional terms to land or sea mammals, birds, fish, or gathering acorns or hazelnuts, he thinks that they would only have been exploited on such a scale if they played a vital role in the economy despite their clear drawbacks. An alternative approach would be to see a role for shellfish as fish bait, given the ample evidence for the exploitation of marine resources, as has been suggested for Neolithic Skara Brae on Orkney (Clarke 1976: 22), where there are substantial middens.

Settlements with a generalised economy are not the only type known, as those specialising in the hunting of one or two species are also well attested. Ølby Lyng in eastern Zealand was a camp for hunting Greenland seals and catching guillemots (Brinch Petersen 1970); Aggersund was a base for hunting whooper swans, ignoring the available ducks and geese, occupied in the late autumn and winter (S. H. Andersen 1978; Møhl 1978). Even the white-tailed eagle was a preferred prey at the inland site of Øgaarde (Grigson 1989b). These more specialised sites are also smaller than those with a wider economic base, as would be expected (Rowley-Conwy 1983). The relationship between the various sites is not clearly established as yet: they could indicate that such specialisation was economically feasible as a way for particular groups to flourish, obtaining other necessary items through exchange relationships; or, more likely, that parties were sent out from the larger, perhaps permanently occupied, sites to carry out specific tasks. That these were not always directly related to the subsistence economy is shown by the eagle-hunting site of Øgaarde (Grigson 1989b).

The overall picture is of a highly organised economy with a significant degree of specialisation on particular prey species. These specialisations in the major animals exploited may well relate to surplus production for gift exchange, either within Ertebølle society itself or with agriculturalists to the south. This is most clear in the emphasis of sites such as Tybrind Vig and Ringkloster on fur-bearing species, but may also lie behind the variation in the kind of fishing carried out and possibly in the emphasis on certain species of birds. Other less common species which may also have been hunted for exchange purposes are brown bear, shark, aurochs and elk. Only at Skateholm were brown bear meat bones found (Jonsson 1988); elsewhere just the teeth are recovered as ornaments in burials (Iregren 1988), for example with a child at Gøngehusvej No. 7, Vedbæk, on Zealand (Brinch Petersen *et al.* 1993). The shark teeth found at Skateholm were nearly all used as grave goods, leading Jonsson (1988) to conclude that they had a special meaning and might have been exchanged from elsewhere as gifts. Also at Skateholm, the burial of a young woman was accompanied by a row of perforated tooth beads around her waist; this included some of aurochs, which is thought to have died out in southern Scania some time before (L. Larsson 1989a). These too would seem to represent the product of gift exchange, as aurochs bones were absent from the settlement (L. Larsson 1988a). Perforated aurochs teeth were also found with an adult burial in the Vedbæk Bøgebakken cemetery on Zealand (Albrethsen and Brinch Petersen 1976) and the Gøngehusvej No. 7 child (Brinch

Petersen *et al.* 1993), although again the aurochs is believed to have disappeared from Zealand far earlier, probably in the sixth millennium BC. Finally, a perforated elk tooth was one of a group of pendants discovered below the pelvis of a young woman at Vedbæk Bøgebakken (Albrethsen and Brinch Petersen 1976), while another was among the ornaments on the chest of the child at Gøngehusvej No. 7 (Brinch Petersen *et al.* 1993), although there are thought to be no elk surviving in the area by that time.

In the case of aurochs and elk Jutland and northern Scania are possible sources for the teeth (L. Larsson 1988a), while brown bears may have been caught no nearer than central Sweden (Iregren 1988). Lars Larsson (1988a) suggests that the evidence shows either that there was an active trade in teeth, or that marriage partners were exchanged between groups over long distances. If the latter was the case it is highly likely that such marriage alliances would in any case be linked to wider exchange relationships between the groups concerned. The exchange economy certainly appears to operate at several levels, not all of which need necessarily to have been open to every individual or group. The ability to obtain tooth pendants belonging to these exotic and powerful animals may well have been highly significant, especially if something of the strength of the animal itself was thought to reside in its remains. The beliefs of the recipient are thus of considerable importance here, whereas the production of furs for exchange may well have been a more utilitarian activity, except perhaps where brown bear or wolves were concerned.

Pottery was introduced into southern Scandinavia around 4600 BC. It took two forms: large pointed-base jars and flat elongated bowls (see Figure 4.1). The flat bowls have long been interpreted as lamps, in which blubber, probably from seals, was burnt (Mathiassen 1935), which might suggest that some of the jars were used for storing the blubber (Rowley-Conwy and Zvelebil 1989). Another possible use has been suggested by their similarity to vessels used in Ghana for boiling shellfish (Noe-Nygaard 1967). The idea of pointed-base jars as storage vessels is supported by the finds of pits containing the base of pots still in place at Grisby on Bornholm (Vang Petersen 1987); the dominance of seal remains in the animal bone assemblage may point to the storage of blubber (Watt 1983). Charred food remains on pots can provide rare direct evidence of their use. An example from Tybrind Vig was interpreted as a fermented porridge with ingredients that included hazelnuts and possibly blood (Arrhenius and Lidén 1988). Interestingly, remains of herring bones and scales were also recovered from the surface of the vessel, but did not relate to the burnt crust which was analysed. Another vessel had bones, scales and skin from small cod and a number of grass impressions in the remains charred onto it (S. H. Andersen 1987b), while a third had fish remains only. C^{13} analyses carried out on the charred deposits on each of the three vessels showed clearly that the main ingredients were actually dryland, so the marine fish must have been only a small element; S. H. Andersen and Malmros (1984) concluded that the contents were primarily fish soup with a high vegetable content. This is a valuable reminder that plant foods are

Figure 4.1 Ertebølle pottery – storage vessel (top) and blubber lamp (bottom)

a conspicuously under-researched area in southern Scandinavian Mesolithic studies, but the results may also show that the same vessel could be used for quite different purposes at different times in its useful life.

A certain amount of evidence relating to the economy has been obtained through the study of usewear on flint tools. A range of activities has been identified by examining both retouched implements and unretouched flakes and blades (Juel Jensen 1986; 1988a; 1988b). At Vænget Nord butchering and the processing of hides were seen, while many unretouched edges showed plant polish, which Juel Jensen suggests may have been the result of preparing the stems of reeds and rushes for making baskets, mats and textiles. Micro-denticulates (blades or flakes with saw-like edges) may have been used to work plant stems for textile production, although the evidence is not clear (Juel Jensen 1994: 50–68). Some unretouched flakes may also have acquired a gloss through working ochre (Juel Jensen 1994: 74–8).

The main items of surviving perishable material culture are all connected with fishing (see Figure 4.2). Nets seem to have been used from the beginning of the Mesolithic (Gramsch 1987), perhaps to catch both seals and birds. The second main form of trap, a structure with arms leading in towards a wicker cage, only

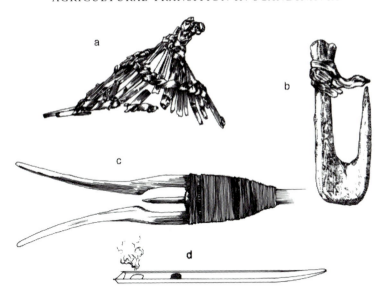

Figure 4.2 Ertebølle fishing equipment – (a) fish trap; (b) fish-hook made from red deer rib bone with plant fibre twine line; (c) leister; (d) 9.5 m long dugout canoe from Tybrind Vig with a ballast stone and fireplace at the stern
(after S. H. Andersen 1987b)

appears after 7000 BC, when it becomes quite frequently used. Bones from small fish show that they were caught in fine-meshed nets or traps (L. Larsson 1990a). Fishing hooks are common through the Mesolithic (S. H. Andersen 1986a), with the variety in size suggesting they were made for catching quite different species. Leisters of wood have also been found on several sites, including Tybrind Vig (S. H. Andersen 1986a), pointing to the close-in spearing of large fish. The frequent boat finds may, of course, also relate to fishing.

An additional source of information on diet is the analysis of the C^{13} content of bones and the trace elements they contain. High C^{13} values are common for skeletons from the Late Mesolithic of eastern Denmark (Tauber 1982), which indicate the consumption of seafish at a level comparable with Greenlanders (Price 1989b). However, two skeletons from the Skateholm I coastal cemetery in Scania had a largely terrestrial diet according to their C^{13} values (Price 1989a), although this may simply mean that they consumed freshwater rather than sea-water fish (Jonsson 1988). Trace element analysis has also been applied to a group of eighteen bodies from Skateholm I and II (Price 1989a), with higher zinc levels, suggesting more meat eating, at Skateholm I, the later of the two cemeteries; this would point to dietary differences amounting to rather more than the origin of their fish. At both Skateholm I and II (Price 1989b) males had higher strontium levels than females, probably signifying a higher marine element in their diet; this would seem to be significant, given the relatively little evidence for seafish; perhaps they were the major consumers of seals.

The case for a diet generally high in fish, at least in Denmark, is supported by the evidence of disease (Meiklejohn and Zvelebil 1991). Danish Mesolithic skeletons demonstrate a high degree of cranial porotic hyperostosis: this condition is usually attributed to iron deficiency anaemia, and correlated with dependence on cereals. This is ruled out for early prehistoric populations, so Meiklejohn and Zvelebil think a more likely cause is infection and/or sedentism; a number of the Danish Mesolithic crania have a very thick vault, so one possibility is infestation by fish tapeworms. This research is clearly at a very preliminary stage, but it does point in the same direction as several other lines of evidence.

One possibility raised some considerable time ago was that there was a minor agricultural element in the Ertebølle economy. As part of the Åmose Project on Zealand the site of Muldbjerg I was examined: here, Ertebølle sherds were found together with pottery of Becker's (1947) Early Neolithic 'A' type. This led Troels-Smith (1953) to conclude that the Ertebølle culture was not purely one of gathering-hunting, but was actually semi-agrarian. He has continued to propound this view (1967 and 1982), arguing that the start of the Ertebølle represents the beginning of farming in Denmark, and that the Elm Decline visible around 4000 BC was caused by Ertebølle farmers pollarding elm trees to provide fodder for their livestock. This model has come under attack from three different angles: Rowley-Conwy (1982) has demonstrated the vast number of cattle which Troels-Smith's model would require; the Elm Decline is now widely believed to be a natural phenomenon (see Chapter 5); and Muldbjerg I has been dated through radiocarbon to c. 3500 BC, long after the end of the Mesolithic, so the thick-walled pottery found there could be residual, or alternatively a Neolithic coarseware, given that the classic indicators of an Ertebølle occupation were missing. The general conclusion (e.g. Zvelebil and Rowley-Conwy 1984) is that Muldbjerg I and the Elm Decline are not evidence of the Ertebølle being a semi-farming society.

There have also been a number of individual claims that domestic cattle remains have been discovered at Ertebølle sites. These have been based on the size of the bones or teeth, with fragments which were thought to be too small to come from the native wild aurochs being classified as domestic. For example, the cattle molars from Dyrholm I in Jutland (Degerbøhl 1963), dating to the earlier Ertebølle, were long regarded as domestic because of their size, but a better knowledge of how small the female aurochs could be has shown that these and other claimed examples fall within the wild size range (Rowley-Conwy 1985).

In recent years, occasional finds of large grass or cereal pollen have been made in pre-Elm Decline pollen diagrams in southern Scandinavia, once more raising the possibility of an agricultural element in the Ertebølle. At Fårups Mosse in the Ystad area of Scania (Berglund et al. 1991) a single grain of a cereal pollen type was found in a level dated to *c.* 5200 BC. Göransson (1988), however, has suggested that at least some of these pollen grains may derive from lyme grass, which is common on the coastal dunes. Two pollen diagrams from Trundholm in northwest Zealand (Kolstrup 1988) provide similar pre-Elm Decline evidence: in one core a layer containing a wheat-type pollen grain was associated with a high level of charcoal, just above this were grains of *plantago major/media* (plantain), and slightly higher again were grains of *plantago lanceolata* (ribwort plantain) and a barley-type grain, although Kolstrup thinks this may simply be a large grass; in the other core a peak of charcoal is associated with a grain of *plantago lanceolata*, and several of cereal type. There is little sign of a decline in tree species, however, so Kolstrup does not believe that the forest was opened up. The alternative, not pursued by Kolstrup, might be that the charcoal results from the fires of nearby settlements. These scattered finds of possible cereal grains can be interpreted in two ways: either they demonstrate a consistent but low-level presence of cereal cultivation in the later Ertebølle, or they are the result of either natural transport or of the difficulty in identifying cereal grains as opposed to those of large grasses (S. T. Andersen 1978). The latter is strongly suggested by the core from Hassing Huse Mose in northwest Jutland (S. T. Andersen 1992–3). Here two wheat-type pollen grains were found in pre-Elm Decline levels: one occurred just prior to the Elm Decline, but the other was in a sixth-millennium level, which would seem to be far too early for an agricultural introduction and is interpreted by Andersen as the result of long-distance transportation. An unpublished review of these early cereal-type pollen finds has been undertaken by Welinder (cited in Juel Jensen 1994: 89), who concludes that only the central Swedish find from Dags Mosse is a completely reliable identification. The distance of this site from definite agricultural activity would make this a likely candidate for long-distance transportation as well.

Pollen diagrams provide better evidence of clearance during the Mesolithic – this would involve cutting down trees and burning off undergrowth. Göransson (1988) records several sites in Scania which appear to show a clearance phase before the Elm Decline. At Fårups Mosse a grain of *plantago lanceolata* occurred in the same level as the claimed cereal grain (Berglund *et al.* 1991) together with a high level of bracken and meadow grasses; all three species are generally associated with clearance. The nearby Herrestads Mosse diagram showed a level dated to *c.* 4300 BC with a layer of charcoal which was succeeded by deposits containing nettles and bedstraw, again indicating clearance. At Kurarps Mosse (Berglund and Kolstrup 1991) the first plantain grains are found in a level dating to *c.* 4300 BC. A series of clearance episodes have been detected by Welinder (1989) on the island of Aspö in Blekinge, southern Sweden, starting in the seventh millennium BC: these consist of charcoal layers, a fall in tree pollen and an increase in herbs. At Lake Skånso in northern Jutland (Odgaard 1989) there were very high amounts of charcoal around 4500 BC, although these are not accompanied by vegetational changes: as at Trundholm this may relate to the existence of nearby settlements. The Holmegård bog in southern Zealand has more definite traces of a human impact on the environment (S. T. Andersen *et al.* 1983): three pre-Elm Decline levels contain plantain, together with an increase in grasses, while cereals appear only after the Elm Decline. Finally, at Hassing Huse Mose (Andersen 1992–3) there are two falls in elm pollen, both associated with a disturbance in the forest cover, before the classic Elm Decline.

What was the purpose of these clearances if not to cultivate cereals? Göransson (1988) speculates that Ertebølle communities may have exploited the fact that bracken is high in both protein and starch by producing bracken flour. Jonsson (1988) has wondered if the rise in the presence of wild boar through time at the Skateholm sites may not reflect clearance activities. Similar clearances in Britain have been interpreted in terms of burning the forest to increase the quality and quantity of grazing and browsing, which would attract both small and large game into the cleared area (Ahlgren 1966; Mellars 1976). The greater amount of light reaching the woodland floor would also encourage the growth of hazel and so hazelnuts, while fruit and berry-producing shrubs might also benefit. Such a model, suggesting of a degree of woodland management during the Mesolithic, does not seem out of place given the nature of the Ertebølle economy (Paludan-Müller 1978).

The general trend through the Ertebølle is one of economic intensification (Price 1991). A wider range of terrestrial species and birds was exploited, and specific hunting camps were developed. Storage facilities may have been improved by the introduction of pottery. Clearances may have been created in forests in order to improve conditions for both hunting and gathering. The exploitation of marine resources increased, with widespread evidence for the catching of cod and flounder, and the hunting of several species of sea mammal: common seal, Greenland seal, grey seal, ringed seal, dolphin, killer whale and porpoise (Price 1991). All this goes to build up a general picture of an economy in which communities were widely engaged in surplus production. In itself this observation does not, of course, provide a reason why there should have been this shift, although the evidence for exchange within and beyond the Ertebølle area is certainly suggestive in this regard.

BURIAL PRACTICES AND TERRITORIES

The second best known element of Ertebølle culture, after the shell middens, is undoubtedly the substantial burial record. This takes three main forms: cemeteries, burials within middens and single or group burials. The first cemetery to be discovered was that at Vedbæk Bøgebakken on Zealand (Albrethsen and Brinch Petersen 1976), on higher ground behind an Ertebølle settlement. Some burials were destroyed by the building work which revealed the site, but twenty-two bodies were located in seventeen graves. There were double burials of women and children, suggesting death in childbirth, but also a triple burial of two adults and a one-year-old child. Not all young children were buried with adults, for there were two graves containing only infants. Notable by their absence were older children, and only a single juvenile was present. The numbers of females and males were roughly even. Several bodies were scattered with ochre, both females and males, and adults, the juvenile and one baby, but not the two infants interred separately. Grave goods included large flint blades (found with seven adults and a baby, the six adults that could be sexed all being definite or probable males), tooth pendants (accompanying four adults, of whom one was female and two probably male), shell pendants (found with one adult female), a bone dagger and a bone spatula (both with adults, probably male), an antler axe and a core-axe (accompanying two adults, one male and the other probably male), and two sets of red deer antlers and a group of red deer jaws and a pine marten jaw (found with an adult male, an adult female and an unidentified adult). There is also considerable variety in the number of grave goods: the young female buried with the ochre-covered baby was accompanied by well over two hundred pendants made from red deer, wild boar, seal and elk teeth and snail shell beads. Other burials had only a single bead or pendant. The baby with this highly adorned young woman was clearly distinguished from other infant burials in the cemetery by being covered with ochre, having a swan's wing laid over it, and possessing a grave good in the form of a large broken flint blade.

A series of cemeteries have been located at Skateholm in Scania (L. Larsson 1989a), although one of these was destroyed by gravel digging in the 1930s, only one of the skeletons surviving to the present day. This has been radiocarbon dated to *c.* 4750 BC. The Skateholm I and II cemeteries were fortunately discovered during archaeological survey (L. Larsson 1988b), the first producing over sixty burials, the second over twenty, although the full extent of the second has not been established. A full listing of burials is not yet available, but some patterns in the material have been identified. The Skateholm II cemetery is the older in date, belonging to the Late Kongemose/Early Ertebølle (L. Larsson 1989a). The site lies on what was a small island, with the graves on the top of the hill and settlement traces of the same broad date on the southern edge. In what is probably an incomplete sample, some twenty burials have been discovered, including a single cremation. Crouched burial was not used, instead many skeletons lay on their backs, and some were seated. Children were rare, although present in small numbers as separate burials – in one case as a double burial of a two-year-old and a four-year-old. Ochre was scattered around both adults and children. Most of the burials had a few grave goods and several were accompanied by a large number. Tooth beads (of red deer, wild boar and aurochs) were found with females and males, while stone and flint axes, flint blades, bone points and knives were found with males only. Despite their small numbers, there were child burials with grave goods: in the double burial of the young children, one was accompanied by a bone point and the other by two flint blades. Animal bones were quite frequently recovered from the graves, including the burial of a woman with a decapitated dog across her shins, and two males each with several sets of deer antlers. There were an equal number of females and males (Persson and Persson 1988), with the vast majority of the males being young, leading Persson and Persson (1988) to suggest that the young males accompanied by large numbers of red deer antlers may have been successful hunters.

At Skateholm I (L. Larsson 1989a) the cemetery lies mostly upslope from the surviving settlement area but was probably originally all covered by occupation debris; so far the cemetery, at *c.* 5100–4900 BC, predates the settlement, at *c.* 4900–4500 BC, but the radiocarbon samples from the settlement deposits came from a quite restricted area, so may well not represent the total date range of the occupation if it spread through time in a similar way to shell midden sites. The presence of scattered human bones and tooth beads in the occupation level strongly indicates that some burials were subsequently disturbed by settlement activities. Both inhumations and cremations (two examples) were found. The inhumations were placed in a variety of positions within the grave: seated, some upright, and from loosely to very tightly crouched. These different burial positions in part relate to the sex of the burial, with two-thirds of the crouched burials being females, nearly all the males being found with their feet close together and the hands of elderly women being placed in front of their faces. There was also some evidence for grave-related structures: a female burial lay in the middle of a large pit, around which were four postholes, perhaps marking the corners of a canopy covering the grave, and just above the skeleton were considerable amounts of charcoal from ashwood logs, presumably derived from the canopy being destroyed by fire; similarly, the cremated bones of an adult male were found in and between a group of postholes. There are apparently groupings of graves, some of which overlap, but only once was an older grave actually disturbed. This could suggest the existence of grave markers, if the cemetery was in use for some time. Most of the burials are of single individuals, the double burials consisting of young adults or children with either older females or males. Extremely few children were found overall, only some 10 per cent of the total burial population. Clearly this would not match any model of the likely mortality pattern, and suggests that here children were generally not accorded a place in the community cemetery. Figures for female and male burials are equal (Persson and Persson 1988).

Ochre is quite frequently found in the graves of both females and males, and on some of the few child burials. In a number of cases the ochre was located below the body, suggesting that it was on the clothing of the deceased, rather than being scattered over the corpse in the grave (L. Larsson 1989a). Overall, there are fewer grave goods per burial than at Skateholm II, suggesting a concentration of grave goods among a smaller proportion of the buried population. The great majority of grave goods accompany younger females and older males: the tooth pendants (from wild boar, red deer and elk) are mainly with females, stone axes with males. There was, however, a well-accompanied child burial (found in the same grave as an elderly male without grave goods) covered in ochre, with two perforated bear teeth, four amber pendants, a bone point and a flint blade knife. Animal remains still featured prominently, with various graves producing jaw fragments from red deer, roe deer and wild boar and a pine marten skull. In several graves there were concentrations of fish bones from different species (Jonsson 1988), which Lars Larsson (1989b) has interpreted as a last meal, because the bones are often in the stomach region; this would, of course, suggest that these bodies at least were of individuals who were known to be dying.

The original interpretation of these concentrations of Late Mesolithic burials was that they were true cemeteries (e.g. Chapman 1981), in the sense of being communal burial grounds set aside from the settlement area. Lars Larsson (1990a), for example, believes that they were originally separate, only later being covered by the settlement as it expanded. However, the Skateholm evidence could be interpreted with a rather different emphasis, as showing that where the preservation conditions were more favourable an occupation deposit survived, so the burials may actually have taken place in the midst of the settlement, at least for part of the life of the site. Again, the Vedbæk Bøgebakken burials were in a higher part of the site with poorer preservation, even before the building work commenced. This would make the 'cemeteries' closer to other settlements with burials, especially the shell middens. Recent discoveries of burials on shell midden sites seem to support this; at Nederst in eastern Jutland the various burials seem to have been situated between the shell heaps (E. K. Nielsen and Brinch Petersen 1993). On the basis of this recent Danish evidence Nielsen and Brinch Petersen (1993) have argued that these large concentrations of burials were really settlement burials, which would match the reinterpretation of the Skateholm sites suggested here.

As suggested, many of the shell middens investigated in modern times have produced burials, together with some of the non-midden sites; it must be remembered that in large parts of southern Scandinavia it is only the presence of the shells which will produce soil conditions conducive to the survival of bone, so skeletons may be absent elsewhere for purely environmental reasons. In many of the middens there are both relatively complete and scattered remains: e.g. at Norsminde (S. H. Andersen 1989) a disturbed grave of a female aged 25–30 years was found, as well as occasional skull fragments, which may come from one or several burials; Tybrind Vig (S. H. Andersen 1985) presents a similar picture, with a grave containing a young female aged 15–17 years and a newborn child, as well as the scattered bones of at least two or three further individuals. At Nederst (Brinch Petersen 1988; 1990a; E. K. Nielsen and Brinch Petersen 1993), among the dozen or so burials found so far are the remains of two adults stained with ochre found in a heavily disturbed grave; an old male with greenstone, flint and antler axes, two large blade knives, six arrowheads and a fine set of tooth pendants, covered with ochre; an adult female with large numbers of tooth beads and a spearpoint; and a child aged about 5 years with a blade knife and several tooth beads of red deer, wild boar and aurochs.

Away from the middens the most remarkable burials found in recent times are those from Gøngehusvej No. 7, Vedbæk (Brinch Petersen 1990b; Brinch Petersen et al. 1993). One of the Late Kongemose graves consists of a group of pits bounded by a circle of stones, which was kept open during the period of the settlement; at the bottom of one was a newborn on a tray with lumps of ochre under the head, another three contained ochre-covered children with flint axes and blade knives, one also possessing two sets of red deer teeth, and in a fifth was a child accompanied by a jaw and other red deer bones and ochre. Of the same date are two cremation graves: one was in a pit, with the collected and cleaned bones of an adult placed on a wooden tray with an unburnt blade knife on top, the bones being only a small part of the original number, although all elements of the skeleton were present; the other contained the bones of two young adults, perhaps of opposite sex, a youth, a 5-year-old and a newborn, with some indications of dismemberment and defleshing having taken place before the cremation, along with the burnt remnants of three duck-feet, a wing from a bird of jackdaw size, a small piece of amber, red deer and fox tooth pendants, with the stomach contents being thought to have been preserved as burnt flounder vertebrae and the clothes as patches of ochre. This clearly represents a complex ritual interment, perhaps with an element of foreknowledge and possibly sacrifice. Another grave belongs to the Early Ertebølle: this contained the burial of a mature female, around 40 years old, with ochre round the head and traces of a roe deer cape on the torso, accompanied by ten severed lower leg joints of red deer, two bone knives, a bone point, and a grebe's beak and tooth pendant decorated cap fixed in place with a bone pin; the child, about 3 years old, had two flint blade knives and on the chest a vast array of items – a naturally perforated stone, two sets of roe deer teeth and one set of red deer teeth, tooth pendants (from wild boar, elk, aurochs and brown bear) and a bird beak, and further roe deer leg bones. The selection of the exotic and the strange as suitable grave goods is notable.

Finally, there are sites with as yet only a single grave, although these may, of course, prove at a later date to have been only part of a larger burial record. Of these, the most noteworthy is the mass grave found at Strøby Egede in eastern Zealand (Brinch Petersen 1990b). This Early Ertebølle grave occurs on a site which is mainly Late Ertebølle in date. The grave contained large amounts of ochre and the skeletons of eight individuals buried at the same time: at the southern end were an elderly female, a young adult female with tooth beads, a bone hairpin and a blade knife, a child (possibly female) with the same set of grave goods, and a newborn with a wild boar tooth bead and deer hooves; at the northern end were an adult male with five blade knives, a bone dagger and a decorated antler axe, a child with two blade knives, a newborn with two blade knives, and a newborn with red deer and wild boar tooth beads. There were no traces of a violent death, so the mass burial may represent death through some epidemic. Certainly it is unusual in containing such a high proportion of children.

A quite different kind of burial practice is revealed by finds from Møllegabet II (Grøn and Skaarup 1991), an Early Ertebølle underwater site off Ærø, to the south of Fyn. A boat, dated to c. 4800 BC, carved from a lime tree trunk, was found off the settlement with the bark floor structure: the central part of the boat had been burnt, in and around the boat were fragments of paddles and bones from the body of a young adult male, and alongside it were pieces of bark which may have been folded over the boat and its contents. An extremely similar burial was found during dredging operations in the harbour at Korsør Nor in western Zealand (Norling-Christensen and Bröste 1945) – an adult male accompanied by a flint flake was discovered in a boat covered by bark.

What overall patterns can be discerned in this mass of material? The most obvious is the enormous variety in burial practice – both inhumation and cremation were practised, with inhumed bodies being positioned in several different ways (crouched, extended, sitting, supine and even face down) and cremation varying from complete to token. Some individuals received burial at sea, others were interred in covered graves. Many had ochre scattered on them or their clothes. The human contents of the graves also demonstrates a wide range of variation. Although most graves contain single burials there are double inhumations, mass inhumations and mass cremations. All ages are represented, but the number of children is low: newborn babies are frequently found, but older children seem to represent a liminal category whose status is not clearly established. Overall there is a general equality in the representation of the sexes, and where figures are available this seems to be true at the local level as well. Most of the adults are quite young, and there is a distinct group of young women buried with newborns or infants, which may correspond to deaths in childbirth. Few elderly individuals are present in the burial record: here as elsewhere, of course, we must remember that this is a selected population, and it may be that elderly individuals only rarely qualified for burial in a grave.

The evidence of grave goods also shows considerable variety, both in number and type. As E. K. Nielsen and Brinch Petersen (1993) suggest, there are three main burial groups with respect to grave goods: those without any (at least half the total individuals buried), those with a few, and those with large numbers of items. There is also a wide range of objects buried, from parts of animals through to stone axes. Most grave goods occur with adults, but there are examples, some given above, of children with quite substantial assemblages. Several grave goods come under the general heading of decorative items, particularly the tooth beads or pendants: many of these could have been attached to clothing, such as caps, tunics, belts and skirts, while others seem to have been worn around the neck or arms. Nielsen and Brinch Petersen (1993) argue that in the case of belts with large numbers of beads found in Scania and on Zealand there was always one exotic tooth. There are also small assemblages of tooth beads which contain exotica, as in the case of the child from Gøngehusvej No. 7 (Brinch Petersen *et al.* 1993) in eastern Zealand, which was accompanied by five tooth pendants from wild boar, elk, aurochs and brown bear. This also makes the point that children were buried with these exotic items as well as adults.

There are some general patterns which emerge concerning sex-related grave goods: Lars Larsson (1990a), for example, thinks that tools, such as knives and axes were typically found with men, while women have ornaments like belts, males also having some tooth beads. On the other hand, Nielsen and Brinch Petersen (1993) believe that blade knives were worn by males, females and children, and that slotted bone points were a female item. However, Albrethsen and Brinch Petersen himself (1976) argued on the basis of the Vedbæk Bøgebakken cemetery that slotted bone points were a male-associated item. Although there are some clear patterns, such as the association between axes made from various materials and males, and the profusion of tooth beads with some females, much of the evidence is not so definite. The sex of the deceased was not the only factor behind decisions of appropriate treatment of the dead; perhaps we may be dealing here with elements of gendered social practice which cannot be reduced purely to biological sex. It is certainly extremely poor practice to follow the line taken by Newell and Constandse-Westermann (1988) for Skateholm, when they alter the sexing of a substantial number of burials in order to make them fit the supposed pattern of absolute differences in grave goods between the sexes. The richness of some child burials acts as a valuable reminder that these Mesolithic funerals will have been social occasions above all, with decisions about the treatment of the dead being taken by a group with mixed motives of rebuilding the community after a loss, commemorating the particular individual (if they are seen as having a separate social existence) and displaying their position, power and wealth.

One final area of general burial practice to be considered relates back to a point made earlier concerning the social role of shell middens. If, as seems to be the case, the middens were either sites of permanent settlement or of repeated seasonal occupation, they will have taken on a considerable degree of significance as a focal point in the social landscape. The middens themselves would steadily build up, especially in the case of the shell middens, becoming more visible from both land and, perhaps more importantly, sea. They would thus become artificial constructions altering the landscape, as they reached the stage of being landmarks which in predominantly flat areas would be the most immediately visible element. They could thus be said to have become monuments. The argument that the cemetery sites were not separated from settlements would imply that burials were one manifestation of the significance that these sites had acquired, as suggested for the Breton middens (see Chapter 3). So the midden heaps with a dual role as settlement and burial site could be seen as an early manifestation of monumental burial rites.

Further ritual activities appear to be tied to burial practices. There is some evidence to suggest that the defleshing of bones took place at Dyrholmen on Zealand, although the interpretation of cannibalism proposed by Degerbøhl (1942) and followed by Lars Larsson (1990a) would need to be confirmed by detailed examination of the formation processes involved at the site. While the cutmarks may be real (although the possibility of root etching should be borne in mind), the fracturing of bones could have had a natural cause, leaving open the possibility that the defleshing formed a stage in the mortuary ritual.

A ritual deposit which seems frequently to be related to burial practices is that of the interment of dog skeletons. At Skateholm (L. Larsson 1989b; 1990b) several dog burials were found in the cemeteries. In general they were distinguished from human burials by their treatment, with six of the eight graves containing dog skeletons at Skateholm I being found in a small area separate from the human interments. They are also found in much shallower graves. Against this, several dogs were found with ochre scattered over them. In one instance a dog was treated in the same way as a more prestigious human burial, being accompanied by grave goods: Skatehom II, Grave XXI, contained a dog with a red deer antler, an ornamented red deer antler hammer and three flint knives (L. Larsson 1989a). This has been interpreted by Lars Larsson (1989b) as a dog being buried as a substitute for its owner, which seems plausible, and suggests that similar symbolism may have operated elsewhere, with items 'standing for' something else. Other sites have produced complete dog skeletons, including Nederst and Gøngehusvej No. 7, but here there were no traces of ochre or graves (E. K. Nielsen and Brinch Petersen 1993).

One final burial-related element of ritual activity may be the construction of special ceremonial houses. At Skateholm II (L. Larsson 1987–8) a rectangular post-built structure was located at the highest point of the site, in the centre of the cemetery. It was bounded by a narrow band of ochre and covered by a thin ochre spread. The postholes were filled with a mixture of soot and sand. Inside the building was found flintwork made from pressure-flaked blades, including arrowheads, and conjoining bones from various animals were recovered from the ochre band outside. The animal bone assemblage was of unusual species, including eel, not generally found in the occupation layer. Larsson concluded that the structure had been used for special meals as part of cult ceremonies. It may be that as more Ertebølle period houses are discovered similar structures will come to light: Larsson suggested in his discussion of the Skateholm structure that the Bredasten building (M. Larsson 1985–6) may have been a ceremonial house, as it contained a puppy buried in a pit. In itself, this is rather slender evidence, and does not seem out of place in a domestic context. Until a wider sample of Ertebølle buildings is published it is hardly feasible to take individual elements as representing sufficiently unusual activities to warrant defining particular buildings as having either a ceremonial or a secular function. The Iron Gates houses (see Chapter 2) show clearly that such definite distinctions may well not be appropriate in the Mesolithic, although the unusual nature of the Skateholm II structure suggests that in southern Scandinavia cult houses of some kind may exist. If feasts were held in the Skateholm building they must have been extremely small-scale affairs, although it is quite possible that the ceremonials were divided into public and private phases.

Lars Larsson has argued that a number of deliberate deposits of objects in bogs may represent hoards or votive deposits (1990a). While in some cases these deposits could be interpreted as caches of items, intended to be retrieved for future use, especially those groups of unfinished objects, other deposits show signs of having been deliberately destroyed before deposition. These are, however, relatively few in number, and Solberg (1989) has argued that they did not exist at all, seeing votive offerings as a Neolithic introduction.

Art objects are far more definitely established (see Figure 4.3). In the Kongemose and Ertebølle periods antler axes and long antler shafts are commonly decorated, and some classes of objects, such as the slotted bone daggers, are almost always decorated (L. Larsson 1990a). Some items have almost the whole surface treated, while others demonstrate in their ovelapping designs that several phases of decoration existed. A number of the patterns seem to be regionally specific (Andersen 1980); the 'sheaf of grain' motif is found carved in groups of four or five on a series of antler objects from Jutland, Fyn and Ellerbek, while an eastern decorative tradition favoured geometric patterns of chessboards, triangles and hatched bands. Another Jutland pattern was the 'net', found on both bone and amber. Amber was carved into animal figurines and into decorated pendants (Mathiassen 1959). The most important discovery of Mesolithic decorated artefacts in recent times is undoubtedly the collection of carved and coloured paddles from Tybrind Vig (S. H. Andersen 1986a). Søren Andersen (1986a) has suggested that paddles may have been decorated in order to make it easy to spot from a distance the group affiliation of the individual in the boat. These decorative items are a predominantly Early Ertebølle phenomenon, argued by Søren Andersen (1980) to have been replaced by pottery around 4600 BC, although the net motif is found on a few Ertebølle sherds (S. H. Andersen 1989).

These hints of regional differentiation are only part of a much larger picture of regional and local patterning of material. Newell *et al.* (1990: 79) have interpreted all Mesolithic ornaments as insignia of group membership, even at the level of individual ornament types, such as tooth beads. Thus they identify a Grooved Incisor band occupying eastern Denmark and southern Sweden, overlapping to some extent with a Ring Bracelet band in Jutland (Newell *et al.* 1990: 370–3). This insistence that ornaments must relate solely to ethnic identity is highly implausible, and indeed is demonstrated to be an over-simplification by the ethnographic parallels adduced by Newell *et al.* themselves. Far more significant is the identification of a series of overlapping artefact distributions (Vang Petersen 1984) for a variety of different types. A division between Jutland and Fyn on the one side and Zealand, the smaller islands and southern Sweden on the other is visible from the beginning of the Mesolithic, but becomes much more clearcut in the Ertebølle period. Bone combs, bird-bone points, bone rings, T-shaped antler axes, and some harpoon types, are found only in the western zone, and polished Limhamn greenstone axes and other harpoon types in the east. There are also differences between southern Sweden and Denmark (L. Larsson 1990a), especially in the decoration on pottery and harpoons and burial positions, but also in particular forms of flint axes. Variation in the shape of flint axes is also seen on a local scale, with Vang Petersen (1984) demonstrating the existence of three groups in one part of eastern Zealand, although

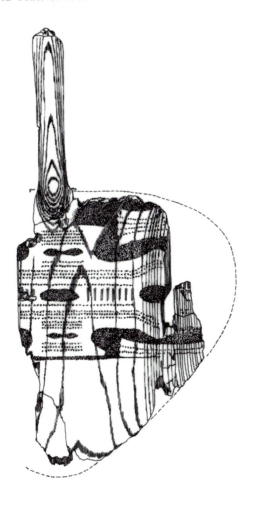

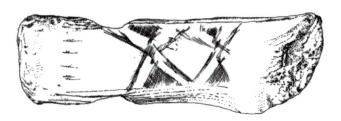

Figure 4.3 Ertebølle art – decorated paddle (top) and antler axe (bottom) from Tybrind Vig (after S. H. Andersen 1985)

one type has a much wider distribution than the other two, suggesting that there may really only be two groups with a territorial significance. Vang Petersen concludes from these local distributions that Ertebølle communities had a limited range and may have been strongly attached to specific areas.

Vang Petersen (1984) has tried to link this greater degree of territoriality in the Ertebølle to the evidence for conflict. The Dyrholmen material could be interpreted in these terms, but, as argued above, it requires further substantiation before it can play a full role in the discussion. More definite indications of conflict come from the skeletal record. At Skateholm I (L. Larsson 1989a) a transverse arrowhead embedded in the pelvis of an adult male was the cause of death; at Vedbæk Bøgebakken (Albrethsen and Brinch Petersen 1976) the adult, probably male (Bennicke 1985: 104), in Grave 19 was killed by an arrowhead wedged between the vertebrae. In her survey of Danish skeletal material Bennicke (1985: 98–101) found that a high proportion of Mesolithic skulls showed depressions, which she thought might in some part be the result of violence. There is thus a plausible case that territorial competition in the Ertebølle period spilled over into violent conflicts between groups.

One possible weapon of the period is the imported Danubian shaft-hole axe (Fischer 1981; 1982). Previous interpretations of these as ploughshares have now been abandoned in favour of the view that they are instead axes, possibly for woodworking (L. Larsson 1988a). Their use by agricultural communities as grave goods suggests that they were symbols of social status, and a similar explanation has been put forward for Denmark (Fischer 1981; 1982). They have been found on a number of Late Ertebølle sites, although not in stratified contexts. The number of axes is not great, but they do indicate a definite pattern of contacts with farming communities to the south over a long period. The other elements which also demonstrate contact of some kind are the T-shaped antler axe, taken up in Denmark presumably under influence from the south, and pottery, introduced around 4600 BC. However, while the idea of a fired clay container was presumably derived from agricultural groups, possibly along with some ideas on pottery decoration (as seen at Ringkloster – S. H. Andersen 1973–4) the form adopted was peculiar to the gatherer-hunter groups along the Baltic and Atlantic coasts. So a product developed from contacts with farmers actually led to the forging of links with similar late gatherer-hunter communities over a wide area. These links may in turn have contributed to the longevity of gatherer-hunter economies by providing external connections. The other area which has been claimed to demonstrate contacts with farming groups are the finds of domesticated cereals and animals reviewed above, together with a number of finds dating to the very end of the Ertebølle which are discussed below.

The question of exports to farmers has been rather less considered, but the most likely item is furs, given the evidence for the exploitation of fur-bearing species. At Skateholm (L. Larsson 1989a) pine marten, otter, wild cat and beaver were trapped, presumably for their fur. The Bjørnsholm midden (S. H. Andersen 1991) contained remains of red fox, badger, wildcat, lynx, otter, wolf, pine marten and polecat which may have been killed for their fur. At Norsminde (S. H. Andersen 1989) wild cat, beaver and wolf are thought to have been killed for their fur. Finally, at Tybrind Vig (S. H. Andersen 1985) a high proportion of fur-bearing animals were killed, including pine marten, wild cat, red fox, otter, badger and polecat, especially after 4500 BC. As noted above, the preservation conditions of the bones from this underwater site were such that careful examination produced strong evidence for the hunting of these fur-bearing species primarily for their pelts, in the form of cutmarks and signs of being held in traps. In itself, this does not of course mean that furs were exchanged outside gathering-hunting society, for the surplus production could be solely for internal consumption. However, the use of pelts as export items seems highly plausible.

THE INTRODUCTION OF AGRICULTURE

The evidence from burial practices, ritual activity, territoriality, and the exchange of status items complements that from the subsistence economy. The general picture is undoubtedly one of a highly complex and differentiated society at all levels, potentially divided both within and between communities. Specialisation, territorial claims, status distinctions and privileged access to ritual activities all point to a degree of social complexity which is far greater than that which can be claimed on present evidence for the societies dealt with in Chapter 3. Given that, it is no surprise that the transition to an agricultural economy was long delayed. When the Neolithic does begin in southern Scandinavia, however, it appears to take hold remarkably quickly. Current evidence from radiocarbon dating suggests that it was achieved in little over a century, between c. 3900 and 3800 BC (L. Larsson 1990a).

The original interpretation of the agricultural transition was naturally that immigrant farmers were responsible for introducing a range of artefactual, economic and monumental developments into southern Scandinavia by moving forward from northern Germany (e.g. Becker 1973; Troels-Smith 1982). Alternative models reviewed below have prompted a restatement of the traditional case for a migrationist interpretation by Solberg (1989). Solberg catalogues the introductions associated with the Neolithic in southern Scandinavia: these are domesticated cattle, sheep, goat and pigs, domesticated wheat and barley; new artefact types, especially TRB pottery, but also battle axes, flint daggers, pointed-butt axes and a flake-based flint industry; small houses; deliberate deposits in bogs of pottery, polished flint axes, animal bones, and even human bodies (Becker 1947); and monumental burial in the form of earthen long barrows.

Many of the elements contained in Solberg's list have, however, been seen from a different perspective by others, suggesting a greater degree of continuity than Solberg would allow. P. O. Nielsen (1986) has concluded from an examination of Ertebølle and TRB pottery that although there were differences in manufacturing technique between the two, the tempering agents used did not change and apparently neither did their function, as larger vessels in both traditions fall into three size groups and were used for cooking. More specific evidence comes from the Bjørnsholm midden in Jutland (S. H. Andersen 1991) and Löddesborg in Sweden (Jennbert 1985). At Bjørnsholm an Ertebølle level was succeeded by a TRB one; at the lowest point of the Neolithic level, below the point at which standard TRB pottery was found, was a single Funnel-Necked Beaker closely related to Ertebølle pointed-base vessels. The obvious conclusion to draw from this is that here at least there was a degree of ceramic continuity. At Löddesborg Jennbert argues that there is continuity from Ertebølle to TRB ceramics in terms of tempering material, clay sources, sherd thickness, vessel-building technique, firing methods and use for cooking; the only real differences she can discern are in decoration and shape. The pointed-butt axes have been suggested as deriving from the Limhamn Mesolithic stone axes, and Jennbert's review of the finds (1984: 108–10) led her to conclude that some pointed-butt axes were of Mesolithic date, thus demonstrating an overlap between the two types. Madsen (1986) has argued that the flintwork assemblages of the Ertebølle and TRB as a whole were very similar. As outlined above, there are now a number of small houses, some rectangular, of Ertebølle date, so no need for external introduction arises there. Lars Larsson's claims (1990a) that some hoards or votive offerings did take place in peat bogs during the Mesolithic would undermine another claimed novelty.

More significant as evidence for an element of local influence on subsequent Neolithic developments is the large number of settlement sites which demonstrate a degree of continuity from the Ertebølle (P. O. Nielsen 1984a). Søren Andersen's work (1991) along the Bjørnsholm Fjord in western Jutland has so far located four shell middens which show continuity from Mesolithic into Neolithic – Bjørnsholm, Lundgård, Åle and Siggård. His investigations of the Norsminde Fjord in eastern Jutland (1989) have produced three middens showing continuity: Norsminde, Store Nor and Kalvø. On Zealand, sample excavations of a number of small settlements in the Åmose bog have demonstrated continuous occupation across the transition at several locations (Fischer 1986; 1993). Among these sites is Spangkonge (Fischer and Asmussen 1988), an apparently short-lived site with Late Ertebølle pottery and a flintwork assemblage which includes a number of TRB types. In southern Sweden Jennbert (1984; 1985), M. Larsson (1985: 77–8) and Wyszomirska (1988) have identified several sites with both Ertebølle and TRB material. There is also a general overlap between the two in terms of the overall distribution of sites, as noted by P. O. Nielsen (1986), so that those areas with Ertebølle settlement have also produced Early Neolithic sites.

Continuity also seems to be demonstrated in terms of burial location by the site of Dragsholm on Zealand (Brinch Petersen 1974). Here a very late Ertebølle or very early TRB double grave, radiocarbon dated to *c.* 4000 BC, contained two adult females covered with ochre, wearing tooth beads of elk, red deer, wild boar and one of cattle (claimed to be from a domesticated animal), and accompanied by a decorated bone dagger, a bone awl and a transverse arrowhead. Only 2 m away is a grave holding the single burial of an adult male with a TRB Funnel-Necked Beaker, amber pendants, transverse arrowheads and a battle axe, radiocarbon dated to *c.* 3700 BC.

The strong evidence for settlement continuity needs to be dealt with by those who favour an immigrant farmer hypothesis, but it is difficult to see how this could be achieved, given that its advocates concentrate their efforts on attempting to demonstrate discontinuities. That there was a shift in the settlement pattern cannot be denied, P. O. Nielsen's survey (1984a) of eastern Denmark and southern Sweden showing, for example, that only some 30 per cent of TRB sites in that area were preceded by Ertebølle occupations. The significance of this, and other evidence of discontinuity such as new pottery and lithic styles, is another matter, however. The overall picture is of a considerable degree of continuity, sufficient to suggest that the Mesolithic population was not pushed aside or killed off by immigrant farmers. The only migration model which seems at all plausible is one which involves a relatively small group of incoming farmers merging with an existing gathering-hunting population. However, once the input from a new population is reduced to this minimal level there is no real need to posit a population influx at all. There is nothing about the changes involved which requires that they were introduced by a movement of agriculturalists. Given the long period of stability on the agriculturalist/gatherer-hunter frontier, it seems highly unlikely that such a dramatic shift in the border could have come about without the cooperation of the indigenous population.

One general theory of local development which has been applied to the southern Scandinavian material is that of Binford (1968), in which sedentism led to population growth. Paludan-Müller (1978) suggested that with an improved climate after 6000 BC estuarine environments became highly productive. Population rose there, and by 5500 BC a local population surplus existed. This surplus population moved inland to set up new settlements, but the carrying capacity of these areas was soon reached. It became necessary to take action to improve the productivity of the land. The only area where a significant increase in production could be achieved was the forest, so inland forest clearance took place to improve browsing for game, as suggested above by analogy with Britain. Continued population growth eventually led to the need to boost production again, this time by the introduction of domesticated species of animals and plants. While it is generally agreed that there probably was an increase in population during the Ertebølle (e.g. Blankholm 1987), in itself that need not have led to any surplus of population over resources. The territorial behaviour seen in regional and local artefact styles and the evidence of violent conflict could support the population pressure theory, but other factors could equally well lie behind it. Against Paludan-Müller's interpretation is the cumulative evidence of a lack of exploitation of resources which were well known, such as fish, as discussed above. This absence of desire to maximise production points clearly to overpopulation not being a major problem for Ertebølle communities, in which case it could hardly be a factor behind the adoption of agriculture.

A theory which has received more substantial support is that of a severe resource shortage triggered by events beyond the control of the gatherer-hunter inhabitants of southern Scandinavia. The specific sequence of events proposed (Rowley-Conwy 1984) is that the postglacial rise in sea level led to the creation of a rich habitat of marine resources; communities exploiting these resources became sedentary, thus requiring local resources throughout the year; although such resources were plentiful during most of the year, there was a shortfall in food supplies in late winter and early spring (February to April); this gap was filled by the gathering of shellfish, which gave a poor calorific return for the labour expended in collecting them, but were at least readily available. After 4000 BC falling relative sea levels brought about a decline in the oyster population, thus producing a crisis in the food supply between February and April; it was not possible to fill this gap by intensifying the exploitation of other wild resources, as land mammals were at their least meat-heavy in spring, while other shellfish, such as cockles, vary far more in their food content throughout the year, and are at their worst in the spring; the only alternative left was to take up the domesticated plants and animals familiar from contacts with agricultural communities to the south.

Objections to Rowley-Conwy's explanation have been on a number of grounds (Madsen 1986). First, it is difficult to see why a shortfall in the supply of oysters could not have been replaced by increasing the role of fishing, perhaps with the storage of fish, rather than necessitating a complete social and economic transformation. Second, the use of oysters was limited to Atlantic coasts, so the impact on inland areas and the Baltic coast is unclear (Blankholm 1987). Finally, some research has been carried out on the seasonality of shellfish collecting at Ertebølle (Madsen 1986; Brock and Bourget 1989). The most detailed study was on cockles rather than oysters, because the growth lines used to estimate the season of the shells survive bettter on cockles. The examination of the cockles showed that they were collected mainly in May and July, with other specimens dating to April, June, August, September, October and December. While these results could be argued not to apply to oysters, a preliminary study undertaken on oysters did indicate a similar pattern (Madsen 1986), and it also seems highly unlikely that mass collections of oysters should take place in late winter and early spring, during which cockles were ignored, while cockles alone should be collected later in the year. Brock and Bourget (1989) conclude that shellfish were a supplementary item of diet collected during the summer, and the evidence presently available would tend to support their argument. The specific significance imputed to oysters in Rowley-Conwy's model is unsupported at the moment; along with the limits placed on their importance by geographical factors, this must lead to the view that an oyster shortage could have been only a partial catalyst for events, if it had any long-lasting impact at all. A less specific model, which sees the oyster shortage as only one element of the changes brought about by shifting sea and land levels, could be produced by combining Rowley-Conwy's suggestions with evidence of a continuing rise in relative sea levels in Scania. Here previously productive lagoons and estuaries were flooded or blocked from the sea by new beach ridges, bringing about dramatic local shifts in productivity (M. Larsson 1985; L. Larsson 1990a; Berglund and Larsson 1991). Lars Larsson has argued that the existing social structure broke down completely under this pressure and new social arrangements came into being. This combination model represents little improvement, however, as evidence for this breakdown in the social order is difficult to discern, and in any case this would again only relate to a coastal situation.

A recent theory which has led to a considerable debate is the notion of the 'fertile gift' (Jennbert 1984; 1985; 1988). The Danubian shaft-hole axes found on Ertebølle sites as surface finds are reasonably seen as prestige items acquired from agricultural communities (Fischer 1981; 1982). Fischer went on to speculate that livestock, grain and the knowledge necessary for agriculture arrived in Scandinavia through the same trade networks which were used to import the Danubian axes. Jennbert (1984; 1985; 1988) has extended this argument to suggest that a number of sites in Scania show clear evidence of continuity from Mesolithic to Neolithic, with the presence of domesticated cereals at the end of the Ertebølle being interpreted by her in terms of a 'fertile gift'. Agricultural products were a luxury good for gatherer-hunter communities, obtained through exchange relations involving both gift-giving and marriage alliances. Grain was imported to be made into porridge, bread or alcoholic drinks, consumed on special occasions, while domestic animals were imported to be killed at feasts (Jennbert 1988). Although the later stages are not entirely clear in Jennbert's model, it seems as though this gradually led on to local production of domesticates.

The specific evidence presented by Jennbert in support of her interpretation (1984; 1985) concerns a number of Scanian sites where there are layers containing a mixture of Ertebølle and TRB pottery, two of which have produced Ertebølle sherds with grain impressions. At Löddesborg these are of both wheat and barley and at Vik of wheat (Jennbert 1984: 93–4). Jennbert interprets this as demonstrating a lengthy period of transition from the Mesolithic to the Neolithic. While many of Jennbert's points, such as the evidence for a degree of settlement continuity and the presence of cereal grain impressions on sherds, are accepted by others, the idea of transitional sites has met with considerable resistance (e.g. M. Larsson 1986; Madsen 1986; P. O. Nielsen 1986). The general view is that Jennbert was mistaken in arguing that the stratigraphic integrity of her sites was high; indeed, at the shell middens of Jutland and Zealand discussed above, there is a clear degree of continuity but very little sign of any transitional levels. Certainly, it is difficult to imagine that a long transition occurred in Scania, but not among the sedentary resource-rich communities of Denmark. Also, as has been noted above, the record of domesticated animals in Ertebølle contexts is extremely weak. Exchange practices which brought domesticated cereals to Mesolithic Scania are seen as plausible, but not a long period of gradual replacement of fertile gifts by local production.

If a swift transition be required by the evidence then a major role for gatherer-hunter communities as decision-makers is strongly indicated. External factors such as incoming farmers or sea-level changes seem inadequate to account for the continuity evident in the material or the scale of the changes, while models of gift exchange need to account for the demands of gatherer-hunter societies. Recent explanations have therefore been situated within the social competition model (P. O. Nielsen 1986). The two most detailed explanations have been put forward by Blankholm (1987) and Madsen (1986). Blankholm suggested that economic intensification led to the development of storage facilities and exchange practices, which in turn produced an unequal distribution of wealth and a social pressure to intensify production even further to accumulate more wealth and control the community. Intensification of production meant over-exploitation and diminishing returns, hence the recourse to agriculture to maintain levels of production. There is certainly ample evidence of social complexity and therefore the possibility of significant inequalities of power and status, an argument also presented by M. Larsson (1991) in terms of the ability of older men to control access to significant resources through exchange. However, the archaeological record does not support the notion of over-exploitation, although it does not rule it out at a local level.

Madsen (1986) has produced a more specific geographical model, which emphasises the role of inland communities. He also sees power within Ertebølle communities as related to food resources, and seen in territorial behaviour such as the violent deaths of the Mesolithic. He sees a distinction between coastal and inland Ertebølle communities, with the coastal groups as being under no pressure of lack of resources, but the sedentary inland occupants of major settlements as having developed a similarly complex society to their coastal counterparts but without the subsistence base to sustain it. The instability of the situation led to the adoption of agriculture. In Madsen's model the adoption of agriculture therefore takes place initially inland, possibly mainly in Jutland. While there probably were differences between different areas of south Scandinavia, it is not at all clear that these were related to a coastal/inland dichotomy. The near-simultaneous transition appears to have shown a considerable degree of continuity at both major and minor sites, on the coast and inland, as outlined above. Madsen instead argued that base camps should have been deserted during the transition, which was not the norm.

Madsen also argues that if power involved the control of resources, then resources which lay outside traditional structures would not be welcomed, so that farming was not adopted for a considerable period. This appears highly probable, but may also suggest an eventual reason why an agricultural economy was taken up. A lengthy period of social competition, during which domesticated species were known, must have offered many possible occasions on which domesticates could have been introduced, but social rules kept them at bay. However, a long period of social competition is in itself likely to lead to the undermining of traditional structures of power and authority. The presence of domesticated cereals on Ertebølle vessels in Scania, as documented by Jennbert, may reveal the first breakdown of social rules, as might some of the disputed pollen evidence for cereals. If clearings were being established in the forests to encourage animals or plant growth, this may already have dealt a blow to existing notions concerning the proper relationship between the community and the landscape, and would also have increased notions of territoriality, which were already developing through the permanence of settlements and the development on the coast of cumulative monumental constructions in the form of shell middens. A conceptual shift may have taken place in the relationship between human action and the environment, as the notion of a cultural landscape came into being. The degree of intervention required by agriculture and the construction of Neolithic communal monuments would not then have seemed so alien. In these circumstances, rules which sought to draw a line between acceptable and unacceptable food resources would have weakened. Once domesticates in the form of grain became acceptable exchange items, then such traditional controls were further undermined, and the idea of cultivation no longer seemed out of the question. The initial adoption of agriculture may have been the work of a few communities, but with the cultural barrier to the adoption of agriculture removed there was nothing to prevent other groups taking up this now acceptable and useful resource.

The transition to agriculture in southern Scandinavia was thus the product of a shift in thinking rather than an economic development, for with it came the whole paraphernalia of the TRB Neolithic. The time of limited and partial acceptance of the Neolithic package was therefore at an end, as Neolithic material culture offered new scope for drawing social distinctions using a wider range of status objects. Previously, items which had crossed the farmer/gatherer-hunter barrier had to be interpreted in local terms, because their full significance in their place of origin was lost in translation. Those whose meaning defied translation were ignored or deemed inappropriate and unacceptable. With a new conceptualisation of the relationship between the community, the environment and the landscape, the Neolithic world now became full with meaning and all its many and varied facets became acceptable.

5

THE INTRODUCTION OF FARMING TO BRITAIN AND IRELAND

The adoption of an agricultural economy in Britain was traditionally seen as merely one example of a continuous process of invasion and migration from continental Europe. Since the questioning of this general model, however, (Clark 1966) there has been an increased willingness to consider alternative theories of local development.

A PIONEER NEOLITHIC

The first issue which needs to be examined is the timescale involved in the transition to agriculture. Many authors have followed Case's (1969) suggestion of a long prologue of Neolithic activity, perhaps starting as early as *c.* 4850 BC (Jacobi 1982), before the establishment of a developed Neolithic around 4000–3800 BC, associated with the construction of funerary and ceremonial monuments. In Case's original model this prologue was intimately connected with his theory of immigrant farmers. In his view the pressures on the colonists of maintaining a farming economy in this new land were so great that social ties between communities broke down to leave a series of small isolated groups. These settlements of individual households were incapable of organising labour on the scale necessary to construct large monuments, so these had to wait until communities had grown larger.

While the specific model put forward by Case has not been followed by others, there are still many who believe that the weight of archaeological evidence favours a long period of trial and error before a fully fledged Neolithic economy developed around 3800 BC. (e.g. I. F. Smith 1974; Fowler 1983; Cooney 1987–8; Williams 1989). This would thus involve a lengthy period of small-scale settlement and minor impact on the environment, which would be difficult to detect. Nevertheless, it is argued that there are three lines of evidence, one negative and two positive, which support the argument for a pioneer Neolithic.

The negative evidence is that of the dearth of fifth millennium BC dates for Mesolithic sites in Britain (Bradley 1978: 7–8). This has been seen as a national pattern, but is now more tightly confined to southern Britain (Mercer 1990a). The excavation of a number of midden sites on the island of Oronsay (Mellars

1987) has produced a series of radiocarbon results which firmly anchor these sites in the fifth millennium BC, with Cnog Sligeach definitely still occupied close to 4000 BC. The recently excavated surviving fragment of a midden on the west coast of Scotland at Carding Mill Bay near Oban had even later dates, at around 3800 BC (Connock *et al.* 1991–2). This substantial Mesolithic presence in Scotland has been suggested as pointing to a discrepancy between northern and southern Britain (Zvelebil and Rowley-Conwy 1986) in terms of Mesolithic activity. An alternative possibility is that the isostatic uplift which occurred in northern Britain at the time, together with the rise in sea level, has meant that while Late Mesolithic coastal sites survive in large numbers in the north, they have largely been destroyed in southern Britain. Inland areas certainly appear to be less intensively occupied during the Late Mesolithic (Bradley 1990: 64). The relatively blank picture inland is gradually being filled in, however, as more settlements are located, some of which belong to the fifth millennium BC. For example, sites in the Pennines with microliths and built hearths are dated to the mid-fifth millennium BC (Stonehouse 1990). Even in the South of England there are now at least a few sites dated to the fifth millennium BC. At Chesham in Buckinghamshire (Stainton 1989) a small flint-working area for the production of microliths has given a date of *c.* 4700 BC; further south, in Hampshire, Wakeford's Copse (Bradley and Lewis 1974) contains a number of pits within a small activity area, and dates to *c.* 4500 BC. The most significant inland settlement site of the Late Mesolithic in southern England promises to be Bowman's Farm, also in Hampshire (Bewley 1994: 42–3): it is sited on the edge of a floodplain, and appears to date to *c.* 4800 BC. Two pairs of houses were discovered, the structures consisting of shallow ring ditches in which the walls were set. Although the fifth millennium BC in southern Britain is therefore not overly well supplied with Mesolithic settlement, there is now sufficient to narrow any gap to the second half of the millennium, while further discoveries may remove it all together.

This theory of a fifth millennium BC hiatus in Mesolithic occupation has never applied to Ireland, as some of the first settlement sites to be given radiocarbon dates were seen to fall after 4500 BC. This included both coastal sites such as Rockmarshall and Sutton and inland sites such as Newferry (O'Kelly 1989: 27–8). Further excavations have continued this pattern, with sites like Ferriter's Cove on the coast of Co. Kerry (Woodman and O'Brien 1993), which has some fifteen radiocarbon dates spanning the fifth millennium, and other less well known Late Mesolithic occupations, as at Moynagh Lough, Co. Meath (Bradley 1991).

The first positive element in favour of a pioneer phase of agricultural economy are the claimed fifth millennium BC Neolithic sites. These are interpreted differently in Britain and Ireland – as evidence of the early replacement of a Mesolithic by a Neolithic economy in Britain and of a long period of overlap between two societies in Ireland. Unfortunately, the British examples are nearly all single dates on unsatisfactory materials such as the heartwood of old timbers, which are liable to produce results which are misleadingly old. The most important of these claimed fifth millennium BC British Neolithic sites is the Briar Hill causewayed enclosure in northamptonshire (Bamford 1985), which the excavator has argued dates back to *c.* 4600 BC. However, a close contextual review of the evidence (Kinnes and Thorpe 1986) reveals that it is highly likely that residual material has produced these early dates, and that the true date of the site lies in the early part of the fourth millennium BC, as a number of the radiocarbon results would suggest.

In Ireland the case for a pioneer Neolithic being reflected in radiocarbon dating is bound up with the interpretation of the house at Ballynagilly (see Figure 5.1) in Ulster (ApSimon 1976; Cooney 1987–8). There is no difficulty in identifying Ballynagilly as an Early Neolithic domestic structure, with a range of associated finds of clear Neolithic type, but it has become increasingly apparent as time goes on that the site stands in isolation at a date of 4600–4400 BC. This is not only as a Neolithic site of such an early date, but also as an assemblage of plain bowl Neolithic pottery (Kinnes 1988; J. Thomas 1988a). To accommodate it within a model of immigrant farmers (e.g. Green and Zvelebil 1990) is difficult, for why would they head straight to Ulster, missing out Britain? It falls no more happily within a hypothesis of indigenous contact with farming groups leading to a local initiative to adopt an agricultural economy, for where could the nearest farming groups have been? It is also surely significant that the dates for later phases of the site, such as those associated with Beaker and Early Bronze Age pottery, are the earliest known in Ireland for these assemblages. Recently, the excavator is reported as having decided that the early dates for Ballynagilly have to be abandoned (Monk 1993), as twenty years of further radiocarbon dating have failed to produce sites of a similar age.

Figure 5.1 Reconstruction of Ballynagilly house (after Parker Pearson 1993)

The developed, or mature, Neolithic, of larger communities opening up more of the landscape to agriculture, could at one time have been associated with the Elm Decline. The dramatic and almost universal decline in elm pollen across northwest Europe occurs around 4000 BC. Its significance has been much debated ever since Iverson (1941) first suggested that climatic deterioration was the cause of the Elm Decline he had observed in Denmark and which Godwin (1940) had noted in Britain. The argument (charted in A. G. Smith 1981) has concentrated on two alternative models: climatic factors against human activity. Those writers who favour anthropogenic models (often employing multi-causal models, e.g. Walker 1966; Birks *et al.* 1975; Godwin 1975) have tended to have the best of the argument. The evidence that other trees declined at the same time as the elm, the possible use of elm leaves for fodder (Troels-Smith 1960) and above all the extensive archaeological evidence of Neolithic activity contemporary with the Elm Decline have all become planks in this interpretation. Although a number of authors have raised the possibility that disease was a factor in the Elm Decline (e.g. Troels-Smith 1960) this has generally not been considered due to the complete lack of positive evidence in its favour.

Recently, however, the case for a Neolithic outbreak of Dutch Elm Disease has become much more convincing. Although Dutch Elm Disease is thought to have spread from Asia to Europe in the early part of this century, and to Britain in 1927, Rackham (1980) has collected evidence pointing to instances in the nineteenth century and earlier. A crucial piece of evidence was provided by the discovery of two specimens of the elm bark beetle (*scolytus scolytus*) (the main carrier of the fungus causing the disease) in a pollen core taken at West Heath Spa, Hampstead Heath, at a level just below that at which the Elm Decline was evident (Girling and Greig 1985). Further, a pollen diagram from modern woodland which had suffered from Dutch Elm Disease showed a progressive decline in elm pollen accompanied by an increase in the representation of *plantago lanceolata* (ribwort plantain). This pattern is characteristic of Elm Decline pollen diagrams (Perry and Moore 1987).

This British evidence for a natural cause underlying the Elm Decline is strengthened by a find from Denmark (Kolstrup 1988). In the Åmose bog on Zealand a piece of elm wood with a gallery system made by the elm bark beetle was discovered at the level of the Elm Decline. The most likely interpretation of the Elm Decline is therefore now seen to be a prehistoric outbreak of Dutch Elm Disease which coincided with and aided a major period of clearance activity.

Now that the Elm Decline is agreed to be of no real relevance to the question of the beginning of the Neolithic in Britain and Ireland, attention has switched to pollen bearing deposits which lie below this horizon. In particular, there is the vexed question of pre-Elm Decline finds of cereal grains. Edwards and Hirons (1984) originally noted eight sites (five in Ireland) from which cereal grains have been reported in deposits which pre-date the Elm Decline, with the earliest dated to *c.* 4600 BC. Many more such occurrences have been documented in the last decade (Simmons and Innes 1987; Edwards 1989a; Zvelebil 1994). Some of these, for example at West Heath Spa (Greig 1989), may pre-date the Elm Decline only slightly, in which case they would fall within the Neolithic on any chronology, but many lie in the fifth millennium BC. On the other hand it should be noted that, as in Scandinavia, considerable problems exist with the definite identification of such grains (see Chapter 4). Worries have been expressed that contamination can occur in the sampling process and that the mounting medium used for pollen samples can cause the pollen to swell (O'Connell 1987; Monk 1993). A more significant problem is that occasional mutations of grasses such as *Molinia caerulea* (Purple moor-grass) can produce features similar to cereal pollen, leading to misidentifications (O'Connell 1987; Monk 1993). However, while such factors may have contributed to an over-estimate of the number of instances, Zvelebil (1994) is probably correct to argue that contamination or misidentifications are more than balanced by the likelihood that older analyses would have ignored cereal-type pollen occurrences in pre-Elm Decline deposits on the grounds that there could not be cereals in such early levels.

An additional issue which needs to be resolved is that 'cereal' grains have been noted from sites which are clearly too early to be influenced by agricultural practices, for example Oakhanger VII (Rankine *et al.* 1960) in Hampshire, which dates to before 8000 BC, among many others in both Britain and Ireland (Woodman 1992a; Zvelebil 1994). While Williams (1989) is confident in arguing that the Oakhanger sample was clearly contaminated and can therefore safely be discarded, the grounds for such a definite position are not established by her. While it may be legitimate to question the sampling procedures in such an old case, it is more difficult to throw into doubt the seven cereal-type pollen grains found at Willow Garth in Yorkshire in contexts predating 6000 BC (Bush and Flenley 1987).

If these very early finds of cereal-type pollen are instead accepted as plausible, then they require an explanation. The most likely is that much of the cereal-type pollen identified belongs to large pollen grains of wild grasses. One possible reason for their increase in frequency during the Late Mesolithic would be climatic (Kinnes 1988); another would be that they reflect human activity (Caseldine and Hatton 1993; Zvelebil 1994). This would not be so much in creating conditions in which large-grained grass pollens could flourish as in the way that opening up the forest to produce clearings would allow grass pollen to spread more widely and so reach more pollen sampling sites (Edwards 1993).

Sufficient doubt therefore exists as to the positive identification of cereals in pollen diagrams to make these fifth millennium BC 'cereals' of questionable relevance to the discussion concerning a pioneer phase of agriculture. Until actual carbonised cereals are recovered from Neolithic sites securely dated to the fifth millennium BC there can be no real certainty about the earliest signs of cereal cultivation (Edwards 1989b). This would apply no matter whether this material is taken as evidence for the presence of Neolithic farmers (Cooney

1987–8) or Mesolithic independent cultivation of wild grasses, turning them into domestic species (Zvelebil 1994).

In conclusion there is a lack of compelling evidence for a pioneer stage to the Neolithic. The hiatus in the Mesolithic has largely been filled in northern Britain and is starting to be narrowed further south. The claimed fifth millennium BC Neolithic radiocarbon dates dissolve on close examination to leave a pattern in which the Neolithic appears to begin in all aspects, including monument construction, by 4200–4000 BC (Kinnes 1988; J. Thomas 1988a). The pollen record of early cereals still has not been confirmed by finds of actual cereals on site (Monk 1993). The weight of the evidence is in favour of a relatively sharp transition to the Neolithic rather than a long drawn out period of experimentation in a largely empty landscape. This thus necessitates a consideration of the role of the existing Mesolithic population, whether as opposing an influx of farmers or as adopting the idea of agriculture from the continent.

NEOLITHIC COLONISTS

The standard explanation of the introduction of agriculture into Britain and Ireland has, since the nineteenth century, been that it was brought there by immigrant farmers. One element in this explanation was that it dealt with the clear parallels between Neolithic material culture in Britain and Ireland and on the Continent, in terms of pottery, stone and flint axes, and the monument types of long barrows and chambered tombs and causewayed enclosures. A second was the general tendency to ascribe all change to the arrival of newcomers from the Continent (Clark 1966; Waddell 1978), but even when this paradigm was challenged it was still seen as unarguable that agriculture must have been introduced by immigrant farmers. Reinforcing this view was a negative perception of the Mesolithic population, in which they were seen as children of nature, conditioned by the environment (e.g. Godwin 1975: 465). They were seen off by the more vigorous Neolithic newcomers, either directly in warfare, more indirectly through disease, or a fragment surviving in the tenuous shape of Piggott's Secondary Neolithic (1954), eventually to be absorbed.

One of the major difficulties of the immigrant hypothesis has always been the problem of identifying the region from which these immigrants would have come to Britain, before moving on to Ireland (Piggott 1955; 1972). While the LBK cultures of the Rhineland and northern France seem the most likely source of inspiration (Whittle 1977: 238–44), there are wider links with Scandinavia and eastern Europe which cannot be ignored, and there is as yet no satisfactory 'homeland' from which a Neolithic package was transferred. Case (1969) attempted to circumvent this problem by proposing that the original homeland was now submerged, but a better understanding of sea-level changes has ruled this out. Neither has it proved possible to identify different groups of colonists arriving in different areas of Britain and carrying with them different material culture traditions. There are also some elements of the Neolithic of Britain which appear to lack convincing ancestors on the Continent: for example, the leaf-shaped arrowhead, a significant item in many Early Neolithic flint assemblages in Britain and Ireland, is a rare find on the Continent (Green 1980; Kinnes 1988). Finally, the use, at least in Ireland, of both flint axes and ground stone axes is now clearly established within the Late Mesolithic (Sheridan *et al.* 1992), so no Neolithic colonisation is needed to explain their presence.

A major divide also exists between those who see agriculturalists as constantly moving to new lands, and those who view them as static and largely tied to their existing fields. Case (1969: 183) argued that the early farming communities along the coast of northwest Europe would have been 'adaptable, sea-going and restless', and thus ideally suited to colonising the offshore islands. Dennell, on the other hand, sees these groups as focused almost entirely on cultivating crops and rearing livestock (1983: 174). While it may well be, as Whittle (1990b) has argued, that areas in the western part of the loess distribution proved to be less fertile soils than commonly thought, this in itself would seem scant reason to uproot and set out for an unknown land and an uncertain future. One would imagine that only a substantial land shortfall, caused by overpopulation or declining soil fertility, would impel communities who relied on their intimate knowledge of a particular landscape for their economic survival to take such a drastic risk. No real evidence suggests that either factor had become significant by 4000 BC, and in any case the most obvious step for large areas of the Continent would have been to push further north into Scandinavia, which must have been fairly well known through long-established exchange networks (see Chapter 4).

There are relatively few archaeologists who have in recent years argued in favour of the immigrant hypothesis, and those who have done so have tended to base their conclusions on the lack of convincing alternatives (e.g. Fowler 1983: 3; Bradley 1984: 10–14; Cooney 1987–8). Thus Cooney believes that an infilling process occurred, in which Neolithic settlers gradually came to occupy all available areas of Continental Europe before spreading into Britain and thence Ireland. He suggests that this pattern is visible in Ireland itself, with the areas occupied by early farmers being those which were only sparsely settled by the indigenous Mesolithic population. There is, however, no convincing chronological evidence to support this model within Ireland, and it becomes impossible if the late date around 4200–4000 BC for the inception of the Neolithic in Britain is accepted, as this would allow very little time for Neolithic colonists to run out of room in Britain (e.g. Hunt 1987: 11–12) before turning their sights to Ireland.

The alternative possibility is that the indigenous Mesolithic population decided to take up agricultural production, either to cope with a shortfall in the subsistence economy or as an additional source of material to be used in status competition. In both theories the idea of food production and some of the domesticates themselves would have to be obtained from Continental Europe by the local Mesolithic population, presumably through a process of exchange.

There is little doubt that Mesolithic populations in Britain and Ireland could have been in contact with Neolithic Europe. Ample evidence exists for Mesolithic seafaring (Clark 1975), and clearly there could have been cross-channel contacts between southwest England and Brittany. Further, there is nothing which should have prevented Mesolithic communities from gaining the materials and knowledge necessary for the development of an agricultural economy in this way, as it is difficult to see any good reason why Neolithic groups would have refused to enter into trade.

The oldest secure evidence of Mesolithic seafaring is the settlement of Ireland around 7000 BC, after the drowning of the land bridge which had connected the island to Britain and the Continent of Europe. Further seafaring can be seen in the arrival of communities on the islands off the western coast of Scotland (Dennell 1983: 185). It is also apparent from a number of finds that Orkney, off the north coast of Scotland, was settled during the Late Mesolithic (Colin Richards pers. comm.), which would have involved crossing one of the most difficult stretches of water in Britain and Ireland.

There are also a number of finds made in Scotland which point strongly to the development of deep-sea fishing during the Late Mesolithic. At the shell midden on Risga, in the mouth of Loch Sunart, on the west coast of Scotland, excavated in 1920, the bones of various seafish were recovered, including skate, conger eel, grey mullet and haddock, indicating the use of a boat for line-fishing or netting (Wymer 1991: 37). At Morton, on the east coast of Scotland around 5000 BC (Coles 1971), there were hearths, stakeholes forming temporary structures and a midden. In the midden were over a thousand fish bones, 90 per cent of those identified being cod. As both heads and tail vertebrae were found, it seems as though whole cod were caught. As cod are difficult to catch from the shore, their presence in such large numbers must imply the use of boats. The excavation also recovered the remains of a massive sturgeon which may have been three metres long, and weighed 250 kilograms. This enormous fish would have to have been taken at sea. A more recent piece of evidence is of the transport of hard stone from Arran off the west coast of Scotland. Pitchstone from Arran has been found on Mesolithic sites in the Tweed Valley in central Scotland and on the Isle of Jura (Affleck *et al.* 1988).

But despite this variety of evidence pointing to seafaring there is no real sign of contacts between Britain and Ireland apart from the Isle of Man (Woodman 1989). The later 'heavy-bladed' industry on the Isle of Man is comparable to Late Mesolithic flintwork traditions in Ireland and different to those of Britain (Cooney 1987–8), but did not appear to involve the actual exchange of items. Perforated antler mattocks, which appear to be an important item in Late Mesolithic Britain (see pp. 103–4), seem to be missing from Ireland and the Isle of Man (Zvelebil 1994). This could be interpreted in terms of the deliberate and overt expression of cultural barriers, but the rarity of evidence for contacts with the Continent is rather more worrying. After the land bridge was drowned around 7500 BC, Britain and Ireland became steadily more separated from continental trends, such as the development of bone and antler artefacts of Maglemosian type (Jacobi 1982). Almost no artefacts seem to have been imported from the Continent, or exported to it. One possible exception is the find of domestic cattle bones at Ferriter's Cove, Co. Kerry, in Ireland (Woodman and O'Brien 1993). The bones themselves are dated to *c.* 4350 BC, and come from a site with a Late Mesolithic lithic assemblage (older excavations have produced similar associations). There is a single Neolithic find from the settlement, a plano-convex knife, so Woodman and O'Brien consider three possibilities: first, that part of the site is Neolithic, but the cattle bones were found near to Mesolithic stone tools with a very similar radiocarbon date; second, that the cattle had been obtained by exchange or theft from nearby Neolithic communities, but there are no good candidates for local Neolithic sites at this early date; the final suggestion is that the cattle were obtained through gift exchange with Neolithic societies outside Ireland (presumably on the Continent), which seems the most likely interpretation in the absence of plausible alternatives. The possibility of local domestication seems to be ruled out by the absence of Irish cattle intermediate in size between wild and domestic forms.

The other element which could point to continental connections is the claimed construction of megalithic chambered tombs in Late Mesolithic Ireland. At Carrowmore, Co. Sligo, a series of small passage tombs were excavated (Burenhult 1980; 1984), producing cremations of adults of both sexes with grave goods of bone pins and rings, stone beads, chalk balls and fragments of pottery, with radiocarbon dates in the Early Neolithic, including one early example around 4100 BC. This would seem to support the theory that passage tombs were the earliest Irish burial monuments, and that the type began with small, simple, structures (Sheridan 1985–6). However, Grave 4 has produced a date of 4600 BC on charcoal incorporated in a stone hole of the small central chamber (Burenhult 1984: 64). The chamber itself had been disturbed at a later date, the backfill containing a large amount of cremated bone, some fifty fragments of antler pins and a scraper made of chert (Burenhult 1980: 68–82), so nothing which absolutely has to be Neolithic in date. It is therefore possible to claim Carrowmore Grave 4 as a Late Mesolithic passage tomb, and possibly even the other sites as well, which must lead on to the question of influences from the Continent in terms of tomb type, but the reaction against this notion has been universal. The strongest critic has been Caulfield (1983), who rejects the claim on the basis that the tombs contain no Late Mesolithic material, that the shell middens excavated in the vicinity were of Neolithic date, so there is little sign of Mesolithic settlement in the area, that the radiocarbon dates are from contexts and on materials that are less than ideal, and that a number of the megaliths are firmly set in the fourth millennium BC. It seems surprising with hindsight that such an important claim could be made on the slender basis of a single radiocarbon date, using a material and a context which could be guaranteed to produce a date older than the structure built above it. The Carrowmore date can therefore at present add nothing to the debate concerning the possibility of sea-borne contacts with the Continent as a mechanism for the transmission of ideas, objects and livestock.

POPULATION PRESSURE

Dennell (1983: 174–85) has suggested that population pressure was a factor in the Late Mesolithic of Britain, caused either by an increasing population, or by a decreasing resource base with the expansion of forests making it harder to hunt. The influence of Rowley-Conwy's work on Denmark on the second proposed cause is clear (see Chapter 4). Dennell does not choose between the two causes, but restricts himself to considering a series of developments which he argues took place in response to an ever-increasing imbalance between population and food supply. These involved a more systematic use of inland resources, especially the increased clearance of woodland, a greater exploitation of marine resources and as a final development, when earlier measures had failed, the acquisition of cereals, sheep and pottery from Continental Europe, knowledge of which had been gained through contacts acquired through greater seafaring. These new items, such as cereals, sheep and pottery, were gradually introduced as the Mesolithic communities transformed their economy into one based on agricultural production. There is little role in this model for monuments, couched as it is in terms of economic rationality (J. Thomas 1988a).

What traces are there of attempts to increase food production during the Late Mesolithic? Direct evidence of food production other than finds of foodstuffs recovered during settlement excavations is rare, but one artefact type which appears during this period and which may be related to food procurement is the mattock (see Figure 5.2). These are common on Late Mesolithic sites on the west coast of Scotland, where they are made from the beams of red deer antlers. They appear well suited to a variety of heavy-duty tasks, as they are solid bone pieces worked to produce a blade. A more definite view of their use has, however, emerged recently through more intensive study of their characteristics (C. Smith 1989). Smith has argued that antler mattocks were used primarily as digging tools, a judgement based on traces of polish, striations possibly produced by gritty soils, and flaking at the tip. They would have been used along riversides for digging up roots, aquatic plants, small animals, molluscs for bait, setting fish traps and snares and occasionally butchering stranded marine mammals. The last is mentioned because of the one clear association of a mattock with productive activity, the example from Meiklewood discovered with the remains of a stranded whale (C. Smith 1992: 153) and now dated to c. 4800 BC (Bonsall and Smith 1990). This interpretation of mattocks as digging tools first and foremost is gaining acceptance (e.g. Zvelebil 1994); this may not necessarily imply the planting of wild cereals, as has been suggested for the Iron Gates sites (see Chapter 2). It does, however, point towards an increased investment in harvesting wild plant resources and possibly also fishing, as bait may have been dug up for line-fishing.

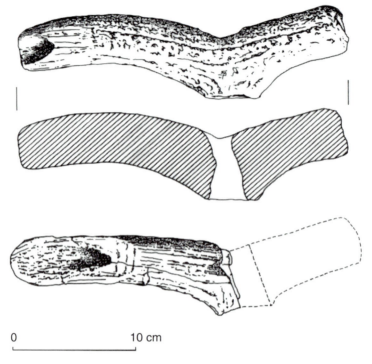

0   10 cm

Figure 5.2 Red deer antler mattocks from Meiklewood (top) and Risga (bottom)
(after C. Smith 1989)

A more indirect source of evidence is the pollen record for the Late Mesolithic. Simmons has put forward an economic model which sees woodland clearance as a response to changing environmental conditions (Simmons *et al.* 1982; Simmons and Innes 1987), at a time of increasing population. He suggests that the Late Mesolithic deciduous forest was less productive than the earlier less densely forested landscape. Woodland canopies were generally dense and continuous, thus reducing the amount of light which reached the forest floor, which in turn meant that the quality and quantity of undergrowth would suffer, providing less plant food for both humans and animals. This would inevitably put pressure on existing subsistence strategies. The expected response (Simmons *et al.* 1982) would be to exploit on a preferential basis those areas which naturally retained a greater degree of vegetational diversity, and second, if this was both technologically and culturally feasible, to encourage this diversity by artificial means. Such human interventions would include the clearance by fire of woodland in favoured locations, generally by the forest edge, spring-heads, lakeside or foreshore, where natural concentrations of game are most likely to be found.

The results of pollen analysis in various parts of Britain and Ireland have been argued to show deliberate woodland fire clearance during the Mesolithic (catalogued in Zvelebil 1994). Areas where this appears to be the case include western and southern Scotland, Cumbria, the North York Moors, Merseyside, North Wales, East Anglia, Dartmoor, Sussex, Hampshire, Dorset and northern and western Ireland. On occasion these disturbances in tree cover are associated with Mesolithic artefacts (e.g. Jacobi *et al.* 1976; Cloutman 1988). If the Late Mesolithic economy were based, at least seasonally, on the exploitation of deer populations then such forest burning would, by increasing the quality and quantity of grazing and browsing plantstuffs available in woodland clearings, attract economically significant concentrations of deer (Mellars 1975; 1976). The same might well apply to wild boar. Birds and small mammals should also be attracted to these areas (Ahlgren 1966). The increased amount of light reaching the woodland floor would also encourage the growth of hazel and therefore hazelnuts, the exploitation of which is commonly noted in the archaeological record (Zvelebil 1994). Greater productivity of other fruit and berry producing shrubs would also be expected. The burning of woodland would therefore have made a significant contribution towards raising the productivity levels of the forests which covered much of Britain in the Late Mesolithic, perhaps doubling output (Mellars 1976).

However, in some areas this would have been an ultimately destructive process, as Simmons and Innes (1987) have argued for the North York Moors. They note that sites where such environmental disturbance has been noted are concentrated on the high watershed areas of the moors, generally at the headwaters of streams, at heights of over 300 m above sea level. They also note that the frequency of such fire clearances appears to increase through time. They believe that the cumulative effect of frequent burning was disastrous, as it prevented the recovery of soils in many places, accelerating their acidification and causing upland woodland to turn into unproductive heathland, moorland and blanket bog. They go on to suggest that their proposed 'ecosystem failure' would have led to increased stress on a subsistence regime which was over-dependent on specialised resources such as the management of game populations as in inland Yorkshire or declining marine resources as elsewhere. Using Dennell's suggestion of an increasing population combined with Simmons's ecological catastrophe one could see this as an attempt to raise subsistence production to meet new demands, which in the longer term went wrong to leave a situation in which supply fell as large tracts of land became unproductive. This moment of catastrophe would then appear to be the point at which agriculture was introduced to meet the subsistence needs of a rising population.

Against the Simmons model, however, it should be noted that Christine Williams (1985: 118), in her detailed analysis of the Soyland Moor peat deposits in the central Pennines, does not see burning as a major tool for environmental modification. Instead, the clearances recorded at this site seem to range from extensive to small-scale, which suggests that a mosaic of clearances, perhaps for different purposes, may have existed, rather than the consistent pattern of the creation of small-scale clearings related to encouraging concentrations of game which the Simmons model would seem to require. Such detailed comparative pollen analysis, when carried out elsewhere, might well reveal an equally complex picture of Late Mesolithic environmental exploitation. Similarly, comparison of the Hockham Mere and Quidenham Mere deposits in East Anglia (Bennett *et al.* 1990) led to a discussion of the role which small domestic fires could have played in charcoal production. These would give erratic records which would vary from site to site, thus making more general patterns difficult to discern. While it is clear that in some areas at least there was a definite increase in the intensity of clearance through time, it may well be that part of this was related to the creation of clearings for settlement or industrial activity, or to subsequent domestic fires, rather than food production.

In addition, it is possible for factors other than human agency to bring about a disturbance phase visible in the pollen record. These include natural fires, windthrows of trees and geological changes (Edwards 1982). A number of pollen analysts have argued that the presence of plants outside their normal habitat, high amounts of anthropogenic indicator species, long-lived disturbance episodes, and the repeated burning of the same area, are in themselves insufficient to be sure of the human origin of the disturbance episode, and that only the presence of cereal pollen can show beyond doubt that these burning incidents were not produced by natural causes (e.g. Edwards 1989a; 1989b). This brings us full circle, and if accepted widely this line of thought would mean that it would never be possible to identify fire clearance which was unrelated to cereal production. This seems an unnecessarily pessimistic view to take, for it is not only the individual pollen cores which need to be assessed, but also the overall pattern. No convincing reason involving natural causes has yet been put forward as to why there should be an increase in fires through the Mesolithic, so the simplest course of action at present is to interpret it as reflecting human impact on the landscape.

Zvelebil (1994: 62) concludes from his recent review of the material that the proposed burning of the landscape, the use of mattocks for soil preparation or root harvesting and the presence of large-grained grasses, probably due to fire-assisted forest clearance, together made up a system of plant food management. He argues that the environment was being manipulated to raise the productivity and predictability of food resources. This certainly seems plausible on the current evidence.

However, need this mean that there was pressure on resources brought about through rising population or a decline in the subsistence economy? A population pressure model certainly does not match the chronology presented above. Unless there was a long pioneer Neolithic in the fifth millennium BC, then the overall lack of sites belonging to that period hardly suggests a burgeoning population, or even a food shortage if the population remained stable, given the probability of a managed environment. The falls in production envisaged by Simmons would have been a severe problem on a local scale, but need not have adversely affected the subsistence economy overall if productivity was raised elsewhere. While there is no longer a case for a Late Mesolithic hiatus, that does not mean that the evidence will support a diametrically opposed position. The number of sites dating to the fifth millennium BC is still sufficiently small to rule out any possibility of a population which had expanded beyond its ability to feed itself. Moreover, in Ireland the population pressure model has never been a realistic possibility, given that until recently large areas of the island were thought to be unoccupied before the advent of an agricultural economy. Systematic survey and excavation work (e.g. Woodman and O'Brien 1993) is beginning to fill in the picture, but even work which specifically targets Mesolithic sites, such as the Bally Lough Archaeological Project in Co. Waterford (Green and Zvelebil 1990; Zvelebil *et al.* 1992), has located few sites. A Late Mesolithic Ireland in which large regions were only sparsely populated thus seems an unlikely candidate for a population rate which is outstripping the availability of food resources.

SOCIAL COMPETITION

The other possible explanation of the agricultural transition in Britain and Ireland is that of the social competition model, as discussed in earlier chapters. While an approach rooted in models of social inequality among gatherer-hunters has not been explored in any detail for Britain and Ireland, it has influenced the views of a number of writers (e.g. Kinnes 1985; Zvelebil and Rowley-Conwy 1986). If there was a competitive society in the Late Mesolithic of the Islands, in which status was enhanced by the holding of feasts, then the attraction of a storable resource that could be used to generate surpluses for distribution at feasts, thus enhancing the status of individuals or groups, would be obvious (Dennell 1992).

What form could the evidence for social competition take in Britain and Ireland? The range of factors to be considered in a consideration of the Late Mesolithic as a complex society is much the same as in southern Scandinavia (see Chapter 4) – burials, personal ornaments, economic intensification and specialisation, sedentism and continuity into the Neolithic. In many areas the picture is far less clear than in southern Scandinavia, but where it is possible to make comparisons there are some clear contrasts.

The usual starting point in any discussion of social complexity is burial practice. The most substantial evidence of Mesolithic burial comes from the only definite cemetery of that date, Aveline's Hole in Somerset (Jacobi 1987). Some 70–80 skeletons were found in 1805, and then between 1919 and 1933, in a cave which may have been artificially blocked. The only grave goods found were perforated winkle shells. This would therefore seem to be a potentially important site in terms of the question of emerging social complexity and settlement stability. However, the radiocarbon dates on human bone show the site to fall at the time of the transition from the Early to Late Mesolithic, as they range from *c.* 8000–7500 BC. This major site therefore cannot be drawn into any discussion of the nature of Late Mesolithic society.

Given the existence of the Aveline's Hole cemetery at such an early date it is surprising that there is a lack of burial evidence for the Late Mesolithic in Britain. The midden sites of western Scotland have produced fragments of human bone in small numbers. At the sites on Oronsay (Mellars 1987: 290–300) bones, mainly of fingers and toes, from a few adults and children were recovered as isolated and relatively dispersed finds. C. Smith (1992: 152–3) has suggested a possible explanation for the selective nature of the bones recovered: that corpses were exposed on platforms as one stage in funerary rites, during which the flesh decomposed; afterwards the clean bones were collected for burial elsewhere, with small bones being missed in the collecting up of the cleaned bones for burial elsewhere. This is a quite plausible reconstruction of events, and a similar interpretation has been put forward to explain comparable patterns in the British Neolithic (see Chapter 7). As yet, however, there are no good candidates for the final resting place of such bodies. Similarly, the recently discovered rock shelters at An Corran on Skye (Saville and Miket 1994) and Carding Mill Bay on the west coast of mainland Scotland (Connock et al. 1991–2) have both produced a small amount of human skeletal material.

One other possible cemetery site was uncovered at Dounan on the west coast of Scotland in 1879. Given the date of the discovery, it is not surprising that records are sketchy, but they record the finding of seven skeletons close together, with an eighth, that of a 10- to 12-year-old child, just below. They were all located in a small area, lying on shingle at about 12–15 metres above sea level, covered by a layer of sand, then pebbles and finally a thick midden deposit of dog-whelk shells (Morrison 1982). In the absence of radiocarbon dates this must remain only a possible Mesolithic site, but it is undoubtedly an intriguing discovery.

A final piece of evidence bearing on Late Mesolithic burial practice is the dating of some cave burials to the period, through the use of direct radio-carbon accelerator dating. At Paviland Cave on the Gower Peninsula in South Wales the Paviland II burial (a single leg) is now dated to c. 6200 BC (Stringer 1986), while a human jaw from Caldey Island off the southern Welsh coast has been dated to c. 6000 BC (Hedges et al. 1994). This discovery of a new facet to Mesolithic burial practice does not, however, mean that all unaccompanied burials or stray bones in caves can be attributed to the Late Mesolithic, thereby solving the lack of human remains, as there are a number of well-established Early Neolithic examples of the practice, e.g. King Alfrid's Cave, Ebberston (Lamplough and Lidster 1959) and Selside, Ribblesdale (Gilks and Lord 1985), both in Yorkshire.

The Late Mesolithic burial record of Britain is thus extremely scanty when set against that of southern Scandinavia, and demonstrates no trend towards increasing social complexity and differentiation. The largest site in terms of numbers, Aveline's Hole, occurs at the beginning of the sequence, although the scattered finds from Oronsay and elsewhere may have a greater significance than is usually assumed, if they are the remnants of a complex burial ritual of exposure and secondary burial. The absence of the major body parts may mean, however, that such rituals did not end with burial, but with the casting of the bones into the sea. In this instance, therefore, the lack of evidence could be interpreted as a consequence of highly structured rituals, rather than the absence of them. The burial record from Ireland is even more insubstantial, setting aside the claimed early dates from the Carrowmore tombs (see pp. 102–3). It is clear that midden sites in Ireland played no major role in the disposal of the dead.

The absence of complete bodies from the Late Mesolithic of Britain and Ireland also means that there is an absence of grave goods. While items which may have acted as grave goods in one stage of the mortuary ritual could have been recovered during excavations, it is not possible to identify them as such. There are, however, examples of the kind of objects which are used in southern Scandinavia as grave goods, such as axes and jewellery. The number of perforated shell and tooth beads, one of the most common grave goods in southern Scandinavia, is small compared with Scandinavia, but they have been recovered from shell middens in western Scotland and Dorset, and other sites in Wales and western England (Newell et al. 1990: Appendix V). The most significant recent find comes from the Madawg rock shelter in the Wye Valley of Wales (Barton 1994). Here there were Late Mesolithic microliths around a spread of ash containing hazelnut shells, together with eleven perforated shell beads of the European cowrie (Trivia monacha), probably brought from the Bristol Channel, found in a tight cluster, suggesting that they formed a necklace. While some of the sites where beads have been found have also produced human skeletal material, the majority have not, including recent excavations.

An area of economic activity which has implications for the question of social complexity is the exploitation and exchange of raw materials. In the Late Mesolithic this involves the use of hard stone, flint and chert. While there is little if any evidence of this involving the transport of material between Britain and Ireland, or to or from the continent of Europe, there is a considerable body of evidence which points to the movement of lithic items on a more local scale, within both Britain and Ireland.

As already noted above, pitchstone from Arran, off the west coast of Scotland, has been found on Mesolithic sites in the Tweed Valley in central Scotland and on the Isle of Jura (Affleck et al. 1988). Similarly, bloodstone from Rhum, also off the west coast of Scotland, was being exploited and presumably transported in the Mesolithic (Mercer 1990a). In southwest England pebbles from hard stone sources in Cornwall have been found as far away as Hampshire and Sussex (Care 1982). In the North of England the Staple Crag Early Mesolithic site in Teesdale has produced a group of flakes which appear to be made of Langdale rock from Cumbria in the Lake District, some 60 km distant (Coggins et al. 1989). No definite examples of Late Mesolithic exploitation of what was to become the largest axe production site in Neolithic Britain have, however, yet been found.

In Ireland the Bally Lough Project in the southeast has recovered evidence pointing to Late Mesolithic quarrying for rhyolite (Green and Zvelebil 1990). Rhyolite was an important raw material locally, as it provided the only source of pieces large enough to fashion into blades and axes. Some 20,000 rhyolite fragments were recovered during the excavations near Tramore, although the presence of Late Mesolithic, Neolithic and Bronze Age artefacts on the site indicates that the outcrop was exploited over an extremely wide time range. Surface survey work and excavations in the surrounding area have produced surprisingly little rhyolite, so either the vast bulk of material was transported out of the area altogether, or there was a very high wastage rate, leaving behind large amounts of quarrying debris for every usable roughout produced. At present it is not possible to distinguish between these two suggestions.

Also in Ireland, ground stone axes were a common tool of the Late Mesolithic (Woodman 1978: 108–14; Sheridan *et al.* 1992), although the scale of production is unclear. Both shale and mudstone were, however, transported from sources at least 60 km distant to major Late Mesolithic sites. The mechanism for this movement of material is not established, as the distances are not too great to represent the movement of groups or individuals to the sources, rather than the exchange of axes, as in the Early Neolithic. At least one example of a hoard of axes is known from the Late Mesolithic, at Ferriter's Cove (Woodman and O'Brien 1993). A group of five mudstone axes was located in the silty soil making up the site, between finds which both produced radiocarbon dates of *c.* 4350 BC; there seems little possibility that these represent objects which had been lost or forgotten, so a deliberate deposit of axes appears to be the motivation. Another five axes were found on the rest of the site. It is difficult to interpret the Ferriter's Cove axe cache in strictly economic terms, leaving open the possibility of an act of offering and deliberate withdrawal of items from circulation.

The dominant raw material in the Late Mesolithic of Britain and parts of Ireland was flint. There are a number of sites which appear to represent specialist production sites, at which a surplus was created, presumably for exchange with other groups. One of the most intensively examined is Broom Hill in Hampshire (O'Malley 1978; O'Malley and Jacobi 1978), first discovered as a flint scatter some 50 × 40 metres in extent, on a small sand patch. Subsequent excavations produced a series of pits, some containing material which gave radiocarbon dates ranging from *c.* 7600–5500 BC, one of which has been claimed to be a 'dwelling pit' as it is surrounded by fourteen possible postholes, but this has been doubted (Boismier 1991). Some 89,000 lithic pieces have been recovered from the site, almost all of flint. The flint source was a substantial outcrop only a few hundred metres from the settlement. Axe and adze production was undoubtedly an important activity on the site, with over a hundred tranchet axes and adzes being found, more than any other Late Mesolithic site, along with sharpening flakes. Many of these are unfinished, as the tranchet flake had not yet been removed, while the sharpening flakes found do not match the finished tools recovered, so the axes and adzes to which they relate have already been removed. It has been widely argued that the scale of production at Broom Hill suggests that this high quality flint was the spur to the development of specialist production for exchange (e.g. Cunliffe 1993: 29). It is unfortunate that present day methods of analysis do not enable us to trace the distribution of the products of the Broom Hill site.

The positioning of sites relative to the availability of good surface flint sources has been established to be common practice on those chalkland areas in southern England which are overlain by superficial deposits of clay-with-flints. A number of smaller tranchet axe production sites in such locations have been noted by Care (1979). The ready availability of nodules of a size suitable for axe manufacture appears to have been a significant factor influencing site location in the Late Mesolithic. Some idea of the scale of production at these sites is given by the finding of considerable numbers of large crude picks, which were probably used for quarrying or grubbing flint nodules from the subsoil (Care 1982). Other small tranchet axe production sites have been found outside this area, e.g. Cliffe in Kent (Ashton 1988). Given the importance of flint production, it is perhaps surprising that there is little evidence of flint being found in hoards, although there are occasional examples, as at Dalkey Island of the east coast of Ireland (Liversage 1968), where a group of blades and flakes was found below a Late Mesolithic midden.

The clearest evidence for the production and movement of lithic raw material comes from the Isle of Portland in Dorset. This is the main source of chert in southern England, and this was exploited from the Late Mesolithic onwards. The Culverwell site (Palmer 1989; 1990) is dated to c. 6100–5400 BC. The main feature of the site is an extensive midden deposit 0.45–0.6 metres in thickness, made up of limpet and winkle shells. Above and beside this midden deposit are various hearths and cooking pits and areas of possible stone paving, a small hollow in one containing an axe, a pierced scallop shell and a smooth round pebble, interpreted as a foundation deposit. The artefacts from Culverwell include several hundred picks made from the limestone bedrock and many pebble tools, as well as flint microliths. The limestone picks (see Figure 5.3), 4–5,000 of which have been found on the Isle of Portland as a whole, are interpreted as quarrying tools (Palmer 1970), used to obtain Portland chert from thick veins in the limestone. It has been argued that sites on Portland were seasonally occupied, as the peninsula, which may even have been an island at this time, lacks the resources necessary to sustain a large permanent population (Evans 1975: 87). Identical picks to those found on Portland, made of coarse chert and limestone, have been recovered from Late Mesolithic sites in Cranborne Chase (Care 1979), where they may have been used for working flint nodules free from the clay subsoil, as suggested above. This similarity may point to the existence of a group engaged in a seasonal round, as some 50 km separates the two groups of sites. Most of the fine Portland chert found in Cranborne Chase occurs in the form of cores and flaking debris, which suggests that chert nodules rather than finished products were brought from Portland (Care 1979).

Portland chert moved beyond Cranborne Chase, reaching Hampshire in quite large quantities (Jacobi 1981) and even further afield. While the local transport of chert may be explicable in terms of the movement of people, the more distant

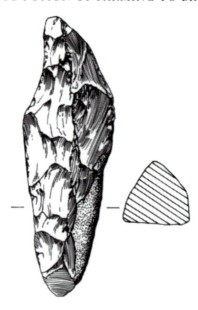

Figure 5.3 Portland chert pick from Culver Well, Portland (after Wymer 1991)

finds are less easy to interpret in this fashion. While it used to be thought that the widespread occurrence of chert could be seen as a result of roving groups of hunters, current models of Late Mesolithic economic practices suggest a greater degree of sedentism (see pp. 115–17) than this would allow, making the presence of an exchange system through which chert passed rather more likely. Given the strong possibility of an exchange system operating in the Late Mesolithic, it is significant that chert is in no way a superior raw material to flint, so its movement into areas with an ample flint supply is apparently rather mysterious. This exchange system therefore has no clear economic rationale, and may be better interpreted in terms of the attractions of exotic and thus potentially controllable materials, and the role of exchange in cementing good relations between neighbouring groups, who may have been involved in the exchange of less visible items including people.

Specialisation in the field of lithic production can thus be demonstrated quite clearly. It has long been argued that there was also a degree of specialisation within the subsistence economy, represented by the 'Obanian Culture' of western Scotland. This is found in a series of caves near Oban and at shell midden sites on a number of offshore islands, including those on Oronsay mentioned above (Mellars 1987). The unusual feature of these sites is that they contain large numbers of implements made of bone and antler, such as barbed points or harpoons, awls, pins, mattocks and 'limpet scoops', along with flat, elongated, beach pebbles seen as 'limpet scoops/punches' or hammers (see Figure 5.4). The distinctive microlith forms used elsewhere in the Late Mesolithic are generally

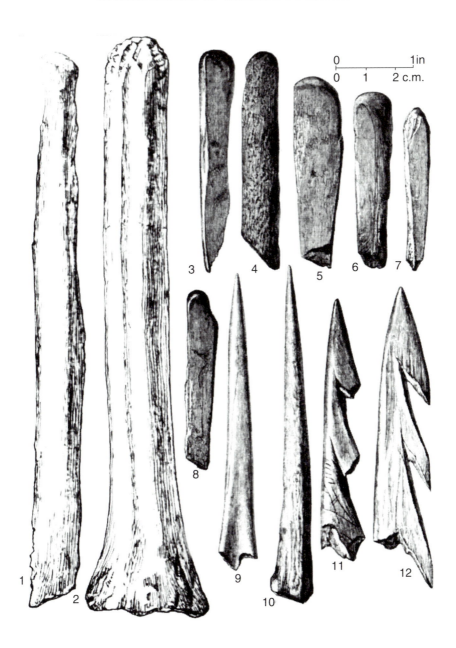

Figure 5.4 Late nineteenth-century drawings by Anderson of bone and antler
implements from the Druimvargie rock shelter, Oban

scarce on Obanian sites, making them difficult to place until the advent of radio-carbon dating. As recently as 1982 it was possible to argue that the Obanian represented a facet of the Early Neolithic economy (Jacobi 1982), but the fifth millennium BC radiocarbon dates from Oronsay (Mellars 1987) and those from a programme of dating bone and antler artefacts (Bonsall and Smith 1990) have demonstrated the Late Mesolithic nature of the sites. While some of the older excavations may have produced microliths (Woodman 1989), more recent work has produced firmer associations. At Staosnaig on Colonsay both typical Late Mesolithic flintwork and stone 'limpet hammers' were present (Mithen *et al.* 1992), dated to *c.* 5800 BC by thermoluminescence, although it is not yet clear if these were contemporary. A more secure association occurs in the An Corran rock shelter on Skye (Saville and Miket 1994), where over eighty Obanian bone and antler tools were found together with a typical Late Mesolithic lithic assemblage, including microliths, made from both flint and basalt, the latter using beach pebbles and flakes from mountainside scree. The site dates to *c.* 6400 BC. The Obanian can therefore be seen to be a consistent element of western Scotland from early in the Late Mesolithic.

The economy of the island shell midden sites is dominated by shellfish, fish, and sea mammals (see Figure 5.5); although land mammals and bird remains are found they are relatively scarce. This is still true for the mainland sites, but the dependence on fish and shellfish is not so complete, for example at An Corran. This economic evidence has undoubtedly influenced the interpretation of the bevel-ended antler, bone and stone tools found in such large numbers on Obanian sites as 'limpet hammers' or 'limpetcoops'. The significance of these to the subsistence economy is suggested by the lack of animal bones, despite the presence of large numbers of tools made from antler and deer and pig bones. It seems possible that the deer and pig remains found were brought to the islands as sources of raw material for tool manufacture, rather than for food (Mellars 1987: 284). Limpets were perhaps gathered to use as fish bait rather than as food in their own right; the limpets could have been hooked on lines, or scattered on the surface of the water (C. Smith 1992: 152). Reflecting the importance of limpets to the subsistence economy, the large pebbles have been interpreted as limpet hammers, with which limpets could have been knocked off rocks, and the small pebbles and pieces of bone and antler as scoops for removing the limpets from their shells.

These traditional interpretations have in recent years been thrown into doubt by alternative suggestions. As Chris Smith (1992: 153) has argued, it is not particularly difficult to remove limpets from their shells, especially if they have been heated, so a specialised tool may well have been unnecessary. At present the favoured alternative use is as an aid to skin working, for softening up hides (e.g. Finlayson 1993), as the ends show signs of rubbing, polishing and abrasion (Morrison 1980: 157). The larger stone pebbles have also been interpreted as hide preparation tools (Finlayson 1993), although C. Smith (1992: 153) has suggested that they are suitable for detaching limpets from their rocks with a swift blow.

Figure 5.5 1882 engraving by Grieve of the Caisteal-nan-Gillean midden on Oronsay

What is the nature, then, of the Obanian sites? Are they normal settlements, or some sort of specialised camp for exploiting marine resources? The first question to be addressed must be the issue of sedentism and year-round settlement versus seasonal occupation. The clearest evidence on the seasonality of occupation comes from the Oronsay sites (Mellars and Wilkinson 1980). The otoliths (or 'ear-stones' – chalky nodules found in the inner ear) of saithe (coalfish) grow rapidly along with the fish in the first three years of life, and can therefore provide a fairly accurate indication of the time of year when they were caught. From the otolith size it is argued that fishing took place at Cnoc Sligeach during July and August and at Cnoc Coig from September to November. Some confirmation of autumn occupation at Cnoc Coig is given by the presence of hazelnuts and a predominance of grey seal bones, some very young, as seals form breeding colonies on land during the early autumn. There are also indicators of a lower level of activity at Cnoc Coig during the summer and winter. At Priory Midden, a more sheltered site, fishing was undertaken from the beginning of winter to early spring, and only young saithe were caught. The low numbers of fish bones relative to shells at Priory Midden would support this interpretation, as present-day older saithe retreat into deep waters over the winter months, putting them beyond the reach of Late Mesolithic fishing technology. At Caisteal nan Gillean II fishing was carried out over a longer period of the year, with the main emphasis during the summer months. This suggestion of seasonal occupation is perhaps supported by the relatively scanty evidence of structures at the middens: at Cnoc Coig, the only major recent excavation (Mellars 1987: 234–40), there are a couple of small stake-built structures with central hearths, but nothing with a very permanent look.

The idea that Obanian sites post-date microlithic assemblages (Woodman 1989), while once attractive, can now be shown to be wrong. It is therefore now generally agreed that the Obanian represents a coastal economic adaptation to a rich marine environment (e.g. Armit and Finlayson 1992), but the exact mechanics of the situation remain to be established. What is the relationship between the various Oronsay sites and between them and those on larger neighbouring islands or on the coast of the mainland? Are they specialist fishing camps, occupied by groups sent out from base camps on the larger islands or the mainland, or are they elements of a seasonal round, merely moving from one site to another as the time of year allowed (Davis 1987: 83)? The presence of bones from the larger land mammals such as red deer and wild boar certainly points to contacts with the outside world, but these could have been obtained by exchange, rather than being brought with them by mobile groups of gatherer-hunters engaged in fishing expeditions. At present it is not possible to decide between these two alternative settlement patterns, but either of them indicates a considerably greater degree of economic planning than other writers have allowed in the past.

Finally, although the emphasis of discussion of the Obanian midden sites has always been in terms of the subsistence economy, it is possible that they may have a wider significance. Finlayson (1993) has argued that the Obanian bone and stone tools (limpet scoops and hammers) were primarily related to hide production, a view which he claims is upheld by preliminary experimental work. From this he hypothesises that the predictable marine resources of western Scotland were exploited to allow the time for industrial activities in the form of the manufacture of fine leather clothing. This fine clothing could then be a vehicle for social display and a status good, possibly also with the beads found on many Obanian sites being sewn on to this clothing to add to the elaboration of the garments. While this interpretation is undeniably speculative, it does represent a more favourable view of the potentiality of Late Mesolithic communities in Britain and Ireland than the prevailing view that they were concerned almost entirely with the subsistence economy.

Elsewhere, there are varying opinions of the degree of sedentism represented at different sites. Woodman takes a generally negative view for Ireland as a whole, arguing that at Ferriter's Cove the lack of structures, well-built hearths, the animal bone and artefact assemblages all point to the site being an accumulation of several short-term episodes of deposition (Woodman and Andersen 1990). He sees Ferriter's Cove as typical of Late Mesolithic settlement in Ireland, and suggests that of the coastal sites only Sutton, Co. Dublin, might have been occupied for a larger part of the year. On the other hand, Armit and Finlayson (1992) favour the idea of base camps in western Scotland, along with more specialised sites, such as the shell middens, although their grounds for this view are not stated. They are here following Bonsall in his interpretation of the Williamson's Moss site in Cumbria (Bonsall *et al.* 1989); Bonsall's view of the site is that it was permanently or semi-permanently settled, based on the efforts made to provide firm living surfaces in this wet location. Stone pavements were thrown down as makeup (although some may date to the beginning of the Neolithic), and a series of wooden foundations were set into the wet ground, on which were laid bark floors. The effort invested implies to Bonsall that something rather more than fleeting visits occurred at Williamson's Moss. This seems a reasonable conclusion, and it is therefore unfortunate that the lack of artefactual associations must render the deliberate nature of some of the deposits open to question, and the reasons for undertaking such work unclear. The overall impression of this un-satisfactory body of evidence is that the possibility of sedentary communities existing in Late Mesolithic Britain and Ireland is there, although the sites where detailed examinations have taken place tend to point towards groups engaged in a regular seasonal round of movement between sites.

The final aspect of the assessment of the social complexity of Late Mesolithic Britain and Ireland is the question of continuity of occupation. The evidence is not so fine-grained as is the case in southern Scandinavia, but some specific obser-vations can be allied to general patterns in a number of different areas. In Ireland the Dalkey Island midden (Liversage 1968) was occupied from Late Mesolithic times into the Early Neolithic, with pottery and the bones of domestic animals present in upper levels; the sites at Newferry and Curran Point also seem to demonstrate continuity (Green and Zvelebil 1990). It has also been suggested that hunting, fishing and food collection remained important in the Neolithic (O'Kelly 1989: 29–30). On a broader scale, the results of the surface survey carried out as part of the Bally Lough Project in southeast Ireland (Green and Zvelebil 1990; Zvelebil *et al.* 1992) strongly point to continuity from Mesolithic to Neolithic. The major sites from both periods are in the same geographical location, set back from the present coastline, and in three instances Mesolithic and Neolithic sites adjoin each other. More detailed evidence from these sites will only be available on excavation.

As in southern Scandinavia and Ireland, the evidence for continuity in Scotland and Wales comes mainly from shell middens. At Ulva Cave on a small island in the Hebrides, and in the Forth Valley in eastern Scotland (Sloan 1984) there are middens which were used in both the Mesolithic and Neolithic (Armit and Finlayson 1992), while the continued formation of new shell middens in the Neolithic suggests a degree of continuity in the subsistence economy. A similar picture can be seen at Prestatyn in North Wales (D. Thomas 1992), where two Early Neolithic cockle shell middens are located next to two mussel shell middens of probable Mesolithic date. More general changes in the subsistence economy with the advent of the Neolithic will be considered below (see Chapter 7).

Some of the factors pointing towards a degree of social complexity which were identified in southern Scandinavia can thus be isolated in Britain and Ireland as well, although not so clearly. The social competition model could therefore apply in both areas. There do, however, also appear to be real differences between the two, with a much less substantial burial record and less evidence for personal ornamentation in Britain and Ireland. Exchange practices did move items over quite long distances, but did not involve contacts with farming groups on any scale – if anything, there appears to have been a deliberate avoidance of such contacts, and there was certainly no question of the adoption of items of Neolithic material culture such as pottery. There were, though, distinct regional material culture traditions, as noted for southern Scandinavia. The largest body of evidence for Britain and Ireland comes in the form of the pollen record showing environmental impact during the Late Mesolithic, on a scale which seems to surpass that in southern Scandinavia. The significance of these variations is not clear, but it has been suggested that even within Scotland there may have been different regional responses to the Neolithic (Armit and Finlayson 1992). Within a model of social competition the various elements making up the Neolithic would have represented a new source of potential economic surplus and a new range of material symbols, which could have been drawn on differently by the various Late Mesolithic communities encountered (as already argued for southern Scandinavia in Chapter 4).

These indications of the potential significance of Late Mesolithic social and economic variability for differing responses to the Neolithic echo Bender's (1992) response to the model presented by Julian Thomas (1991). Thomas rightly stresses the importance of the Neolithic as being far more than simply an economic adaptation, with the central role played by monuments in the reproduction of society. However, he has also argued (1988a) that the point at which a Neolithic economy was adopted in northwest Europe was primarily determined by changes in Neolithic society itself, rather than in Late Mesolithic communities. Bender (1992) rightly sees this as implying that the gatherer-hunters of the region reacted in a uniform fashion to a Neolithic package, denying the possibility of significant differences existing between Mesolithic communities. These differences created variations in the degree of resistance to change, and therefore led to different patterns of acceptance and modification of all elements of the Neolithic. It is these differences which can be explored in the subsequent development of Neolithic societies in both southern Scandinavia and Britain and Ireland.

6

EARLY NEOLITHIC SOUTHERN SCANDINAVIA

The main issue to be addressed in this consideration of the Early Neolithic of southern Scandinavia will be the degree and significance of Late Mesolithic influences on subsequent developments. These will be explored within a consideration of the nature of Early Neolithic social organisation as revealed by the evidence from economic, settlement, monumental and ritual practices, and end with a discussion of regional differences and the relationship between these and the regional variation noted for the Late Mesolithic.

THE SUBSISTENCE ECONOMY AND SETTLEMENT

As elsewhere in Early Neolithic Europe, discussion of the subsistence economy of southern Scandinavian early agriculturalists has traditionally been in terms of slash-and-burn or swidden agriculture. In southern Scandinavia the slash-and-burn theory is particularly associated with the work of Iverson, who proposed his *landnam* (land clearance) model of forest clearance in 1941 (1941: 25). He proposed a three-stage sequence, starting with a fall in tree pollen and an increase in herbs and grasses, often accompanied by charcoal; followed by a phase of farming; finally there was a recovery in tree pollen, together with a fall in birch and hazel, which were thought to have occupied the cleared area, showing that the clearing had been abandoned and the forest was now growing back. In this model of shifting cultivation the settlement would move to a new location every fifty to one hundred years.

The theory has been successfully challenged for central Europe and the LBK (see Chapter 2) on archaeological grounds. In southern Scandinavia the main basis of opposition (e.g. Rowley-Conwy 1981) has been the productive capacity of the soil. It has been suggested that even long-term cropping of the soil would produce only marginally poorer yields and therefore there was no need for an agricultural system in which land was cleared by fire, only to be cultivated for a short time before it was left to lie fallow for a much longer period (e.g. Midgley 1992: 364). In addition, experimental work in Denmark has pointed to efficiency problems in slash-and-burn farming in temperate woodland (Steensberg 1957). Finally, radiocarbon dating has shown for some time that at least some of the clearances lasted for centuries rather than decades (Tauber 1965).

Recently, however, pollen analysis has been used to argue for the existence of swidden agriculture in Early Neolithic Denmark. Pollen samples taken from the mound of the passage grave of Klekkendehøj on the island of Møn, south of Zealand, suggested to S. T. Andersen (1988) that hazel and alder groves had been felled, the land lightly burnt and barley and wheat sown for a short time before the passage grave was built. A similar sequence can be detected in the pollen preserved in one of the vessels found in the façade trench of the long barrow at Bjørnsholm (S. T. Andersen 1990), dated to *c.* 3900 BC (S. H. Andersen and Johansen 1990). Here a recently burnt birch woodland showed signs of the growing of cereals. Andersen has recently summarised the evidence from Denmark as a whole (S. T. Andersen 1993): at Klekkendehøj, Bjørnsholm, Bygholm Nørremark (Jutland) and Strandby Skovgrave (Fyn) cereals were cultivated in small clearings in recently burnt birch (or hazel) woodland; at Rude (Jutland), Hassing Huse Mose (Jutland) (S. T. Andersen 1992–93), Mønge Havregard (Zealand) and Næsbyholm Storskov (Zealand) lime forest was cleared for pasture, generally by felling rather than burning. This clearly suggests that the burning was not simply a tool for forest clearance, but, as in slash-and-burn, an important precondition for the cultivation of cereals. However, this need not imply the existence of a full cycle of swidden agriculture. Although these particular fields evidently were shortlived, the fact that they were all succeeded by burial monuments may mean that the sequences being studied are not typical of Early Neolithic agriculture. If further detailed analyses could show the whole cycle of burning–cultivation–abandonment to occupy only a short time then a model of shifting cultivation would certainly have to be revived, although not as the only agricultural regime. If this is the case then it would suggest not that the Early Neolithic farmers of Denmark were incapable of maintaining clearings, but that the nature of society was such that short-term field clearance was more appropriate within the wider economy as determined by the nature of society.

What crops were grown in these clearances, and how far were wild plant foods still important? Unfortunately, the direct evidence available virtually all derives from sites dating well into the Early Neolithic, and from contexts such as causewayed enclosures (e.g. Jørgensen 1976; 1981) which may not be at all representative of the more general subsistence economy. Exceptions are the Norsminde shell midden (S. H. Andersen 1989), where a few charred grains of emmer wheat and naked barley were recovered, together with hazelnut shells, and Sigersted on Zealand (P. O. Nielsen 1984a) where a small number of seeds of six-rowed barley were found. There is plentiful evidence from pollen diagrams of the cultivation of cereals, but the scale of production cannot easily be estimated, except that it is generally agreed to result in a relatively minor impact on existing woodland (e.g. Gebauer and Price 1990).

The main source of evidence concerning early agriculture has been indirect, in the form of impressions of cereal grains on pottery. A survey of the Danish material (G. Jørgensen 1976) showed that emmer wheat accounted for 55 per cent of cereals, einkorn wheat 18 per cent, barley 17.4 per cent and bread wheat 9.4 per cent. A similar pattern appears to apply in Scania, with emmer wheat being more common than einkorn wheat or barley, although the detailed suggestions made by M. Larsson (1985) concerning wheat- and barley-growing regions in southeast Scania seem premature, given the tiny sample of grain impressions on which they are based (Midgley 1992: 365). Apple pip impressions have also been reported from sites in the Hagestad area of Scania (Strömberg 1987–8). This, of course, does not say anything about the importance of cereals, or indeed apples, to the subsistence economy as a whole. This dearth of evidence renders any interpretation difficult, although it certainly need not point to a complete and utter switch to a fully agricultural regime with the beginning of the Neolithic.

Other indirect sources of evidence concerning crop cultivation point to a fairly low level of activity in the Early Neolithic. Ard marks have been preserved below the mounds of a number of TRB burial mounds (Thrane 1989), sometimes covering quite large areas, and in a number of cases running beneath the walls of burial chambers (e.g. Ebbesen and Brinch Petersen 1973). It seems likely that a rip-ard was involved in many cases, which was particularly suited to opening up new ground or reclaiming fallow ground (Reynolds 1981), as the standard crook-ard would not normally leave any traces. The relevance of these marks to the agricultural economy has, however, been questioned by Rowley-Conwy (1987) by reviving the original interpretation of the ard marks as 'ritual plough-ing' connected with ceremonies undertaken during the construction of burial mounds (Ørsnes 1956). This argument has been effectively undermined by the pollen analyses, which show that crop cultivation took place on the site before mound construction (Juel Jensen 1994: 102). The ard marks therefore do appear to be a phenomenon related to breaking up the soil for crop cultivation. It is thus of significance that they are all of final Early Neolithic (Fuchsberg) date or later, and none have been found below unchambered long barrows (Thrane 1989). This would suggest a degree of intensification of woodland clearance at the end of the Early Neolithic compared with a relatively minor impact before that.

The other major potential source of information concerning early agriculture in southern Scandinavia is the examination of flint tools used in the subsistence economy. This has been undertaken through microwear analysis of the edges of a range of different flint types. Microdenticulates are blades or flakes with a saw-like edge formed by a series of notches. They occur on both Late Mesolithic and Early Neolithic sites, but have a geographically limited distribution (Juel Jensen 1994: 50–68). The Ertebølle examples are found in western Denmark, both on the coast and inland, but are not common on the many sites along the Limfjord. They continue in use into the Neolithic, when they spread into Zealand, but are still rare in eastern Denmark and Scania. In Mesolithic contexts they have been interpreted as saws, and in the Neolithic as sickles or harvesting knives.

However, the microdenticulates from both Ertebølle and TRB contexts show the same pattern of wear traces, so they should be fulfilling the same function (Juel Jensen 1988b). This might suggest that the Mesolithic examples were also harvesting implements, but the microwear traces do not show signs of sawing through cereal stems, but instead of scraping or peeling. Their use is therefore more likely hackling the fibres of plant stems for textile production. This leaves only a few sickles proper in the Early Neolithic, and may therefore point to cereal production being of relatively low importance in the subsistence economy (Juel Jensen 1988b).

Furthermore, the small number of genuine sickles from the Early Neolithic have only a modest degree of usewear (Juel Jensen 1994: 150). Classic examples completely covered with gloss do not appear until the Middle Neolithic. This could mean that Early Neolithic sickles were replaced more frequently, but traces of hafting show that even the earliest examples were securely mounted in a style which did not change with time, so that does not seem likely. Experimental work by Juel Jensen suggests that the degree of gloss found on Early Neolithic sickles would have been created by the harvesting of some six or seven kilograms of grain. If Juel Jensen is also correct in her belief that each sickle generally represents a season's work by a single individual, then this would clearly point to only small-scale cereal production in the Early Neolithic (Juel Jensen 1994: 150–60). The evidence from grain remains, pollen analysis, ard-marks and usewear on flint tools combines to produce a picture of an agricultural economy in which cereal production was undoubtedly present, but of relatively little significance.

Direct evidence relating to the subsistence economy from the study of animal bones is unfortunately almost as rare as that from preserved plant remains. This is because the generally acid soils in southern Scandinavia do not allow for the survival of faunal material. A few Early Neolithic settlements in Scania have produced small samples of animal bones, as at Nymölla III (Wyszomirska 1988: 196–8), where the commonest animal was red deer, followed by wild boar or domestic pig (it was not possible to decide which), seal, a few fish and just seven cattle bones, only one of which was definitely from a domesticated animal. Small assemblages also came from Soldattorpet – sheep and pig – and Gränsstigen – red deer, wild cat, cattle and white-tailed eagle (M. Larsson 1985: 77–8). The main assemblages come from shell midden sites, where the presence of large numbers of shells alters the acidity of the soil sufficiently to ensure bone survival. The most significant are a group of sites along the Limfjord, all with both Ertebølle and TRB phases of occupation. At Aggersund (S. H. Andersen 1978), a small site produced wild and domestic pig, domestic cattle, red deer, sheep or goat, dog, swan and codfish. At Norsminde (S. H. Andersen 1989) domestic animals were present in the form of pig, cattle, sheep or goat and dog; wild animals were well represented, with seal, wild boar, fox and red deer; cockles, mussels, periwinkles and oysters were gathered (the growth rings of the cockles showing that this took place in the spring and summer), although, significantly, there were no fish bones. A similar pattern of evidence prevails at Bjørnsholm (S. H. Andersen 1991; Bratlund 1991), with domestic sheep, cattle and pig, wild boar, fox, pine marten, red deer, roe deer and swan; although fishing did take place at Neolithic Bjørnsholm it was greatly reduced from the scale of operations in the Mesolithic (only 250 bones against 11,000), but eel still dominated the catch, as it had done earlier.

This material does not in itself suggest that any intensive scheme of animal husbandry operated in Early Neolithic southern Scandinavia, but does demonstrate the regular occurrence of domesticated animals, at least on a certain type of site. Pollen analyses support this picture, as they document the existence of clearances for pasture in both Denmark (S. T. Andersen 1993) and Scania (Berglund and Larsson 1991), although these do not appear to be of any great size, or always of long duration. Low lying, wetter, areas with a varied and open vegetation would already be suitable for pasture (Gebauer and Price 1990), so fairly substantial numbers of animals could have been grazed without the need to alter the environment.

This paucity of evidence has not prevented the production of general models of animal exploitation. The most influential has been the suggestion of Madsen (1982) that in Jutland pig were initially more important than cattle, as early TRB sites were located in a heavily forested environment which would have limited the potential size of herds of cattle or sheep/goat but would have been able to support large numbers of pigs. Only after several hundred years of further clearance of woodland did cattle begin to become more important at the end of the Early Neolithic. M. Larsson (1985: 92) has gone on to apply Madsen's model to Scania. However, Madsen's main faunal evidence was the assemblage from the causewayed enclosure at Toftum (Madsen 1977) in Jutland (see pp. 137–8). Not only is this assemblage dated to c. 3400 BC or later, and thus several hundred years after the beginning of the Neolithic, but it comes from a site which may well not be typical of normal domestic animal bone assemblages. They may relate to ceremonial meals (for which pig are eminently suitable, as they can be killed off and bred back up to former numbers again much more quickly than cattle) or ritual deposits of a kind well known at causewayed enclosures (Midgley 1992: 381). The importance of pigs in the Early Neolithic may well therefore be somewhat exaggerated in Madsen's model.

This all suggests that there may not have been that much of a gulf between the Mesolithic and Early Neolithic subsistence economies. However, one other piece of information points in the opposite direction. A group of eight skeletons from the Early Neolithic had the C^{13} content of their bones measured. These were clearly lower than the results for Late Mesolithic skeletons (Tauber 1982), which indicate the consumption of seafish at a level comparable with Greenlanders (Price 1989b). Despite the Neolithic skeletons being chosen for their coastal location, the lower C^{13} content would mean that they had a more terrestrial diet (Tauber 1981), or ate freshwater rather than seawater fish. The lack of evidence for Early Neolithic fish consumption noted above would tend to suggest that the former is a more likely explanation, and does denote a significant alignment of the coastal subsistence economy away from marine resources. This was not a complete change in diet, however, as the majority of the Early Neolithic skeletons had C^{13} figures which would point to a mixed marine and terrestrial consumption pattern. Given this qualified confirmation of traditional models of the agricultural transition the continued use into the Early Neolithic of many Mesolithic shell middens requires investigation, and will be considered below in the analysis of settlement patterns.

An overall picture of the shifts in the subsistence economy from the Mesolithic to the Neolithic cannot be produced at present, due to the lack of detailed site-based dietary evidence for both plant and animal exploitation. It can, however, be argued that there are a number of indications that there was not a complete economic transformation. At some sites, indeed, there is very little indication of a new subsistence basis. At Nymölla III in Scania the scanty domesticated animal bone remains and the absence of both cereal impressions on pottery and quern fragments led Wyszomirska (1988: 198) to conclude that there was no crop-growing at Nymölla and possibly not even animal husbandry, although TRB pottery, polished stone axes and a typically Neolithic flint assemblage were present. The current data thus certainly hints at the possibility that the advent of a Neolithic society was not especially significant in terms of the subsistence economy.

The settlement record of Early Neolithic southern Scandinavia is rather more substantial than that relating to the subsistence economy, if only in terms of negative evidence. Although many apparent settlement sites of this period have now been investigated, the majority have been poorly preserved, producing few traces of structures, for example at Nymölla III there were only two hearths and a posthole (Wyszomirska 1988: 188–95), at Norsminde (S. H. Andersen 1989) the TRB level of the midden produced no hearths or postholes at all, and at Kabusa in Scania three Early Neolithic sites produced only a few features between them, and no definite structural elements (M. Larsson 1990). Structures have been found, although their identification as houses has often been a matter of debate. At both Barkær in eastern Jutland (Glob 1949) and Stengade on Langeland, to the south of Fyn (Skaarup 1975), excavations revealed two timber structures which were originally interpreted as longhouses. At Barkær both were c. 85 metres long, at Stengade they were 33 and 36 metres long. Re-examination of the excavation results has, however, led to a new interpretation of the structures as the remains of timber and stone-built long barrows (Glob 1975; Madsen 1979; Liversage 1983; 1992). It is, however, still the case that settlement debris was found at both sites and quite possible that some parts of the structural remains could well relate to this phase of activity rather than to the long barrow (Midgley 1992: 325).

Similar questions have arisen concerning the interpretation of some potential major settlement sites. Eriksen and Madsen (1984) suggested that the sites at Knardrup Galgebakke on Zealand and Troldebjerg on Langeland were better interpreted as causewayed enclosures. The three structures at Knardrup seem to be set on stone platforms with a few postholes enclosing areas of *c.* 6–7 m by 3.5–5 m (Larsen 1957). Only in one instance did the postholes form a roughly rectangular shape. Eriksen and Madsen may well be correct to criticise the standard of the excavation, but their reinterpretation of the houses as ditches seems highly speculative (Midgley 1992: 325); the location of the site on a clear promontory is typical of causewayed enclosures, but this need not mean that only enclosures could be constructed in such topographical situations. At Troldebjerg some twenty-five house sites, both large longhouses and small horse-shoe- or D-shaped huts have been argued to exist within an area of 250 × 100 m (Winther 1935: 6–13). The two features of the site which aroused suspicion that Troldebjerg might be a causewayed enclosure were its location on a ridge between two areas of boggy land and the main longhouse discovered by Winther. This involved a continuous bedding trench 0.5 metres wide, 0.3 metres deep and 71 metres long. Some one to two metres from this trench was a row of stone-packed postholes, which did not run in a straight line but in three or four arcs. Winther's rather forced interpretation envisaged a longhouse with a roof resting on a post and wattle-and-daub wall on the lower side and against the ground on the upslope side.

Re-excavation of the site to examine the possibility that it was a causewayed enclosure showed that the bedding trench was not merely the top layer of a ditch fill, and this part of the site has been reinterpreted as a palisade with a row of posts outside (Eriksen and Madsen 1984; Madsen 1988). Inside the enclosed area was a very rich settlement of Middle Neolithic date with a series of small houses. This interpretation would therefore retain the smaller buildings but discard the longhouses. Midgley (1992: 326–7) has objected to the reinterpreta-tion on the grounds that it does not explain the rich culture layer which runs up to the claimed palisade, but as Madsen has suggested (1988) that the settlement material inside the enclosure could be of the same date then this would only show that the culture layer built up at a time when the palisade and post setting were standing, either still in use or in a state of decay. The overall thrust of Eriksen and Madsen's reconsideration of the evidence seems eminently reasonable: at the time the sites concerned were excavated there was a strong expectation that the normal house form in the TRB would be the longhouse (a view which undoubtedly also lay behind the interpretation of Barkær and Stengade), while the alternative interpretation of sites as enclosures was not possible before the first example in the region was identified at Büdelsdorf in Holstein (Hingst 1970).

It is surely significant that recent excavations have only produced small houses from the Early Neolithic (see Figure 6.1); although larger rectangular houses are known, they date to the Middle Neolithic. Among the sites where small rectang-ular houses have been found are Bygholm Nørremark in Jutland, Ornehus (Eriksen 1991) and Skræppekærgård (Kaul 1988) on Zealand and Mossby in Scania (M. Larsson 1991). They range in size from ten to eighteen metres long and four to six metres wide, with a single central row of roof-supporting posts,

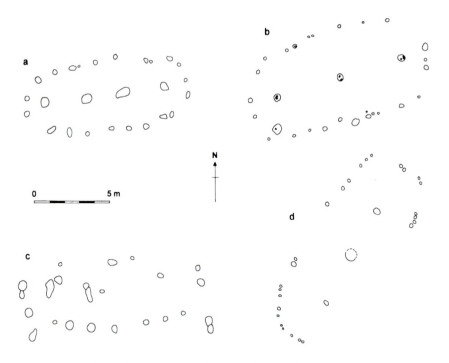

Figure 6.1 Early Neolithic southern Scandinavian houses – (a) Bygholm Nørremark, below long barrow, (b) Mossby, (c) Skræppekærgård, (d) Ornehus (after Eriksen 1991)

slightly curved walls of smaller posts and rounded ends (Eriksen 1991). D-shaped houses of clear Early Neolithic date have also been uncovered: at Holmegård on Zealand four or five small structures up to eight metres long were excavated (P. O. Nielsen 1991). Small circular huts are thought to be present at Mosegården in Jutland (Madsen and Juel Jensen 1982; Madsen and Petersen 1982–3), although the interpretation of certain of the pits as postholes is not particularly secure.

Occasional sites exist where different house shapes occur together, suggesting some functional variation. At Tygapil in Scania (Strömberg 1977–8) three houses of late Early Neolithic date were identified, although this was mainly on the basis of the shape of the culture layer rather than clear patterns of postholes. There were two rectangular buildings, 6 × 3 m and 7 × 4 m, together with a smaller circular building interpreted as a workshop, which contained a considerable amount of flint debris. Unfortunately, surviving culture layers which represent house floors are a rare occurrence, and in general there is little information available on the activities carried out inside houses (Eriksen 1991); more material would be available if artefacts in the ploughsoil were not routinely discarded.

Better information is often available concerning overall activities at the settlement. At Mosegården, for example, while the structural remains were slight and difficult to interpret, there was also a fireplace in the centre of the settlement area and to the side of this a dump of flintwork including scrapers, knives, fragments of axes, and pottery beakers, jars and discs (Madsen and Petersen 1982–3). This material had been preserved below a long barrow. The interpretation of the site as a whole is as a small base camp for about fifteen people occupied for a relatively short time. A rather different interpretation has been presented for the Muldbjerg site, which occupied a small island in the middle of the large Åmose bog on Zealand. A hut with a bark floor, some 7 × 3 m in size, was associated with Early Neolithic pottery (Troels-Smith 1959), with the site being interpreted as an activity camp (e.g. Jensen 1982: 119).

The interpretation of some sites as special activity camps brings us to the question of the overall settlement pattern. Here the most influential model has been without doubt been that developed by Madsen for East Jutland (1978; 1982) following survey work. Settlements were placed in one or other category. Residential sites were small (less than 500 m²) and with relatively little cultural material; they were located near open water, with easy access to both better drained soils on higher ground (for cereal cultivation), and lower-lying land suitable for grazing and hunting game. This would include sites such as Mosegården. Catching sites were situated on coastal or lakeshore positions, particularly by narrows in the fjords ideal for net fishing and where the tides built up banks of shells; the animals exploited at these sites were very close to those found at Ertebølle sites in the vicinity. Muldbjerg would fit here, as would a number of coastal sites. The small island of Hesselø, north of Zealand, was an important sealing site, occupied during the winter (Skaarup 1973: 13–58). Sølager on Fyn was used mainly to catch migrating birds, along with other hunting activities, including sealing (Skaarup 1973: 59–117).

Madsen concludes that this demonstrates a subsistence economy in which farming took place only on a small scale and was much less important than foraging, and a settlement pattern of mobile family groups occupying small farms for short periods and hunting sites for specific activities, perhaps on a seasonal basis (Madsen 1991). Similar arguments have been presented for Zealand (Kristiansen 1982) and for Scania by M. Larsson (1985). Within this model, only towards the end of the Early Neolithic do larger settlement sites appear, along with causewayed enclosures (Madsen 1988). This general model has been widely accepted, although it is beginning to come under rather more critical scrutiny. The most significant aspect of this is the suggestion that the hunting sites of Madsen's model may have been rather more important than the current model allows. While the faunal assemblages from sites such as Hesselø and Sølager do support the notion that they were special-purpose hunting camps occupied on a temporary or seasonal basis, at Hesselø there were also large numbers of flint blanks for tool production, showing the exploitation of local flint supplies during visits to the island (Skaarup 1973: 18–19; Midgley

1992: 322), so even here the emphasis on hunting was not total. More seriously, the special-purpose interpretation does not seem to fit the evidence from the major coastal Ertebølle sites which continued into the TRB. Juel Jensen has argued (1994: 160) that these were residential sites during the Mesolithic and that the evidence for continuity in the subsistence economy at these locations does not provide any reason to suppose that they were downgraded to mere hunting stations. As we have seen, the presence of domesticates on newly founded Neolithic sites is often minimal, so the varied animal bone assemblages of sites such as Norsminde and Bjørnsholm could well represent debris from a permanent settlement.

Even when the specific division of sites into residential and catching types is not followed, there is still a general agreement that Early Neolithic settlements were all small (e.g. Berglund and Larsson 1991; P. O. Nielsen 1993). This may not, however, be entirely correct. Despite attempts to move large sites such as Troldebjerg into the category of causewayed enclosures, there are still some potentially anomalous sites (Midgley 1992: 317–18). The Havnelev excavations, some 3 km inland from Sølager, produced over 4,500 sherds of pottery and some 800 flint tools (Mathiassen 1940), which seems an excessive breakage rate for a single family in less than ten years (Madsen 1988). In Scania the Oxie site appears to occupy an area of some 10,000 m^2, several orders larger than the norm, although here we must acknowledge the difficulty of defining the boundaries of such sites (M. Larsson 1985: 80). Midgley has therefore produced at least a prima-facie case that there were some larger settlement sites during the Early Neolithic, although it is unclear where these belong chronologically, and their numbers certainly appear to be small.

Overall, it does seem likely that settlement was small scale, probably at the level of the single household, given the economic and settlement evidence. The argument that these small communities were also highly mobile, shifting settlement every few years, would certainly tally well with the slash-and-burn model for the agricultural economy, but is only really supported in the settlement record by the negative evidence of flimsy house constructions and small accumulations of settlement debris. This certainly does not argue for lengthy episodes of occupation, but need not be incompatible with a life for sites rather longer than a decade. It may also be that while settlement did shift, it perhaps did not move very far, establishing a more permanent presence within a fairly restricted area. The general picture, however, does not show a dramatic transformation from the Mesolithic, and if the suggestions made concerning the monumental role of shell middens are correct (see Chapter 4) then it may be that the primary element of permanency of occupation was the monument in both the Late Mesolithic and the Early Neolithic.

MONUMENTS AND BURIAL PRACTICE

The 'earth graves' (*jordgrav*) or non-megalithic graves of Denmark show clear resemblances to the earthen long barrows found across much of northern Europe, including Britain. They are the earliest agriculturalist monuments, occurring in the earliest phases of the Neolithic. At Bjørnsholm charcoal from the façade trench of the mound gave a date of *c.* 3950 BC, confirming its early date (Andersen and Johansen 1990). In the fill of the façade were three deliberately placed vessels. The presumed grave (no bone survived) contained a polished thin-butted flint axe, a diabase axe and a group of transverse arrowheads. The mound had been constructed over a settlement, a pattern already noted for Barkær, Stengade and Mosegården, which in this instance was the successor to a major Late Mesolithic occupation.

There are large numbers of non-megalithic graves (see Figure 6.2), with a wide range of variation in terms of structure (Madsen 1979; Kristensen 1989; Liversage 1992: 79–84). The simplest type is a grave without stones or signs of related structures, and is found all over Denmark. Closed graves sealed by wood or stones are the most common type found throughout Scandinavia, in which the bodies could not be disturbed after their interment. The Konens Høj type (Stürup 1965) with a solid timber structure at both ends of the grave is found throughout Jutland, with single examples on Fyn at Toftlungard (Thomson 1984) and on Zealand at Asnæs Forskov in the western part of the island (Gebauer 1988). The Troelstrup type (Kjærum 1977) with a rectangular timber box with a single entrance, and sometimes a short passage, enclosing the grave is particularly frequent in northern Jutland, although it also occurs in southern Jutland. Examples of planked coffins come from the Bygholm Nørremark site (Rønne 1979) and from Morup Mølle and Storgård in Jutland (Bech and Olsen 1984; Bech 1985; Kristensen 1989). The significance of this variation is unclear at present, except that it does appear to have a geographical element.

One distinct problem in interpretation is the general lack of survival of skeletal material, which makes it difficult to draw conclusions concerning the selection of individuals for burial in graves. Rare exceptions (Madsen 1991; 1993) are at Skibshøj (E. Jørgensen 1977) on Jutland, a Troelstrup type grave containing an adult and four children together with a heavily worn flint axe and a few amber beads, and Bygholm Nørremark where the first grave contained an adolescent with an amber bead and an arrowhead (possibly the cause of death), and the second four adults buried in pairs with the heads in opposite directions and without grave goods. We can therefore say that there were both single and multiple burials, and that both adults and children were buried, apparently at the same time, but little beyond that.

Some information can also be gained from the grave goods found in earth graves. There is some variety in items and materials used, even within individual sites. At Barkær, for example (Liversage 1992: 23–5), Grave 2 in the southern mound had pits at each end and contained two groups of grave goods at either

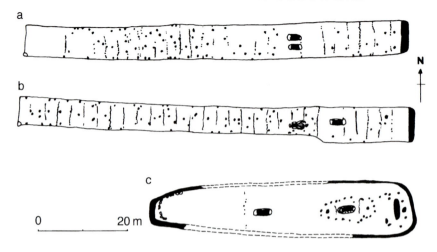

Figure 6.2 Southern Scandinavian non-megalithic graves – (a) and (b) Barkær, (c) Bygholm Nørremark (after Madsen 1979)

end of the grave: a pottery flask, rolled sheet copper ornament and 30–40 amber beads; and a handled pottery beaker and around forty amber beads. In the northern mound Grave 3 also had pits at each end, and grave goods of a collared pottery flask and four amber beads; Grave 4 again had pits at each end, and about forty amber beads and fragments of a copper spiral. The other common grave goods are flint items (as found at Bjørnsholm), mainly thin-butted axes, but also transverse arrowheads and blades. Pottery, flintwork and metalwork are found only in small numbers, but there may be considerable amounts of amber. At Storgård, for example, a plank coffin contained a thin-butted axe, a transverse arrowhead, a string of thirty amber beads, two perforated pieces of amber and seventeen smaller amber beads which may have formed a bracelet. Two graves at Sejlflod in North Jutland (J. N. Nielsen 1982) contained a collared pottery flask, a thin-butted flint axe, 220 amber beads and two fragments of copper, and in the other two thin-butted flint axes, six transverse arrowheads, a blade-knife and pieces of amber. At the same time other graves, even in Jutland (the amber source), may be lacking amber, as at Bjørnsholm.

Madsen (1988; 1991) has concluded from a review of the evidence that the long barrow burials do not represent an elite. He suggests that there are no real status differences apparent in body treatment or grave goods and therefore the earth graves were open access tombs. However, he does admit that there are far too few earth grave burials to represent the total population and that a number of mounds appear to cover single individuals, which implies a special case for erecting the barrow. He suggests that this was not related to the status of the individual but had far more to do with social obligation and competition between social groups. While the erection of a monument was undoubtedly a community undertaking and almost certainly played a part in competition for prestige between communities, there seems no good reason to deny the possibility of individual status distinctions. Given the importance of the mound as a community symbol it must have been important to ensure that the right people were interred below one, perhaps those from a particular family or lineage (Damm 1991).

It may indeed be that some of the earth graves which were not covered by mounds when excavated may relate to such circumstances. Although the mound may of course have been ploughed away over the last 5,000 years, there are also traces of palisades and façades at many sites which have survived ploughing. Those instances, as at Morup Mølle (Bech and Olsen 1984; Bech 1985), or at the type site of Konens Høj (Stürup 1965) where no trace of a mound, palisade or façade trench survived, could be seen as sites which were not deemed important enough for mound construction (Whittle 1985: 228). However, it has to be noted that the grave treatment and grave goods do not clearly distinguish Morup Mølle from other sites: Grave 1 was stone-filled, probably originally covering a wooden coffin, with 170 amber beads; Grave 2 was stone-lined and had probably held a wooden coffin and contained a string of amber beads; Grave 3 had a similar stone lining and contained two amber pendants; Grave 4 had a single row of stones around the grave edge and contained no grave goods. The grave goods were certainly not rich, but other than that there is no obvious difference between Morup Mølle and other earth graves covered by mounds. The possibility certainly exists that a turf mound was scraped up and has been ploughed away to leave no trace, but this would still represent a rather less monumental undertaking than a mound provided with a wooden façade. A rather more definite example of non-monumental burial is provided by the Dragsholm grave in Zealand, away from the distribution of earth graves and non-megalithic barrows (Brinch Petersen 1974). As noted in Chapter 4, this is a grave holding the single burial of an adult male with a beaker, amber pendants, transverse arrowheads and a battle axe, radiocarbon dated to c. 3700 BC, found only two metres away from a very late Ertebølle or very early TRB double grave, radiocarbon dated to c. 4000 BC, contained two adult females covered with ochre, wearing tooth beads of elk, red deer, wild boar and one of cattle (possibly domesticated), and accompanied by a decorated bone dagger, a bone awl and an arrowhead. It is difficult to establish the significance of the Dragsholm find in the absence of comparable material from other sites in Zealand or Scania.

The other form of Early Neolithic burial is the dolmen, or megalithic grave (see Figure 6.3). These have to be distinguished from passage graves, which appear only in the Middle Neolithic. Following the original formulation of Worsaae in the nineteenth century there is a general distinction which can be made between *langdysse* (dolmens in long mounds) and *runddysse* (dolmens in round mounds). There is unfortunately no recent study of the dolmens, as efforts have been concentrated on the passage graves, but a number of general

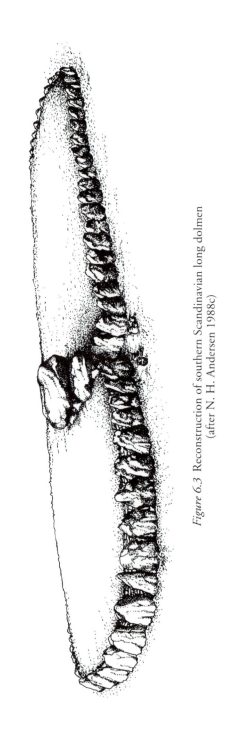

Figure 6.3 Reconstruction of southern Scandinavian long dolmen
(after N. H. Andersen 1988c)

observations can be made (Kaelas 1981; Midgley 1992: 424–8; Skaarup 1993). As Thorvildsen noted (1941), simple small closed dolmens (*Urdolmen*) were concentrated in southeast Jutland and the Danish islands, while more elaborate chambers were particularly common in northern Jutland. The dating of the long and round dolmens is mainly after 3500 BC (P. O. Nielsen 1984b; Skaarup 1993), although some of the *urdolmen* are earlier. As with non-megalithic graves there are few burials, often only a single individual, although there are a number of examples of double burials of a male and a female, and children are also represented. The common idea that dolmens were intended for single burial is thus only true for some sites (Kaelas 1981; Midgley 1992: 449–50). Pottery vessels are common as grave goods, either flasks or beakers, along with amber, bone wristguards and copper ornaments.

No clear differences seem to exist between long and round dolmens. At Kongenshøjvej in Jutland (Schmidt and Sterum 1986) a round dolmen contained the skeletons of nine individuals together with seven amber beads and a spiral copper tube. At Grøfte on Zealand (Ebbesen 1988; Bennicke 1988) the long mound contained two megalithic chambers, one with two males and two pottery flasks and a flint halberd, the other with a female and a pottery flask. There is also no very clear distinction between non-megalithic and megalithic graves, except that the non-megalithic element appears to be restricted to long mounds. At Barkær, in the southern long mound, Grave 1 was an *urdolmen*, robbed before Glob's excavation and thus containing only a broken amber bead, while Grave 2 was an earth grave with a substantial inventory of grave goods listed above (Glob 1949; Liversage 1992: 22–3). There is, however, a difference of emphasis on the interpretation of the status of the individuals buried. Skaarup (1990) has argued that the dolmens contain petty chieftains buried together with their families and items symbolising their status. This would allow a greater degree of social differentiation than Madsen (1988; 1991) favours for earthen graves. They are not perhaps that far apart though, if Skaarup's petty chieftains are seen as symbolising the power of the lineage to which they belonged rather than personal power achieved as individuals.

The other element which the two forms have in common is, of course, their monumental status, which manifests itself in their continuing presence in the landscape. In the case of the long mounds and long dolmens the area of the mound was vastly greater than that required to cover the burial zone. Palisades or stone kerbs were built around a number of examples to retain the mound material and thus ensure that the mound would continue to have the maximum possible visibility. There is also a clear emphasis on linear arrangements, not surprisingly commented on by Hodder (1990: 186). When several graves were present they were set out in lines before the mound was constructed to cover them. At the eastern end of the long mounds a façade was often constructed, although there was no access to the burials. This façade was often the scene of what are interpreted as offerings of pottery (beakers and bowls) and thin-butted flint axes (at dolmens) when the mound was constructed and after the tomb was no longer in use for burials. These seem to have been deposited with care, for example at Onsved Mark I long dolmen in Zealand thirteen out of fifteen beakers found in front and to the side of the entrance were placed on the northern side (Kaul 1987). Similar offerings were placed against the kerbs of round dolmens. These offerings were sometimes in pits near the mound rather than directly next to them. These offerings attest to the continuing importance of tombs within the landscape, and prefigure the massive episodes of pot-smashing seen at some passage graves in the Middle Neolithic. The significance of the façades is also seen in the practice of deliberately destroying them, and the timber chambers enclosing graves, by burning (Madsen 1993). At Skibshøj (Jørgensen 1977) the bodies and grave goods were quite heavily burnt. This presumably acted as a closing ritual, marking the transformation of the site from burial place to monument.

We should not forget that other non-monumental forms of burial existed, as well as those earth graves which were not covered by mounds. There are occasional finds of human skeletal material on settlements, as in the mound at Norsminde (S. H. Andersen 1989), although it is possible that these derived from the lower Ertebølle midden deposit on the site, which had contained a number of burials. Far better known are the bog burials of the Early Neolithic. The two Boldkilde bodies (Bennicke *et al.* 1986) were found in a small bog on Als, off southeast Jutland, at different heights but near to each other. Skeleton I was a male about 16 years old; Skeleton II, a male *c.* 35 years old, had pieces of cloth nearby and a rope near the neck, with which he was presumably strangled or hanged. The bodies date to *c.* 3400 BC. At Sigersdal in northern Zealand (Bennicke and Ebbesen 1986) two adolescents, 16 and 18 years old, were discovered together with a large pottery jar. The older individual, possibly female, had a cord wrapped round the neck, and may have had a skull wound (S. T. Andersen 1987), although this has also been attributed to the peat cutters who found the body (Bennicke and Ebbesen 1986). Radiocarbon dates place these bodies around 3500 BC. There seems no real doubt that these finds are best interpreted as sacrifices.

Other skeletons found in bogs could be viewed similarly. The two adult males from Døjringe and the adult male from Vibygårds Mose, both on Zealand, had all been trepanned (Bennicke 1985: 67–72, 90), although the trepanation holes had healed up, so there need not be a connection. However, it may be significant that three of the four Danish Early Neolithic trepanations were bog bodies. The Porsmose skeleton, also on Zealand, dated to *c.* 3450 BC, has two bone arrowheads lodged in his body, one in the face and one in the breastbone; nearby were the bones of a small child (Bennicke 1985: 110–12). He may have been sacrificed or murdered (Bennicke and Ebbesen 1986). Finally, a rather more mixed deposit of bones was found at Myrebjerg on Langeland, south of Fyn (Bennicke and Ebbesen 1986). Here there was a heap of bones belonging to domestic cattle, sheep, pig, horse and five humans (two small children, two adolescents and an adult female), dated to *c.* 3400 BC, together with late Early Neolithic or early Middle Neolithic pottery. This last deposit has more in common with the other bog deposits of the Early Neolithic discussed below.

ENCLOSURES AND OFFERINGS

The final context in which Early Neolithic burials occur is causewayed enclosures, although burial practice is only one facet of the activities undertaken at these major sites. As noted above, the category was recognised in southern Scandinavia only in 1970, but an impressive number of sites have already been identified, some from new work, others as a result of the reinterpretation of old excavations. By now some twenty-five examples are known from Jutland, Fyn, Ærø, Zealand, Bornholm and Scania (N. H. Andersen 1993). They are a relatively short-lived phenomenon, from c. 3400 to 3200 BC, within the Fuchsberg pottery phase between the Early and Middle Neolithic and the first part of the Middle Neolithic (Madsen 1988).

There are common features of location and layout (Madsen 1988; Midgley 1992: 341–3). The vast majority are on promontories surrounded by wetland or open water, although more sites not naturally circumscribed are now coming to light. They have a ditch layout which is mostly single, although double lines of ditches are known, with the ditches separated by causeways. This relatively open barrier either cuts off a promontory or forms a boundary around the whole site. At some sites the ditches are supplemented by a timber palisade. In general, however, the layout of the sites is fairly simple, with the notable exception of Sarup on Fyn (N. H. Andersen 1988a–c), where in the Fuchsberg phase enclosure there are two lines of ditches, with individual ditch segments fenced off, fencelines and a palisade behind the ditches and small enclosures tacked onto the outside of the palisade, with two formal entrances (although one only gave access to a fenced area) but a number of apparent gaps in the palisade and fences (see Figure 6.4). It is thus not entirely clear how far attempts were made to control entry into the enclosure.

Sarup is by far the most intensively explored of the enclosures, having seen an almost total excavation. Deliberately placed deposits are a clear feature of both phases, although they are far more numerous in the first enclosure, which is the focus of discussion here. In the ditches there was Fuchsberg pottery, two complete vessels, flintwork, human adult and child jaws and skulls, stone settings near the ditch base with pottery animal bones and charcoal in and below the stones and layers of charcoal and burnt soil, suggesting that the charcoal was sometimes still smouldering when it was buried in the ditch. Even the more mundane potsherds and flintwork are interpreted as deliberate deposits rather than settlement debris, as small sherds and flint waste from tool manufacture were largely absent (N. H. Andersen 1988b). The soil conditions were not conducive to the survival of bone, so far more human and animal bone may have been deposited originally. The flint tools were examined for microwear traces, which showed that they had mainly been used to work wood, but also hide and bone, and that tools used to work different materials tended to be found in different areas of the site. The palisade trench contained considerable amounts of pottery, far more than in the interior of the enclosure; it appears that

Figure 6.4 Reconstruction of Sarup Phase 1
(after N. H. Andersen 1988c)

complete vessels were placed along the palisade at some parts; some areas also have concentrations of burnt flint and bones. Neither the ditches nor the palisade are believed to have been in use for long (N. H. Andersen 1988a) – the ditches for a single year before they were deliberately backfilled and the palisade also for as little as a single year, but in any case rotting within a generation.

Inside the enclosure were nearly a hundred features, most of them small post-holes and pits, but some twenty are larger and are interpreted as offering pits (N. H. Andersen 1988b). Nine of these contain complete vessels; one large vessel contained two smaller pots and a large quantity of carbonised emmer wheat grain with a tiny amount of barley and no weed seeds (Jørgensen 1976). Nearby was another pit containing burnt wheat grains, together with sherds from one of the same pots as in the other pit. Other pits produced flint tools but only a little flint waste; for example, one contained ten scrapers used for scraping wood and only seven pieces of waste. From the purity of the flint and plant assemblages Andersen (1988b) has concluded that the flint was brought in to the site and only selected grain buried.

Other sites have produced similar traces of placed deposits of various kinds (N. H. Andersen 1993). The bases of ditches at many sites contained deliberate deposits, including whole pots at Bjerggård, Bårse, Lønt, Sarup, Sjørring, Store Brokhøj and Toftum; piles of flint tools at Bjerggård and Sarup; heaps of animal bone, sometimes with human skulls, at Bjerggård, Hygind and Sarup; and parts of human skulls at Hygind, Sarup, Stävie and Åsum Enggård. Traces of fire were noted in the ditches at Bjerggard, Toftum and Sarup. Another activity undertaken in enclosure ditches appears to have been pottery manufacture. At Hevringholm in eastern Jutland (Madsen and Fiedel 1987) one of the ditch segments contained parts of Fuchsberg-style pots and nearly complete vessels, heavily burnt clay daub with wattle impressions, a group of large rounded stones and a massive charred tree trunk. The stones and the tree trunk made up a construction which ran below the area of pottery and daub, and is interpreted as a pottery kiln; nearby ditch segments contained large amounts of pottery and daub which are believed to be the remnants of unsuccessful firings. The signifi-cance of this activity being carried out at an enclosure is difficult to gauge, as so little of the enclosure has been excavated. Similar activities were, however, carried out at Sarup, Stävie and Büdelsdorf in Holstein, although at a rather later date.

Relatively few sites have seen the exploration of large areas of the interior of the enclosure, but some have produced offering pits as at Sarup (Madsen 1988). At Lønt in Jutland, a very large enclosure, many pits have been found, some including complete vessels; at Årupgard, also in Jutland, pits have produced complete pots and a hoard of copper and amber. At Toftum (Madsen 1977) the site is constructed and abandoned within the Fuchsberg pottery phase, but the ditches show a series of activities involving natural and deliberate infilling, recutting and final backfilling. Some backfilling included the deposition of complete vessels, but other areas of the ditches were backfilled with cultural debris including heaps of shells, flintwork and potsherds. Madsen has argued that the sheer volume of this material must imply the presence on the site of a settlement, but an alternative would be to interpret it as a mass of feasting debris.

A model of the development of these major enclosures has been put forward by Madsen (1988). He argues that around 3500 BC there was increased forest clearance, denoting a growing population, and greater rivalry between communities. This was dealt with by an increasing ritualisation of society, providing a framework for both competition and cooperation within and between groups, ensuring the stability of society. Two aspects of ritual were particularly important: the rituals of the dead, and the shared investment of labour in building enclosures. The idea of enclosures already existed, and was drawn upon at this crucial time. The enclosures were not neutral, but belonged to specific groups, who brought in members of other communities to participate in the construction and subsequent rituals; the success of the enclosure thus reflected the importance and strength of the group itself. However, the continued growth in settlements led to greater permanency in occupation sites, which rendered the enclosures unnecessary.

While there are a number of important elements in Madsen's case, it has a highly functionalist tinge to it, in which enclosures arose to fulfil a specific social function, then disappeared once that need was met elsewhere. It is difficult to accept that Early Neolithic society employed such typically twentieth-century thinking. The enclosures certainly did appear at a specific moment, and their importance was undoubtedly in part due to their monumental character compared with the very low-key settlement remains. However, the major excavations at Sarup and Toftum have produced a picture of highly ephemeral sites, undergoing extremely rapid change, and therefore unlike the fixed burial mounds. They seem to represent sites of conspicuous consumption, which rapidly exhausted a particular location, although presumably leaving it with a considerable amount of ritual significance, rendering it a powerful place in the landscape, which may be why many large Middle Neolithic settlements occupy the sites of enclosures. Rather than achieving harmony through labouring towards a common goal, it may well have been the display of effort and the destruction of specially chosen items in sight of representatives from other rival communities which was the main motivation behind this short-lived burst of construction. Tensions between communities could well have been exacerbated by enclosure building, rather than dampening them down.

On a smaller scale we can see the theme of conspicuous consumption emerging again when we consider finds from bogs. These constitute an important class of evidence which has been studied for a long time in Denmark (Becker 1947). The finds include pottery, polished flint axes (mainly thin-butted), and domesticated animal bones, along with occasional human bones (see Figure 6.5). Other flintwork, and bone or amber jewellery are much rarer, with possible settlement

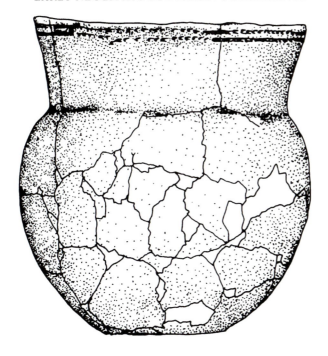

Figure 6.5 Reconstruction of Early Neolithic sacrificed vessel from Danish bog
(after Koch 1990)

rubbish not occurring. Some of the deposits can contain quite large numbers of objects, as in the case of the hoard of thirteen thin-butted axes from the Sigersdal bog (Bennicke and Ebbesen 1986). They can also contain very high quality axes, too long and finely polished to be for practical use (P. O. Nielsen 1977; 1984b). In a number of instances the axes can be shown to have been carefully arranged. The bog finds were interpreted by Becker as sacrificial or votive offerings in bogs or small lakes, sometimes deposited from platforms, as part of a fertility cult. The pots are thought to have contained food offerings, and are often found with animal remains (Skaarup 1990). One vessel with preserved contents held the bones of fish, duck and beaver, along with eggshells, which may not suggest a straightforward food interpretation. We should also not forget that a beaker accompanied the Sigersdal sacrificial burial (Bennicke and Ebbesen 1986). Koch (1990) has argued that at the brushwood platform sites the pots were set out on the platforms as offerings in the course of communal rituals. There seems to be a significant difference between pots and axes. Becker (1947) noted that of 150 pottery deposits only seventeen had axes associated with them. They also differ in their findspots, in that pots appear to have been placed in what was open water at the time, while axe hoards were deposited at the water's edge (Bennicke and Ebbesen 1986). The two groups do, however, both occur across the whole of southern Scandinavia (Bradley 1990: 57–9). The bog deposits may have operated at several levels: while there may have been an element of fertility cult in the offerings, it is likely that motives of communal display and competition through conspicuous consumption were paramount. Whether this actually took the form of sacrificing members of the group is not really clear (a theory involving punishment is also possible), but this would have brought the two aspects of the offerings together at an ultimate level of commitment.

PRODUCTION AND EXCHANGE

Discussion of the wetland flint axe hoards brings us to the question of the production and exchange of flint. Flint is available everywhere on the surface, but good quality flint is more restricted in distribution. Jutland Sennonian flint is found in seams in chalky deposits across northern Jutland, and was mined at Hov and Bjerre in the northwest (Becker 1958; 1959; 1966; 1980). Zealand Sennonian flint occurs in the cliffs of eastern Zealand (Becker 1980), on Møn, southeast of Zealand, and in Scania (Olaussen *et al.* 1980; Rudebeck 1987), where it was mined at Kvarnby. Simple shafts have been explored at Hov and Kvarnby, up to thirty in number, which reached a few metres into the ground and followed the seams of flint for a short distance. Radiocarbon dates suggest that the mines were in operation from the beginning of the Neolithic. They were dug with antler picks and cattle shoulder-blade shovels. Kvarnby seems to be unusual in that all stages of axe manufacture were carried out at the mine site, even final grinding and polishing.

The main products of these early mines were undoubtedly axes, which were produced in a series of regional types (see Figure 6.6). Point-butted axes (P. O. Nielsen 1977) are found in Zealand and Scania with occasional examples in northern and eastern Zealand. Thin-butted axes (P. O. Nielsen 1977) are believed to develop from the point-butted type. Nielsen has divided them into a series of types based on shape. Types I–III are made from Zealand Sennonian flint and not surprisingly are mostly found in Zealand. Types V and VI are generally made from Jutland Sennonian flint and are found widely. Type IV is rather different in that it is made from both types of flint and is found across Denmark, although with a definite concentration in northern Jutland (where they are common grave goods), being produced in large numbers at the Hov and Bjerre mine sites.

Flint was undoubtedly exchanged, and the visible difference between the better and poorer quality flint allows this to be established. At Nymölla III in northeast Scania, for example, local flint was available in large quantities, but the better quality flint from western Scania was imported in the form of finished tools, especially blades (Wyszomirska 1988: 188–95). It is significant that the flint axes in this area are clearly shorter than those from southwest Scania (M. Larsson 1988). However, this pattern does not apply to axes found in hoards, suggesting a different treatment of the larger axes. Long distance exchange is

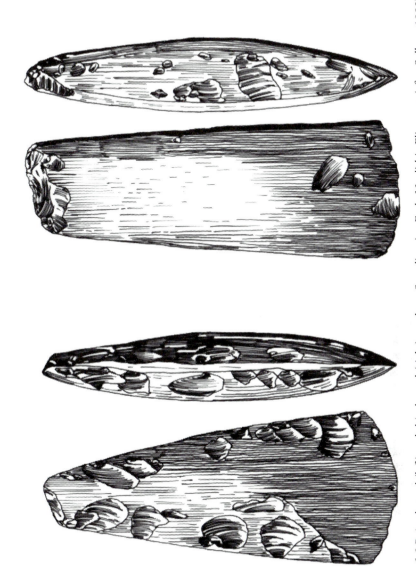

Figure 6.6 Point-butted (left) and thin-butted (right) southern Scandinavian Early Neolithic Flint axes (after Solberg 1989)

shown by the two hoards of thin-butted flint axes from the island of Gotland in the Baltic (P. O. Nielsen 1984b). Nielsen has argued that the axes were primarily objects of exchange, and that this explains the large number of axe hoards, with these representing ritual expenditure. Most hoards contain only flint and stone axes, between two and four in number, although amber beads are sometimes found. Most of the axes are fully polished, but only a few show traces of use. The longer and highly polished examples are unlikely ever to have been used. As Madsen (1991) has suggested, these represent a large investment of labour in order to produce objects with a design and a finish far beyond what is functionally required. Frequently, only a single of Nielsen's types is represented, suggesting a close degree of control over decisions as to the appropriateness of objects for deposition. As with the bog deposits, axe hoards are probably best seen in terms of communal acts of deliberate deposition.

As we have noted, stone axes are also present in these hoards, although they have been given far less attention than flint axes. Ebbesen, however, has studied greenstone axes (1984). These are found fairly evenly across the country, although with a concentration on Zealand, on settlements and in bogs. They have a more restricted distribution when used as grave goods, however. Point-butted axes are quite rare, but thin-butted axes common. Compared with flint axes, many greenstone axes show marks of use and wear, resharpening and repair. Ebbesen suggests that they were tougher than flint axes and thus more suited to working wood. The other main type of stone artefact in use was the battle axe (Midgley 1992: 284–90), a general TRB type. These are found on settlements and in burials, although only rarely. Given the lack of associated skeletal material, it is difficult to be sure of the significance of the burial finds, but their rarity must have given them a certain social significance.

The other important local product was amber, found along the western coast of Jutland and Schleswig-Holstein and used from the Early Mesolithic onwards. In the TRB amber is found widely and Denmark is believed to be the main supplier. Brønsted (1957: 184–5) noted the tendency for amber not to move far from its source, with over 90 per cent of Early Neolithic amber finds confined to northern Jutland (see also Beck and Shennan 1991: 109–12). These are found mainly in graves, up to a hundred beads accompanying a burial, and in bog offerings, where thousands can be found in a single deposit. Most amber was made into beads, but amber discs are also found as grave goods, and were exchanged beyond Denmark. The method of collecting amber presumably meant that, unlike flint mining, no complex organisation was required and therefore little possibility existed of controlling it locally. It may have been possible to exert a degree of control over its movement from Jutland and into other areas, however, although this was never sufficiently secure to allow the development of any significant power base.

Offering far more possibilities in this respect was copper, which entered southern Scandinavia, from outside and which there was no prospect of producing locally (see Figure 6.7). Copper artefacts reaching southern Scandinavia took two forms: ornaments (Ottaway 1973; Liversage 1992: 97) and flat axes (Randsborg 1978). Under a hundred Early Neolithic copper items are known altogether, the vast majority being axes. They all appear to be made from the same low-impurity arsenical copper, which is generally thought to originate in the eastern Alps. They do occur together, as in the Bygholm hoard on Jutland, where four axes, three spiral rings or bracelets and a copper knife or dagger were found together inside a pot (Brøndsted 1957: 188), but the ornaments are usually grave goods and the axes single finds or occasionally hoards, but not grave goods.

Randsborg (1978) has argued that the flat axes were distributed from a primary area of east central Jutland, Fyn and Scania to peripheral zones. The axes in these peripheral areas are lighter than those in the primary zone. Randsborg suggests that they may have been exchanged in return for flint and amber, from northern Jutland and Zealand. Midgley (1992: 297) has raised the possibility that these lighter axes may be the product of recasting to make the metal supply go further, although there is as yet no direct evidence to support this hypothesis. This would, however, seem quite plausible in a situation where control over the supply of this rare and desirable commodity was threatened by a shortage of material.

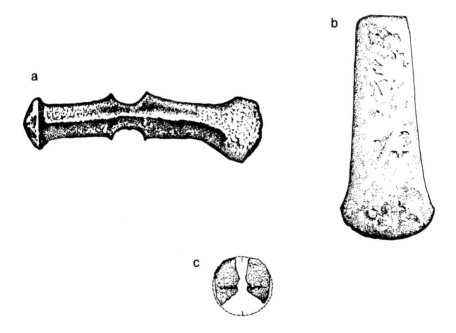

Figure 6.7 Early Neolithic southern Scandinavian copper artefacts – (a) shafthole axe, (b) flat axe, (c) copper disc
(after Stenberger 1967, Randsborg 1978)

The value ascribed to copper items can be seen in the production of imitations, which themselves appear to be highly valued. Thus the amber discs found in dolmens in northern Jutland imitate copper discs (Midgley 1992: 291), while the shape and colour of the diabase axe in the earth grave at Bjørnsholm (Andersen and Johansen 1990) clearly copies copper axes, while another example comes from a cist burial and the remainder are from northern Zealand, outside Randsborg's primary axe area. Some indication of the significance of copper is also given by the Årupgård hoard of eight ornaments and 271 amber beads found in a pot placed in a pit inside this probable Jutland causewayed enclosure (Bradley 1990: 63).

REGIONAL STYLES AND MESOLITHIC CONTINUITY

One of the most significant shifts in thinking about the Early Neolithic of Scandinavia in recent times has concerned pottery typology and chronology. The established system was that of Becker (1947), which divided Early Neolithic pottery into three main groups, Early Neolithic A to C. These were argued to represent a chronological sequence as well as a logical division of the material. The A group was based on a small number of bog deposits and two beakers from the shell midden at Sølager. The B group represented more finds, but as in the case of the A group, was concentrated on the Danish islands. The more numerous C Group was divided into a north Jutland C group, a south Danish C Group (or Megalithic group), a Bornholm and south Swedish group and a south Danish (non-Megalithic) C group (Becker 1949). So by Early Neolithic C there were several contemporary groups in southern Scandinavia, each with their own distinct pottery assemblage.

A new typology has been developed by Madsen (Madsen and Petersen 1982–3), which changes the definition of some groups, but more importantly takes into account the results of radiocarbon dating (see Figure 6.8). The north Jutland C group has been transformed into the Volling group in northern and central Jutland, with a dating from the beginning of the Neolithic up to the Middle Neolithic. The Oxie group replaces the A group in Scania and Zealand. The Svaleklindt group replaces the south Danish (non-megalithic) C group. The B group has been discarded. These pottery groups are thought to be sufficiently different that they may have different origins. Around 3400 BC these groups are replaced by the Fuchsberg group in Jutland and Fyn and the Virum group in the eastern islands (Andersen and Madsen 1977), incorporating material from Becker's megalithic C group. M. Larsson (1985: 15–35) has followed this new typology in a re-examination of the Scanian evidence, dividing the Early Neolithic material there into three groups – the Oxie group, the Svenstorp group (similar to Svaleklindt) and the Bellevuegården group (similar to the later Virum group); he thus confirms the absence of Volling material from Scania, and so the geographical nature of the groups.

Figure 6.8 Southern Scandinavian Early Neolithic pottery – Oxie (left), Svaleklindt (middle) and Virum (right) groups (after Koch 1990)

These distinctions also have a significance in other areas of material culture. The Oxie group flint industry shows a strong degree of continuity with Mesolithic flintworking traditions (Midgley 1992: 109–10, 266–8), as does the Svenstorp material in Scania (M. Larsson 1985: 15–35). The use of a blade technique, flake axes and transverse arrowheads all show continuity, while the point-butted axe, common on Oxie and Svenstorp sites, has often been thought to derive from the Mesolithic core axe. Similarly, Nielsen's Type I and II thin-butted axes are particularly associated with the Svaleklindt group, and Type IV with the Volling group. It has also been suggested (e.g. Gebauer and Price 1990) that the less heavily decorated Oxie pottery and the use of simple inhumation graves, such as Dragsholm, in the Oxie area show further evidence of continuity from the Mesolithic.

How may we best interpret this pattern of relatively clear-cut but overlapping regional assemblages? Madsen (1991) has suggested that the different regional groups correspond to ethnic identities consciously stressing their differences from neighbouring groups. Liversage (1992: 89–90) has questioned this inter-pretation, but put forward no convincing alternative. One area of evidence which could be used to bolster Madsen's theory is that of inter-group violence. A number of the bog bodies could be interpreted in these terms. The Porsmose skeleton from Zealand, dated to *c.* 3450 BC, with two bone arrowheads lodged in his body (Bennicke 1985: 110–12) would be an obvious candidate. Bennicke (1985: 67–98) has argued that three of the four Early Neolithic trepanations (one of the two male bog bodies from Døjringe, the male bog body from Vibygårds Mose, and the male from the Kelderød long barrow, all on Zealand) were carried out as a result of axe blows to the head. Other skulls show lesions which resulted from violence (Bennicke 1985: 98). One recent find is of a skull with slash marks from the causewayed enclosure of Hygind on Fyn (N. H. Andersen 1988d). The interpretation of this evidence is not clear-cut. The Porsmose and Hygind finds could represent sacrifices, given their context of discovery in a bog and a causewayed enclosure. The trepanations did not take place shortly before death, except in the case of the Kelderød burial, so they are less likely to represent part of a ritual of sacrifice, although they may well have been an important factor in the choice of sacrifice. They could, therefore, be seen as evidence for violence, but the number of individuals involved is certainly small, and the ascription of the operation to repairing wounds from axe blows is by no means certain. It seems strange that the flint arrowheads found so widely in Early Neolithic Scandinavia have not been found embedded in individuals, and that no convincing defensive enclosures have been located, if there was conflict between ethnic groups.

One view of this claimed ethnic identity could be that it relates to a division between an eastern part of southern Scandinavia (Zealand and Scania) which through the Oxie group shows a strong degree of continuity with Late Mesolithic practices, and another part where the evidence suggests greater discontinuity. This could then be interpreted in terms of a western zone which saw the actual immigration of farmers and an eastern zone which had continuity of population. However, Madsen (1991) has argued that the divisions visible in the Early Neolithic relate to those in the Late Mesolithic (see Chapter 4), and that they therefore constitute an argument in favour of an overall continuity in population. Certainly the pattern of an east–west split is strongly reminiscent of that recorded for the Late Mesolithic, and the continuity argument seems more plausible than the immigration model, given the rapidity of the transition to agriculture across the whole of southern Scandinavia and the consequent lack of any convincing evidence for an agricultural frontier having developed between the two regions. Instead it seems as though there was a differential adoption of certain items of Neolithic material culture and monuments. It is perhaps significant in this regard that the area with the most monumental of shell middens in the Mesolithic is that where earthen long barrows appear in such numbers. The different social trajectories of the eastern and western parts of southern Scandinavia thus do appear to have had an important influence on subsequent developments into a Neolithic which was in many fundamental ways a continuation of Ertebølle society.

7

EARLY NEOLITHIC BRITAIN
AND IRELAND

As in the discussion of the Early Neolithic of southern Scandinavia the main aim of this chapter will be to assess the extent to which patterns of social action and material culture in the Early Neolithic of Britain and Ireland were influenced by the pre-existing situation of the Late Mesolithic. This will be undertaken through a review of the evidence for economy, settlement, burial, monuments, exchange and warfare, ending with an examination of emergent regional traditions and the significance of this for the origins of the British and Irish Neolithic.

THE SUBSISTENCE ECONOMY AND SETTLEMENT

The direct record of agricultural crops is rather better in Britain and Ireland than in southern Scandinavia, although it could certainly be argued here as well that a number of the most thoroughly investigated sites are far from typical settlements. Early attempts to investigate agricultural practices through the presence of grain impressions on pottery (e.g. Helbaek 1952), as in southern Scandinavia, have foundered on the observation that some of the vessels had themselves been exchanged (Dennell 1976). In southern England direct evidence of grain production has come from enclosures such as Hembury (Moffett *et al.* 1989), Maiden Castle (Palmer and Jones in Sharples 1991: 129–39) and Hambledon Hill (Mercer 1988) where charred grains of wheat and barley have been preserved for study. The problems in extrapolating this evidence to that of the wider subsistence economy are demonstrated by the grain deposits from Hambledon Hill in Dorset (Legge 1981), where the emmer wheat was almost free of processing waste (weed seeds and spikelet fragments), suggesting that only clean 'processed' grain was brought into the site. This would clearly represent a highly biased sample. The Rowden pit in Dorset (Woodward 1991: 43) may represent a different kind of deposit; this contained emmer wheat and barley. The isolated nature of the pit may, however, argue for it being a deliberate deposit rather than a component of a settlement. The same caveat applies, with more force, to the Coneybury Anomaly (Richards 1990: 40–61), a large pit dating to *c.* 3850 BC, discovered on the site of this Wiltshire henge, from which a few cereal grains,

147

probably of emmer wheat, were recovered (Carruthers in Richards 1990: 250–1). A more typical assemblage may be represented by the material found below the Hazleton north chambered tomb in Gloucestershire (Straker in Saville 1990: 215–18). Emmer and bread wheat grains were found together with some barley, hazelnuts and onion couch tubers in a midden, hearth and postholes which also produced pottery, flintwork, pounders and quernstones and animal bones (Saville 1990: 14–22). One exotic element is represented by a grape pip from Hambledon Hill (Jones and Legge 1987), with a direct radiocarbon date of c. 3550 BC. The small size of the pip suggests that it comes from a domesticated grape, but very little can be said on the basis of a single pip.

In Wales the Gwernvale chambered tomb covered a small settlement with postholes, pits and scatters of pottery and flintwork (Britnell and Savory 1984: 138–54). The presence of querns and rubbing stones, together with emmer wheat and barley argues for a significant element of cereals in the diet here. An enormous assemblage of cereal remains (over 20,000 grains) has also come from the Early Neolithic hall at Balbridie in Scotland (Fairweather and Ralston 1993), dating to c. 3800–3700 BC. The cereals were 80 per cent emmer wheat, 18 per cent naked barley and 2 per cent bread wheat; as at Hambledon Hill there was little trace of processing waste. Wild oats, flax, hazelnuts and crab apple were also found. A number of recent settlement excavations in Ireland have also produced cereal remains. At Tankardstown, Co. Limerick, (Gowen 1988: 26–43; Monk in Gowen 1988: 185–91) the postholes and foundation trench of a small rectangular house contained emmer wheat, hazelnuts and crab apple pips. A less well preserved house at Pepperhill, Co. Cork (Gowen 1988: 44–51; Monk in Gowen 1988: 185–91) produced only a few fragments of cereal grains. A more significant plant assemblage is being produced by the excavations at Balleygalley in Co. Antrim (Simpson 1993), where a large amount of grain, mostly emmer wheat, but with a high proportion of einkorn, was recovered from the wall slots. No processing waste was found in the samples from the building, although it was common elsewhere on the site, so only cleaned grain entered the house.

The other area of evidence concerning the agricultural plant economy is the suggestion that ploughmarks have been preserved under the long barrow at South Street (Fowler and Evans 1967). These have been argued to be the result of the use of a rip ard (Reynolds 1981: 102–3), used to cut especially deep into the ground in order to break in new land and stubborn old fallow ground. Alternatively, Barker and Webley (1978) have suggested that light wooden ards of the kind known from prehistoric Europe could not have produced the 15-cm deep furrows found at South Street, and that turf cutting with a hoe or spade may be responsible instead.

The most far-reaching conclusion drawn from the examination of animal bones is the suggestion of Early Neolithic dairy economies. Legge (1981) has argued that at both the Hambledon Hill, Dorset, and Windmill Hill, Wiltshire, enclosures the majority of cattle bones came from female animals, which represented the surplus from a dairy economy based in lowland areas around the sites. Some support for Legge's model comes from the work of Grigson (1982), who has shown for the Windmill Hill cattle that females aged five or more years far outnumber younger animals and bulls, and that all the bulls are young. She refers to the possibility that this pattern may reflect a dairying economy but goes no further. A similar dominance of adult cattle bones is seen at the enclosures of Knap Hill and Robin Hood's Ball in Wiltshire (Grigson 1981) and Maiden Castle in Dorset (Armour-Chelu in Sharples 1991: 139–51). Legge has also suggested that the large enclosures may relate to the management of cattle herds, leading to the notion of a cattle-based agricultural economy.

The dairying interpretation has been questioned by Entwistle and Grant (1989), who find the idea of a cattle economy implausible. They believe that insufficient milk would have been produced for this to be practical, and that dairying economies are a medieval development. They suggest that the high numbers of adult female cattle bones in the ditches of enclosures such as Hambledon Hill, Windmill Hill and Maiden Castle are the result of male animals being killed off for their meat before they reached maturity, while the females were kept for breeding. Legge has replied (1989) by stating that dairying economies did exist before medieval times, while a need primarily for meat would result in steers (castrated males) being kept and killed off at two to three years of age. While the Legge argument is persuasive in terms of pointing out a pattern that requires explanation, it is not possible to assess the significance of the material recovered from enclosures in the absence of background evidence from settlements, as Entwistle and Grant note (1989).

Other assemblages occur outside enclosures, but they are mostly too small in number to allow any conclusions to be drawn concerning the nature of the wider economy. The Coneybury Anomaly (Richards 1990: 40–61), contained over two thousand fragments of animal bone, mainly cattle and roe deer, with smaller numbers of pig, red deer, beaver and fish; together the material represents the slaughter of at least ten cattle, several roe deer, a pig (which could be domesticated or wild) and two red deer. It seems as though a single large feast or a series of smaller feasts within a short time gave rise to this massive deposit, which contains a significant proportion of wild species. A similar, though smaller scale, event, gave rise to the Rowden pit deposit (Woodward 1991: 105), with pig, sheep, cattle and roe deer bones; the emphasis on pig is unusual for Early Neolithic sites, but this may again represent a feasting deposit.

This rather scattered material, together with smaller assemblages of both plants and animal bones, has been used to construct quite different models of the Early Neolithic agricultural economy. Thus the concept of a 'pioneer Neolithic' (see Chapter 5) led to a model in which a low density and mobile settlement pattern must have existed before monuments began to be constructed and sedentism became the norm (Case 1969). The consensus is now that monuments were an important element in Early Neolithic societies from the beginning (Kinnes 1988; J. Thomas 1988a), but there is still considerable debate over the nature of the agricultural economy. Barker and Webley (1978) proposed a model of fairly sedentary mixed farming, with each community exploiting a transect across the landscape from river floodplain via lightly drained soils to upland chalk. This would suggest that a fully developed agricultural economy existed from the beginning of the Neolithic, the surplus from that economy providing the wherewithal to fund the construction of the monuments. Similarly, Mercer (1981a: x), suggests that large areas of the landscape were brought under arable cultivation.

Alternatively, it has been argued that pastoralism was the mainstay of the economy (Legge 1981;1989; Barrett 1994: 139–41). This could be seen as a variation on the Barker and Webley sedentary model, with cattle as the most significant element rather than cereals (Legge 1989). Pryor (1988a) has concluded that cereals and vegetable crops were grown in small plots or gardens around settlements, with livestock kept in the surrounding fields, making livestock the most significant element of a horticultural and pastoralist economy. In itself this need not imply population mobility, but the idea of transient hoe-based horticulture has become popular (e.g. Entwistle and Grant 1989; J. Thomas 1991:18–19; 1994). This is based on the evidence presented by Moffett et al. (1989), that although cereals were present across Britain their importance may have been over-estimated. A number of settlement sites have produced only scant evidence of cereal production, but large quantities of hazelnut shells and occasional remains of other wild foods. They believe it is not feasible to make an accurate estimate of the contribution made by various foods in the diet, but that it is possible that on a number of sites hazelnuts were at least as important a source of food as grain. From this analysis the conclusion has been drawn that the importance of cereals was relatively slight (Entwistle and Grant 1989), in this particular interpretation combined with doubts about the significance of pastoralism.

Julian Thomas (1994) has further suggested that data concerning both plantstuffs and domesticated animals are biased by Neolithic processes of selection, and that the significance of domesticated plants and animals lay more in the symbolic arena than in the subsistence economy. In this view monuments were again built from the earliest Neolithic, but here served to bind together transient communities. Indeed, it might be possible to see the Sweet Track in the Somerset Levels (Coles 1989), constructed in 3807/6 BC (Hillam et al. 1990) in this light. Legge (1989) has defended his model of pastoralism, and also questioned the alternative interpretation of a lower-intensity agricultural regime of plot-based horticulture with a substantial element of wild food collection. He doubts that the nuts available in Neolithic Britain would be a very feasible large scale food resource, as they were unpredictable in the size of the harvest and difficult to store. Storage clearly could have taken place, but little sign of it can be traced in the archaeological record.

Thomas is certainly right about the element of Neolithic selection of material for deposition at major monuments, but other recent sites can also show a high frequency of cereals (e.g Balbridie – Fairweather and Ralston 1993 and Hazleton

– Straker in Saville 1990: 215–18). However, there is no real consensus either on the interpretation of plant and animal bone assemblages and the significance of variation or on the definition of ordinary settlements. Thus the Balbridie hall could well be just as unusual a site in its local context as the enclosures are in theirs. The current situation is undoubtedly one of those unsatisfactory circumstances in which further data are required, particularly from more ephemeral structures and sites, in order to build up a more complete picture of the subsistence economy. It would also be advantageous, however, to attempt to pursue alternative avenues of research, such as the microwear analysis of flint tools, which might shed some light on the extent of cereal harvesting, and the study of diet through chemical analysis of human skeletal material, which could provide a more direct picture of diet, if methodological problems can be overcome.

These two models of sedentary or transient populations clearly have important consequences for the question of continuity from Late Mesolithic to Early Neolithic in economic practices, settlement patterns and thus social organisation, so it would clearly be valuable to attempt a wider approach to the question. One element which has not entered this debate is the continued use of shell middens. Although this does not occur on such a large scale as in southern Scandinavia (see Chapter 6), there are a number of recorded instances (Bradley 1978: 93). In Wales two Early Neolithic cockle-shell middens were found near to two mussel shell middens of probable Mesolithic date at Prestatyn (D. Thomas 1992). In eastern Scotland a number of sites have been located in the Forth Valley, where the middens at Polmonthill, Inveravon and Nether Kinneal date to the Mesolithic and Neolithic, but there is no significant difference in resource use between the two (Sloan 1984). Off the west coast at Ulva Cave on a small island in the Hebrides the midden was used in both the Mesolithic and Neolithic (Armit and Finlayson 1992).

Finally, in Ireland the Swedish project at Carrowmore paid considerable attention to shell middens, not surprisingly given its national origin, and discovered an example consisting mostly of oyster shells which dated to *c.* 3500 BC (Österholm and Österholm 1984). As already noted, the Dalkey Island midden (Liversage 1968) was occupied from Late Mesolithic times into the Early Neolithic, with pottery and the bones of domestic animals present in upper layers. It is also clear from the general settlement pattern in Ireland that hunting, fishing and food collection remained important in the Neolithic (O'Kelly 1989: 29–30). This points to there being perhaps less of a day-to-day difference in the subsistence economy than has often been assumed.

Turning to the evidence of buildings, the actual structures which can be dated to this period are a rather mixed group. A number of sites have produced rectangular buildings of various sizes, such as the Crickley Hill enclosure in Gloucestershire (Dixon 1988), Haldon in Devon (Clark 1938), two examples at Lismore Fields, Derbyshire, (Garton 1987), dating to *c.* 3800 and 3500 BC (Hedges *et al.* 1991), a substantial hall at Balbridie in Scotland (Fairweather and

Ralston 1993), and in Ireland examples at Ballynagilly, Co. Tyrone (ApSimon 1976), Ballyglass, Co. Mayo (O'Nuallain 1972), the earliest Lough Gur buildings (O'Riordáin 1954; Grogan 1988) and Tankardstown (two buildings – Gowen 1988; Gowen and Tarbett 1988) in Co. Limerick, Pepperhill, Co. Cork (Gowen 1988), Balleygalley, Co. Antrim (Simpson 1993), and Knowth (several structures – Eogan 1984; 1991) and Newtown in Co. Meath (Gowen and Halpin 1992).

This might lead us to suppose that a degree of structural uniformity existed, but there are other house shapes, some known from the same sites which have produced rectangular buildings, and also some variety within the group of rectangular structures themselves. At Crickley Hill (Dixon 1988) a group of oval huts was discovered below the enclosure bank, although Dixon suggests that they may be temporary structures, given that they lack both artefacts and hearths; it is indeed possible that they relate to the construction of the enclosure. At Knowth (Roche 1989) a series of five arcs of stakeholes have been claimed to form successive huts, although the selection of particular stakeholes as structural elements has a distinctly subjective air to it. A clearer case of structural variabilty at a single site comes from Lismore Fields (Garton 1987), where the two rectangular buildings were excavated together with ring-slots, a post ring and a D-shaped slot, all of which appear to be Early Neolithic in date.

A number of the rectangular buildings have features which mark them out as being in some way unusual (see Figure 7.1). Building I at Lismore Fields (Garton 1987) was 15 × 5 m, divided into four compartments, with hearths set between compartments, which were partitioned off by lines of postholes. This appears to be quite a complex structure, although the large number of postholes in the central area raises the possibility that two overlapping structures succeeded each other; alternatively, however, this may be a single building which was enlarged. The Balbridie structure (Fairweather and Ralston 1993) is a hall with various internal features, 24 × 12 m in size, which makes it considerably larger than any of the other buildings recorded from Early Neolithic Britain or Ireland, and thus potentially a special-purpose structure. In Ireland, too, there are alternative views of some of the known buildings. The Ballyglass structure (O'Nuallain 1972) was found partly below a chambered tomb, and is argued to have been demolished in order to make way for the construction of the tomb. The building had two rooms, with a fire-reddened area of the floor in each. The siting of the tomb over the building raises the possibility that this was a cult house relating to death rituals, perhaps including storage of corpses, or it may be that this was a house which had acquired sufficient prestige due to its inhabitants that it became an appropriate place in the cultural landscape for a tomb to be built.

A different series of questions have been raised by the Balleygalley site (Simpson 1993); several hundred thousand flint flakes, over 800 cores and 2,000 finished tools (mainly scrapers, but also knives and axes) have been recovered by the excavations, suggesting to the excavator (Simpson 1990) that it might be a flint-working site related to the nearby mines on Balleygalley Hill only 1.5 km

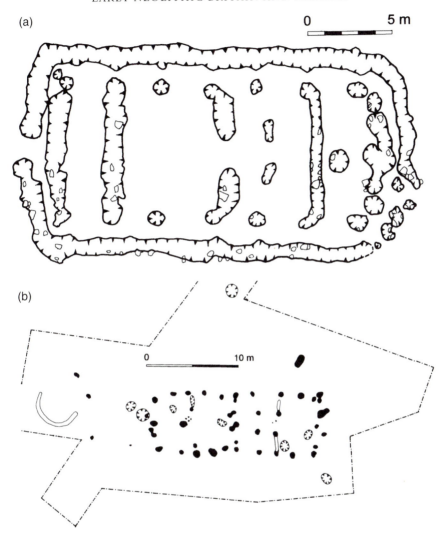

Figure 7.1 Early Neolithic British houses – Balbridie (a) and Lismore Fields (b) (after Fairweather and Ralston 1993, Garton 1987)

away. However, there is also material from the Tievebulliagh stone quarry some 30 km distant, including partially finished axes and beads, and stones which could have been used for final polishing of axes. Other exotic substances were mudstone from the River Bann over 40 km away, crystal from an unknown Irish source, and from across the Irish Sea some 200 pieces of Arran pitchstone (extremely rare in Ireland) and two axe fragments made of Langdale rock from the Lake District. The current interpretation is thus that Balleygalley was a major exchange centre, with exotic and local material being fashioned into finished products on site (Simpson 1993). However, the rarity of Arran pitch-stone elsewhere in Ireland does lead to the alternative suggestion that the site may be more of a destination for exotic materials, in the same way as enclosures, and indeed a possible ditch has been located at Balleygalley (Simpson 1993).

The majority of excavated sites with Early Neolithic material have not produced structures (Holgate 1988: 31–3), which may therefore strengthen the argument that many of the domestic buildings claimed for the Early Neolithic are not ordinary houses, but had some other significance. The smaller rectangular structures, especially in Ireland, where they are by now relatively common, do, however, seem to represent domestic architecture, and suggest there was at least a degree of permanency of occupation in the Irish Early Neolithic.

Taking a different look at the settlement pattern, from the perspective of the lithic evidence, both Bradley (1987) and Edmonds (1987) have suggested that the nature of the Early Neolithic flint toolkit of carefully prepared cores and utilised and serrated blades and flakes points towards communities being on the move rather than settled. They propose that residential foci of a fairly insubstantial kind may have moved frequently within a fairly small area.

Quite different opinions have been expressed on the question of sedentism. Thus the implication of Barker and Webley's (1978) reconstruction of an agricultural landscape would be that sedentary communities existed from the beginning of the Neolithic across southern England. By contrast, Julian Thomas (1991: 18–20; 1994) has followed the views of Entwistle and Grant (1989) on transient hoe-based cultivation and Edmonds (1987) and Bradley (1987) on shifting settlement to conclude that in southern England both diet and settlement patterns changed little from the Mesolithic to the Neolithic. He argues that the food eaten in the Early Neolithic was of Mesolithic character, except on ceremonial occasions, although the use of pottery to eat it from represented a fundamental change in the way in which the food was consumed. Relatively mobile settlements were tied in to horticulture on fixed plots, with seasonal or more frequent group movements possibly determined by the dictates of cattle herding. Holgate (1988: 132) has reached similar conclusions relating to the settlement pattern of the Thames Valley, which he argues consisted of base camps around which were garden plots and browsing cattle, and from which groups went out to other sites in order to achieve specific tasks. The material from the Coneybury Anomaly has been argued by Richards (1990: 43) to demonstrate an essentially mobile economy, with a significant wild element in the animal bones, including river valley resources such as beaver and brown trout, and a flint assemblage with high numbers of blades. He also sees these factors as representing continuity from the Mesolithic. In Scotland Armit and Finlayson (1992) have observed that much Early Neolithic settlement is small in scale with only temporary structures, with many of the same sites reoccupied over long periods. However, they interpret these as representing the existence of sites set up for short periods to exploit particular resources, with these rich resources proving to be a magnet on numerous occasions. They suggest that similar patterns of settlement and economic exploitation existed in both the Late Mesolithic and Early Neolithic, with base camps from which task groups were sent out to subsidiary sites.

Although we need not adopt this model of economic rationality and maximising production, the suggestion that there was little change between the Mesolithic and Neolithic, because the Mesolithic was already a highly structured society with a degree of sedentism, seems to provide a good fit with the evidence. Although the majority of Early Neolithic sites are unquestionably ephemeral in nature, there are sufficient sites which display a larger input of constructional activity and greater degree of permanence to show that this was not the whole picture. The elaboration of sites such as Lismore Fields and Balbridie suggests that they were not merely of greater economic significance, but also had far more symbolic weight as fixed points in a largely fluid cultural landscape than the mass of temporary encampments. In this way they acted in a similar fashion to the enclosures, burial mounds and cursus monuments and perhaps trackways which acted to transform the landscape, although they were designed to dominate the present-day landscape rather than that of the future.

MONUMENTS AND BURIAL PRACTICE

Having seen that there is a good case for continuity in the subsistence economy and settlement pattern, can any such claims be made for burial practices, traditionally one of the main elements which distinguishes the Neolithic from the Mesolithic? As we have already documented (see Chapter 5) there is little evidence of Later Mesolithic burial in Britain and Ireland, so the expectation of continuity must be low. There are, however, a number of possible instances which are worth investigating. Cave burial is a practice which begins in the Mesolithic and is also documented for the Neolithic, although direct evidence for continuity at the sites with Mesolithic examples is lacking. One source of human skeletal material in the Late Mesolithic of Britain is shell middens, and a number of Obanian shell middens occur in caves. Pollard (1990) has argued for a significant relationship existing between these middens and Neolithic burial. There are, however, major difficulties with this argument (Armit and Finlayson 1992): first, the Neolithic cave burials on the Scottish coast are not in middens and come mostly from caves without significant midden deposits; second, the caves may have been chosen as burial places because of their resemblance to chambered tombs, rather than their past history. This latter argument may be overdone, in that by no means all caves were used in this way, and one element in the choice of cave may well have been its previous history as rendered by oral history and folklore. This need not, however, imply any continuity of burial practice from the Mesolithic to Neolithic, rather the continued significance of certain places in the landscape. This is strongly suggested by the Iron Age radiocarbon dates obtained from four human bones from MacArthur Cave (Saville and Hallén 1994).

A similar claim for a direct relationship between Mesolithic practice and Neolithic burials has been made for the Avebury region in north Wiltshire by R. W. Smith (1984). He suggests that at the Horslip, South Street and Beckhampton Road earthen long barrows (Ashbee *et al.* 1979) there were traces of Mesolithic activity. At Horslip this is fairly clear, with a Late Mesolithic assemblage from the old land surface below the barrow mound, pollen evidence suggesting that the resulting clearing was being recolonised by hazel woodland at the time of the barrow's construction; at South Street a similar context produced sherds of plain bowl pottery, bones of domestic sheep and cattle and an assemblage of blades and flakes, which Smith (1984: 113) regards as being of Mesolithic character; at Beckhampton Road the suggestion of a Mesolithic input rests on the existence of a structure below the barrow and the absence of Neolithic type artefacts from lower levels of the site. Horslip, South Street and Beckhampton Road have one further thing in common: they lack burials, being cenotaph barrows. Smith (1984: 114) therefore concludes that these mounds may therefore have been constructed 'by people who had glimpsed the Neolithic lifestyle without achieving a proper understanding of its ritual character'. This specific model has been regarded as both fruitful (e.g. Cunliffe 1993: 39) and highly dubious (Whittle 1990b). A reappraisal of the evidence suggests that there are severe flaws in the argument, particularly on the grounds of date. Horslip probably does belong to the beginning of the Neolithic, dating to around 4200 BC; however, South Street shows occupation around 3550 BC and mound construction *c.* 3400 BC, so is firmly in the Neolithic, with Smith's claim to be able to date a flint assemblage without diagnostic tools to the Late Mesolithic rather than the Early Neolithic being difficult to accept; and Beckhampton Road has produced clear Neolithic material, dated to *c.* 4200 BC from below the mound, while the barrow itself was constructed *c.* 3300 BC. The time gaps involved are too great, and the presence of Neolithic material culture too substantial to allow any role for remnant gatherer-hunter groups living on the fringes of an agricultural landscape any role in the construction of these long barrows.

A rather looser relationship, which acknowledges the importance of certain places within the cultural landscape but involves no Mesolithic survivals, may be a more acceptable model for the Avebury area monuments. Choices were undoubtedly being made on the positioning of major monuments in the landscape with regard to the histories of particular spaces. Similar factors may have been at work in the siting of the Cotswold–Severn tombs at Ascott-under-Wychwood in Oxfordshire, Hazleton in Gloucestershire and Gwernvale in Wales (Britnell and Savory 1984; Saville 1989). Saville argues that the sites may have become ritually important through constant use. The creation of the chambered tomb may therefore mark the monumentalisation of this particular place in the landscape. The same may apply to the Later Mesolithic material found below the Kilham long barrow in Yorkshire (Manby 1976).

A general rather than close tie between the Mesolithic cultural landscape and the siting of Neolithic burial monuments therefore appears to exist. Despite that relationship there is no real doubt that the creation of burial monuments did mark a significant shift in the treatment of the dead in Britain and Ireland. Large numbers of these monuments were constructed and a significant proportion have probably survived to the present day. Looking first at the earthen or non-megalithic long barrows of eastern Britain, these have been studied in depth for over a century (Thurnam 1869; Kinnes 1992a), although as Kinnes notes (1992a: 59–60) the recent concentration of excavation efforts on recording badly damaged sites before their final destruction has produced few informative sites. This leaves us still largely dependent on the results of nineteenth century excavations, incomplete though these are in terms of both scale and recording (Thorpe 1984).

Consideration of possible structures within long barrows has been dominated by Ashbee's (1966; 1970) claims of mortuary houses existing in large numbers, developed from his excavation of Fussell's Lodge and that of Atkinson (1965) at Wayland's Smithy. Ashbee's mortuary houses were substantial ridged roof build-ings using sophisticated carpentry. The number of mortuary houses was soon questioned by Simpson (1968), and indeed some of Ashbee's cases rest on no more than the presence of cut features below the mound. Some at least of these are better seen as pits rather than postholes supporting buildings (Thorpe 1984), but embanked chambers do seem to exist in small numbers (Kinnes 1992a: 81–4), although in a rather simpler form. The walls could be of turf, soil or stone, with posts at the ends. The wetland site of Haddenham has been particularly important in providing a clear example of a timber chamber (Hodder and Shand 1988; Shand and Hodder 1990). The enclosing bank was only broken by a post-linked 'access' to the front part of the plank-built chamber; the side walls and floor were of massive oak planks, the ends made up of two and three posts and access between the two compartments was blocked by a massive D-section post; the posts supported a substantial plank roof, either a lid which could have been removed if needed, or added as a final act of closure. There are no signs of sophisticated carpentry, and the large timbers seem to be the equivalent of large unworked stones in megalithic chambers.

The study of mortuary ritual particularly suffers from the lack of recent excavations of well preserved sites. Crematoria were quite regularly uncovered in the nineteenth century in northern England, but largely lack recent investigation. The burial deposit was contained in a crematorium constructed along a narrow strip within the mound behind a façade trench filled with wood with a large central pit; the bones of disarticulated individuals were placed in this linear zone, then covered by stacked timber and stones; the mound was then constructed; finally, the deposit was fired and the temperature reached was sufficient to convert the surrounding chalk and limestone into lime. The burning was most intense at the façade end of the zone, so that bodies at the back are often only slightly burnt and sometimes not at all. This general picture is not entirely without variety (Manby 1970), although this has not been emphasised. Thus there are both articulated and disarticulated bodies in the barrows, although if the intention was to destroy the bodies then their condition beforehand was presumably not significant.

One much considered aspect of Earlier Neolithic burial practice is the question of whether more than one stage of burial took place. Both Hertz's (1960) distinction between primary and secondary burial and van Gennep's concept of rites of passage (1960) have been applied in the archaeological literature (e.g. Thorpe 1984). The death of the single individual may be denied by concentrating on the dead as ancestors rather than corpses; thus the unsettling effect of the death of one of its members is minimised. The dead have to undertake a passage from the world of the living to the world of the dead. This often involves the decomposition of the flesh, with its unfavourable associations with the individual and discontinuity, until only the purified white bones are left, with their favourable associations with the ancestral group and continuity. However, there is no single recipe for this transformation. Instead a simple process involving a primary burial which is just a matter of disposing of an unpleasantly rotting corpse, and a secondary burial which will merge the purged skeleton into the ideal community of the ancestors, there are a range of options open to any community, as reviewed by Bloch and Parry (1982). It may dispose of all corpses without regard to the ancestors, who play only a minimal role. Alternatively, the body may enter an idealised community of the ancestors, but only after it has been completely destroyed to leave behind just the incorruptible immortal soul. In between these two extremes are the vast majority of societies, which require the body to pass through a number of bounded stages (in some sense a parallel both to the passage through stages in life and the more general passage of time) before interment in the ancestral resting place. Even then parts of the ancestor may be removed, temporarily or permanently, to play a continuing social role.

Communities for whom an ancestral presence in the form of monumental burial sites is central to social life rely on the ancestors to occupy an intermediate position from which they may intervene with the gods in order to favour their descendants by bestowing wealth upon them. In such societies there is a definite tendency towards unequal treatment of the dead: only the bodies of certain individuals may be considered worthy of being received into the powerful and responsible community of the ancestors. Such decisions will be made on the basis of status during life, manner of death and the existence of a community of descendants.

The existence of mortuary houses has played a large part in deliberations on the nature of Early Neolithic multi-stage burial practice. These are generally argued to be buildings found adjacent to burial chambers. Examples occur at earthen long barrows, chambered tombs and early round barrows (Kinnes 1992a: 90–1). In a number of cases the lack of associated finds makes it difficult to be sure of the function of the structure, although this absence of material would make a domestic role unlikely. The most convincing example is that from

Gwernvale (Britnell and Savory 1984: 138–54): beneath the Cotswold–Severn chambered tomb was a rectangular wooden structure loosely associated with both pits containing apparently domestic material and small fragments of human skull. While the finds may suggest a domestic role for the building, the skull fragments would point in the direction of mortuary ritual, although human bone is not unknown on settlement sites.

Separate mortuary enclosures also exist, best known at Normanton Down in Wiltshire (Vatcher 1961) and Dorchester-on-Thames, Oxfordshire (Whittle *et al.* 1992). They are ditched and banked enclosures, and do not appear to be unfinished long barrows (Kinnes 1992a: 90). It is not possible to say whether they were a consistent feature of Early Neolithic burial practice, although their small numbers (Kinnes 1992a: 19, 142–5) may suggest that they were not. In any case, the general lack of finds from claimed mortuary enclosures makes it impossible to say more about their role in the mortuary process except that they may have been one place where bodies were stored on a temporary basis.

Other possible contexts for temporary burial certainly exist, including enclosures (see pp. 171–7), settlements, flat graves and round barrows. A number of apparently ordinary settlements have produced fragmentary skeletal remains, as at Bishops Cannings (Proudfoot 1965), where two cremations in pits under a round barrow were associated with settlement debris, or at South Cadbury (Alcock 1969), where skull fragments occurred in a pit together with plain Early Neolithic pottery. Overall, however, there are relatively few instances, suggesting that this was not a consistent practice. Instead these may have been token deposits of human bone abstracted from monuments, rather than debris left behind from a temporary stay.

Flat graves are a much more common occurrence, and one which may have been underrated, given the problems of dating unaccompanied burials other than through direct radiocarbon dates. The majority are dated by grave good associations with plain bowls or axes (Kinnes 1979: 126–7); these can be single burials, as at Pangbourne, Berkshire (Piggott 1929), or multiple interments, as in the two pits at Winterbourne Monkton in Wiltshire (Hillier 1854; Davis and Thurnam 1865: II, 58). There is a general distinction between southern and northern Britain in terms of treatment of the corpse, which mirrors that in long barrows. In the South nearly all burials are inhumations, while in the North there is a clear group of cremations. In Yorkshire, at both Garton Slack and Raisthorpe (Kinnes 1992a: 40–1) cremation pits were cut into earthen long barrows, while at Bridlington there was an isolated example (Earnshaw 1973). Single cremations in separate pits also occur in Scotland, as at North Mains, Perthshire (Barclay 1983), and Ireland, with a probable example at Killaghy in Armagh (E. E. Evans 1940). One of the most interesting of the flat graves is that at Fengate, Cambridgeshire (Pryor 1976; 1984), containing an intact adult male and child and a disarticulated female and child, with a leaf-shaped arrowhead lodged between the ribs of the adult male (Pryor 1984: 19).

Kinnes (1992a: 127) has suggested that the Park Farm round barrow in

Berkshire (Richards 1986–90) represents a stage of mortuary activity prior to final interment. Three inhumations (an adult female and male and an adolescent) were buried in a shallow slot and covered by sarsen stones; large postholes next to the burials could have acted as markers; the burials have been directly dated to *c.* 3600 BC. While the presence of the postholes might point to a desire to record the existence of the burials for future recovery, it seems unlikely that this would actually be necessary, and the sarsen covering would certainly have made any attempt to recover the bodies in the future extremely difficult. There seems little doubt that most round barrows were definitely final resting places (see pp. 167–9), and indeed there is no strong evidence that flat graves were different, especially cremation graves and more elaborate examples such as Fengate. We may well be in danger of attempting to force the data into a single model of mortuary activity, when variability may have been a crucial element.

However, there is clear evidence from both long barrows and chambered tombs of differential treatment of bones before their arrival at a final resting place. It has been argued that bodies were introduced into some long barrows and chambered tombs in a defleshed state (Wells in Piggott 1962a); the disarticulated nature of many skeletons could be a result of this practice, but it could equally well be the consequence of subsequent disturbance when further bodies were interred. Better evidence is provided by the weathered condition of many bones, as at Fussell's Lodge (Ashbee 1966), suggesting that the bodies had been exposed prior to their interment. In some cases flesh may have been scorched off the bones before their permanent burial. Finally, there is evidence that small bones had been lost from bodies before they reached the monument (e.g. at Fussell's Lodge – Ashbee 1966, and at Giant's Hills 2 in Lincolnshire – Evans and Simpson 1991). This need not be a consistent pattern, for the skeletal material at Wayland's Smithy (Whittle 1991) is equally consistent with the primary burial of complete bodies.

Two distinct attitudes have emerged towards the study of skeletal material in earthen long barrows, what may be described as the optimistic (e.g. Thorpe 1984) and pessimistic approaches (Kinnes 1992a). Kinnes, in his survey of earthen long barrows, admits that the small number of recent excavations provides an inadequate database (1992a: 98), but argues that the inadequacies of older excavations renders their observations unusable (1992a: 98). The alternative approach has been to see if some patterns may be teased out of the available evidence, despite its clear limitations. This is only really feasible for the Wessex area (Thorpe 1984), as many other regions such as Scotland provide a mere handful of sites (Kinnes 1992b), while most of the long barrows explored in Yorkshire have proved to be crematoria, making it impossible for nineteenth-century excavators to achieve even the broadest of estimates of numbers of bodies.

Looking at Wessex (Thorpe 1984) it is clear that nineteenth-century excavations were by no means complete, and that the number of bodies represented by a mass of disarticulated bone was almost certainly underestimated, given that Ashbee's (1966) preliminary estimate of the Fussell's Lodge remains was less than half the number eventually revealed by careful analysis. However, it does appear that the early excavators did pursue their digging until they had recovered a reasonable number of skeletons, which means that instances where no bodies or a single inhumation only were found are quite likely to reflect a real lack of skeletal material. It is clear that a considerable variety exists in the number of bodies present, from 57 at Fussell's Lodge down to none at South Street and Beckhampton Road (Ashbee *et al.* 1979), with single burials at Hambledon Hill (Mercer 1980) and Moody's Down South East (Grimes 1960) among recent excavations, together with several from nineteenth century records. This variety in absolute numbers is related to the state of the bodies (Thorpe 1984): barrows where all the material was disarticulated contain the largest number of bodies, while the single burials were all articulated.

The available evidence for the age and sex of bodies shows that both females and males were buried, although males outnumbered females, and that children were present as well, but were less well represented than adults (Thorpe 1984). Tieing the different patterns together, nearly all articulated burials were adults, and the majority male (Thorpe 1984). Finally, the single burials, where an identification was made, are adults, mainly males (Thorpe 1984). These broad patterns point to a series of choices being made by the burying community of those corpses which should be merged into an undifferentiated group of the ancestors and those which should be kept aside to maintain an individual identity, in some cases this being taken as far as to produce a long barrow with only a single inhabitant.

However, this occasional stress on individual identity did not take the form of burial with grave goods, in Wessex or elsewhere, with rare exceptions (Kinnes 1992a: 108–10). In Wessex only a handful of instances exist of pottery or flint-work being placed with a particular body; significantly, all were articulated adults, and where the sex of the body was established, this was male (Thorpe 1984); the most well known of these is the single burial of an articulated adult inhumation, identified as male, from Winterbourne Stoke, found with a flint core (Thurnam 1869). The most informative recent case is the oval barrow at Abingdon in Oxfordshire (Bradley 1992). Here an adult male was found with a jet belt slider and a leaf-shaped arrowhead and an adult female with a polished flint knife. In Yorkshire there are almost no convincing cases of grave goods in earthen long barrows (Thorpe 1989: 184), as is the case elsewhere in the North.

More common are what may be regarded as offerings of various kinds, both with the burial deposit and occasionally replacing it, and as later deposits in the forecourt or flanking ditches. A variety of items occur in the mortuary deposits of earthen long barrows (Kinnes 1992a: 108–12), including complete pottery vessels, groups of sherds, arrowheads and other flintwork and a single bead. Such associations occur in both southern and northern Britain. More common are deposits of material around mounds. Again this is seen widely, although there may be a regional distinction in the focus of activity. In southern Britain this is mainly in the ditches, as at Thickthorn Down (Barrett *et al.* 1991: fig. 2.11), where a distinct pattern of deposits of animal bone and pottery was noted by Julian Thomas. Material was concentrated in the eastern end of the ditches, particularly near the terminal, and more material was found in the northern ditch. The eastern end of the ditches was also the open end in this U-shaped ditch barrow. Outside Wessex some sites do show substantial ditch deposits, as at Kilham in Yorkshire (Manby 1976), where a rich deposit of pottery, flintwork and animal bones occurred in secondary ditch silts, but more frequent are finds of pottery in and around façade trenches (Kinnes 1992a: 109). The best known example is Hanging Grimston (Mortimer 1905: 102–5), where only a single human femur was recovered, but several heaps of pig bones and a number of plain bowls were found in the central cremation pit, the façade trench, another pit and the barrow mound. The importance of the forecourt was also stressed in Yorkshire by the construction of avenues of posts leading towards the barrow (see Figure 7.2) at Kemp Howe, Kilham and Street House (Brewster 1968; Manby 1976; Vyner 1984). A recent site with a similar emphasis on the forecourt is Haddenham in Cambridgeshire (Hodder and Shand 1988; Shand and Hodder 1990); here the forecourt was paved with gravel brought in to the site and deposits included a complete decorated vessel.

Finally, we may consider the nature of the animal bone assemblages which make up a large part of these offerings. The Hanging Grimston material consisted of some twenty-five pigs, nearly all immature (Pierpoint 1979), but in southern Britain cattle were clearly dominant (Thorpe 1984), with other animals almost absent. Grinsell (1958) suggested that these were the remains of funeral feasts, but this is too limited an explanation. While it is appropriate for the Hanging Grimston material, it would certainly not cover sites where skulls and feet were found, as at Fussell's Lodge (Ashbee 1966); these seem far more likely to represent the surviving parts of hides (Piggott 1962b). Even more

Figure 7.2 Reconstruction of Street House Farm, Yorkshire, long barrow with mortuary enclosure and avenue (after Vyner 1984)

162

difficult to explain in these terms would be the Beckhampton Road long barrow (Ashbee *et al.* 1979); this contained no human remains, but had three cattle skulls and a long bone placed along the axis of the mound in the position which human bones would normally occupy. Here it seems as though cattle have been chosen as substitutes for the human bodies absent from the monument. This all points towards the existence, in the Wessex area at least, of an animal hierarchy, in which cattle were deemed to be more important than other animals; such a hierarchy in the animal world is likely to have been a transformation of social hierarchy, suggesting an attempt to legitimise existing social divisions by painting them as all encompassing, and thus indicating the presence of a social group, most plausibly an aristocratic clan, which stood in the same relationship to other human groups as cattle did to other animals.

Turning to the study of chambered tombs we can see that many of the same questions emerge again in the consideration of a body of data deriving mainly from western and northern Britain and Ireland. One crucial difference is that in some areas of Britain, most notably Orkney and Ireland, chambered tombs were still being constructed after 3000 BC; these late tombs will not be considered here. The main groups of chambered tombs to be considered are Cotswold–Severn tombs in England and Wales; Portal Dolmens in England, Wales and Ireland; Clyde Cairns in Scotland and Court Tombs in Northern Ireland; and Passage Graves in western Britain and Ireland (see Figure 7.3). There are major variations in spatial layout between these different types: thus Cotswold–Severn tombs have a trapezoidal cairn and a forecourt, with chambers leading in from the sides or end of the mound; Portal Dolmens have a chamber made of upright stones topped by a massive capstone, which was probably covered by a stone cairn or earthen mound; Clyde Cairns have a linear chamber divided into segments below a trapezoidal or round cairn; Court Tombs have segmented chambers, forecourts and rectangular or trapezoidal cairns; Passage Graves have a circular mound below which was a long passage leading to a chamber. It is clear that some of these formats have a strong degree of similarity with earthen long barrows, particularly Cotswold–Severn tombs (Kinnes 1992a: 122–3), while others are completely different, most dramatically Passage Graves.

Light may be thrown on this issue by the examination of tomb contents. Unfortunately this is limited to certain groups of monuments, as others (for example Portal Dolmens and Passage Graves) have produced insufficient Early Neolithic skeletal material to enable any patterns of activity to emerge. As with earthen long barrows there are rival approaches to the interpretation of mortuary ritual at chambered tombs. While the notion of secondary burial has been popular here, too (e.g. Chesterman 1977), there have also been suggestions that some sites saw the burial of complete bodies, only for these to be disturbed subsequently by the insertion of later inhumations. While there are many chambered tombs which contain only partial remains, these could result from bones being removed from the tomb rather than being lost on the way. The recent excavations at the lateral-chambered Cotswold–Severn tomb of Hazleton North (Saville

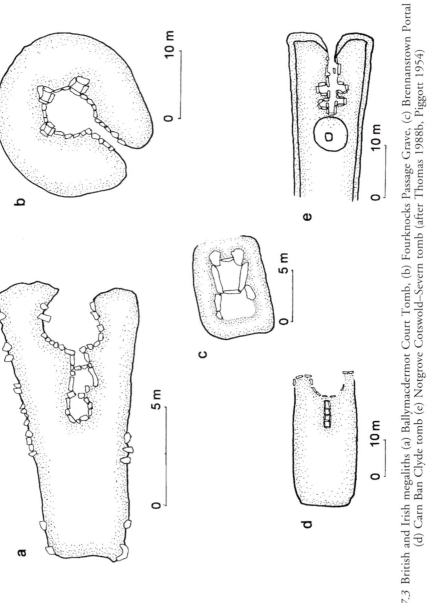

Figure 7.3 British and Irish megaliths (a) Ballymacdermot Court Tomb, (b) Fourknocks Passage Grave, (c) Brennanstown Portal Dolmen, (d) Carn Ban Clyde tomb (e) Norgrove Cotswold–Severn tomb (after Thomas 1988b, Piggott 1954)

1990) have led to the interpretation of whole bodies having been originally interred, followed by their subsequent incorporation into collective disarticulated deposits. Thus the well-known extended burial of an adult male with a flint core and pebble hammer in the passage leading to the northern chamber apparently disturbed a crouched articulated male inhumation (see Figure 7.4). Saville (1990: 250–2) concluded that intact bodies were brought into the interior chamber, only to be rearranged at a later date, as many tiny skeletal parts were present and there were numerous examples of articulation. Other sites recorded in the nineteenth and early twentieth centuries seem to show the same pattern (Thomas 1988b). This is not to say that a completely disordered mass of bones was created inside chambers, for many Cotswold–Severn and other tombs show signs of the careful arrangement of skeletal material (Thomas 1988b). There may have been different patterns of mortuary process at work here, with potentially different social implications, but until the Ascott-under-Wychwood Cotswold–Severn tomb is published, its contribution to the discussion will continue to be an internal debate (Chesterman 1977; Benson and Clegg 1978). It is, however, possible that chronology may play a part, with complete burials representing a later development.

Turning to a consideration of those interred in chambered tombs, once again the highest quality information comes from the Cotswold–Severn group. There is a considerable variety in the number of burials, from two or three up to nearly fifty (Darvill 1982: 11). The overall figures for age and sex (if they can be relied on – Saville 1990: 261) suggest that children are under-represented and adult males over-represented (Brothwell 1973; Rogers in Saville 1990: 197–8), though not to the extent that Piggott (1954: 139) argued. There are, however, a number of specific instances of the sorting of bones within the chambers on the basis of

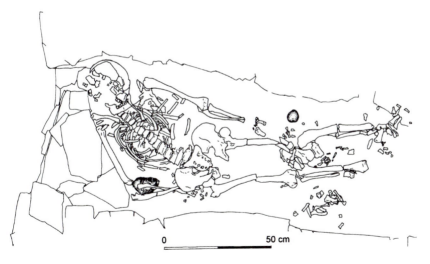

Figure 7.4 Hazleton flintknapper burial (after Saville 1990)

age and sex (Thomas 1988b). At West Kennet (a transepted tomb), for example (Piggott 1962a; Thomas and Whittle 1986), adult males occupied the end chamber directly facing the entrance, while juveniles dominated the southeast chamber (the first on the left after entering the tomb). Similar patterns have been noted by Julian Thomas (1988b) at other transepted tombs; as he points out, the more complex chamber design allowed for the spatial expression of difference to become elaborate. Such divisions are not a universal feature of Cotswold–Severn tombs, and at Hazleton (Saville 1990) adult males and females were present in both northern and southern chambers, along with children and infants. Although there was no spatial separation of the sexes, there was an overall pre-ponderance of adult males among the bones which could be sexed (Rogers in Saville 1990: 187–8). It may be, as Julian Thomas argues (1988b) that there were significant differences between lateral and terminal chambered tombs within the Cotswold–Severn group, but this need not follow inexorably from the different spatial layouts, as local variation may have a role here (Whittle 1991).

The Clyde cairns of western Scotland (Scott 1969) have produced both inhumations and cremations, although inhumations are much more common. Large numbers of individuals have been recovered from some sites, although little analysis has been carried out on this material. In Ireland the information available is also limited, partly due to the presence of acid soils and partly to the low level of recording. However, it is clear that Court Tombs contained only a few cremation burials, with rare exceptions (Mallory and McNeill 1991: 81), such as the double Court Tomb of Audleystown, Co. Down (Collins 1954; 1959), where both cremations and inhumations were present in a series of chambers arranged in two lines running towards each other. There was a dramatic variation in the number of individuals contained within the chambers, from thirteen to zero (two out of eight chambers). Of thirty-five burials only five were children and among the sexed adults males outnumbered females by fourteen to six. There was, however, a mixture of age and sex in the two chambers which produced substantial amounts of skeletal material.

Apart from the Hazleton 'flintknapper' (Saville 1990) already discussed, burials with grave goods are rare in all forms of chambered tomb. There are no certain cases among other Cotswold–Severn tombs of grave goods (Darvill 1982: 20–6), although the stone and bone beads found at Hazleton, West Kennet, Ty-Isaf and Notgrove (Saville 1990: 178–80) may originally have been grave goods, before later activities in the tombs displaced them, and a flint blade may have been associated with a burial at Lugbury in Wiltshire (Thurnam 1856). The Passage Tombs of Ireland may have been an exception, given the presence of some highly elaborate items in later examples, including the famous flint macehead from Knowth, Co. Meath (Eogan 1983), but the survival of skeletal material is too poor to examine this possibility further.

The most detailed evidence available on the question of offerings comes from the Cotswold–Severn tombs. Although other sites probably do have such deposits, little has been revealed through excavation. One exception is the ox burial in a pit outside the entrance of the passage grave at Bryn Celli Ddu (Hemp 1930), although its dating is undetermined. The Cotswold–Severn tombs produce clear evidence of similar treatment of animal bones as in earthen long barrows (Thomas 1988b); in chambers cattle are the most common element, placed along with human burials, while pig dominate in forecourt deposits, which include both pits and hearths. The recent excavations at Hazleton have produced more detailed analyses of such material which enable a deeper insight into Early Neolithic ritual practices (Levitan in Saville 1990: 212–13). In the southern quarry ditch three concentrations of animal bone were noted: a group of miscellaneous cattle bones and one pig bone with several human bones; a large deposit of burnt cattle and sheep bones with a decorated pot; and a group of cattle (mostly skull fragments), sheep and pig bones with a single human bone. These have been interpreted in terms of ritual offerings. In the forecourt a scatter of cattle and pig bones was located, nearly all being cranial fragments; the possibility that these once sat on the forecourt revetment wall has been tentatively proposed. Given that many of the animal remains from other sites are also dominated by skulls, jaws and teeth the suggestion of animal guardians for the tombs could be applied there as well.

The importance of both earthen long barrows and chambered tombs as monuments is crucial to their understanding, for they may have had quite different histories before, during and after construction, which only careful excavation can reveal. It has been argued for Britain that burial monuments often lay on the upland edge of a settled area (e.g. Bradley 1984: 16; Thomas 1988b). This, of course, undermines any argument based on the notion of burial sites as central places (Renfrew 1976). Specific examination of this question has tended to confirm this general impression at both Hazleton and Wayland's Smithy (Saville 1990; Whittle 1991), where both artefactual and environmental evidence suggest little in the way of contemporary settlement. However, in both instances material was found below the tomb, leading to the possibility that the location had already achieved a degree of importance, a suggestion strengthened by Whittle's (1991) observations at Wayland's Smithy that the pre-barrow deposits included exotic axes, which were deliberately broken. Cooney (1987–8) has suggested the opposite relationship for Ireland, with a close tie between settlements and tombs, but this appears to be based largely on the presence of Neolithic material below tombs rather than contemporary settlement.

The other main form of burial below a mound was under round barrows or cairns, without a stone chamber. These are far more common in northern Britain than in the South (Kinnes 1979; Thorpe 1984; Kinnes 1992b), with a notable concentration in East Yorkshire (Kinnes *et al.* 1983; Manby 1988). A considerable variety of burial practices have been recorded, including both crematoria and enclosed inhumations. The general lack of grave goods makes it difficult to see how far round barrows were also present from the beginning of the Neolithic, although a number of early examples are known. The most significant of these may prove to be at Whitwell in Derbyshire (Kinnes 1992a: 143–4; Hedges *et al.*

1994), where a single female adolescent inhumation, direct dated to *c.* 4050 BC, was buried in a timber chamber then enclosed in a round cairn, which was later incorporated into a trapezoidal long cairn together with a linear stone and timber chamber containing at least fifteen disarticulated inhumations, with direct dates of *c.* 4300 and 3900 BC. Here there seems little doubt that a single burial was accorded special treatment at an early stage in the creation of the monument, although the gap between this and the long chambered tomb is not yet clearly established. It is, of course, probable that some of the Carrowmore passage graves in Ireland are as early as this in date (see Chapter 5). The significance of this division into long and round mounds will not be established until a sufficient sample of earthen round barrow and passage graves has been excavated, although there seems little doubt that they represent a minority practice, certainly in Britain.

It may be possible to untangle the picture to some degree in Yorkshire, given the larger numbers of round barrows recorded. A wide variety of burial practice is recorded, although inhumation is far more frequent than in contemporary long barrows, and a number of articulated burials with grave goods are known. A few examples can give an indication of the overall nature of the burial process. Callis Wold, excavated by Mortimer (1905: 161–3) and re-excavated by Coombs (1976), produced a scattered series of inhumation and cremation burials towards the periphery of the mound; more central was a stone pavement on which were eleven (ten adults and a child) tightly packed but articulated inhumations, two of the adults being associated with leaf-shaped arrowheads; around two sides of this platform were post settings. Charcoal has given two dates of *c.* 3800–3600 BC. A similar pattern is repeated at Towthorpe (Mortimer 1905: 9–11), where six crouched articulated inhumations were found in a small area, two accompanied by fine leaf-shaped arrowheads which may well be grave goods; also below the mound were two Towthorpe style bowls (Manby 1988), a group of four leaf-shaped arrowheads and other flint and stonework.

Other round barrows have produced far smaller numbers of burials, but again primarily articulated inhumations. At Aldro (Mortimer 1905: 82) two crouched articulated inhumations had a Towthorpe bowl and an edge-polished flint knife on the ground between them. The first phase of Duggleby Howe, which was to become one of the massive Late Neolithic mounds, saw the excavation of a substantial grave and the burial of a supposed adult male accompanied by a Towthorpe bowl and a deposit of cores and flakes (Mortimer 1905: 23–42; Kinnes *et al.* 1983). The Whitegrounds site (Brewster 1984) has a single burial of an adult male, direct dated to *c.* 3200 BC, accompanied by a polished jet slider and an edge-polished waisted flint axe at the bottom of a shaft-grave dug into an existing linear chamber in an oval mound; this burial was then covered by a round soil mound with a stone kerb. Clearly, then, in Yorkshire we may see the emergence of a tradition of individual ariculated burial with grave goods, showing the selection of certain individuals for a dramatically different treatment after death than those who were subsumed into an undifferentiated mass of fused ancestral bone in the crematorium long barrows. Alternatively, such a process of division may have been operating from the beginning of the Neolithic, as possibly was the case in Derbyshire, to judge by the Whitwell site. In any case, this division of bodies is matched in Yorkshire by a division of pottery styles, with Grimston ware primarily associated with long barrows and Towthorpe ware with round barrows (Thorpe 1989: 185–7).

A development of this kind can also be traced in southern Ireland, with the emergence of the Linkardstown burials (Ryan 1981). Burials, mainly of single adult males, are placed in massive stone cists along with highly decorated bowls, plainer pottery, bone beads, arrowheads and stone axes, below round mounds. These were long dated to the end of the Neolithic, but radiocarbon dating of bones from the burials has shown that they are instead Earlier Neolithic, ranging from c. 3500–3300 BC (Brindley et al. 1983). They thus clearly overlap with the passage graves within circular mounds, which do not contain single burials and have produced collective cremation burials, so again a significant distinction is being made between two groups of the dead, this time apparently divided on sexual and presumably gender lines.

Burials in the Early Neolithic of Britain and Ireland were not entirely limited to settlements, barrows and enclosures, as a small but nonetheless significant body of evidence demonstrates. Cave burials have been known from many areas for some time, although most examples lack clear dating evidence (Kinnes 1979: 126–7). King Alfrid's Cave in Yorkshire produced a series of deposits of disarticulated skeletons associated with Grimston ware, possibly defined by dry-stone walling at the cave entrance (Lamplough and Lidster 1959). Single cave burials are also recorded, such as the probable example from Selside in Yorkshire, buried in a hillside rock crevice (Gilks and Lord 1985). The Oban cave burial deposits (see p. 155) noted by Pollard (1990) may fit here, if they are not later in date. In Ireland a small cave or crevice at Annagh, Co. Limerick, produced four adults, probably all males, two of which were articulated and associated with a large flint knife and a bone pin; above these on a narrow ledge were two complete decorated vessels, with broken pots below this which may have fallen (Ó Floinn 1992). A similar context at the nearby site of Caherguillamore produced a single burial with a flint knife, bone pin, and plain and decorated pottery (Hunt 1967). Ó Floinn (1992) has suggested that these sites may represent a local alternative to chambered tombs, while the English examples appear to mimic chambered tombs in a number of instances, with the provision of internal walling. In cave burials as well, we may therefore see a selection process at work, with a wider variety of burial options open to the community than is generally appreciated.

There are also rare finds of Early Neolithic bodies from wetland contexts. Coastal peat beds at Hartlepool Bay, County Durham, produced the partially disarticulated skeleton of an adult male dated to c. 3450 BC (Tooley 1975). Other undated examples from the coasts of Wales and northwest England may also prove to be Neolithic (Turner 1995). No other definite examples are known from

Britain, although bog bodies from Shropshire and Cumbria are from Bronze Age or Neolithic deposits (Turner 1995). In Ireland the only certain example of an Early Neolithic bog body comes from Stoneyisland, Co. Galway (Ó Floinn 1995), a single unaccompanied burial dated to *c.* 4000 BC (Brindley and Lanting 1995). One should also mention here the skull from the River Thames at Battersea, direct dated to *c.* 3800 BC (Bradley and Gordon 1988). The significance of these wetland burials is unclear, although they were not distinguished from other burials in any additional manner, such as the provision of grave goods.

It is also appropriate to treat here two classes of major monument with close connections with funerary activity. A small number of bank barrows have been recorded (Kinnes 1992a: 70, 144; Barclay *et al.* 1995); these take the form of long and narrow mounds, ranging from *c.* 100 m up to 546 m at Maiden Castle in Dorset (Sharples 1991: 54–6). No proven mortuary deposits are associated with bank barrows. Two post-date causewayed enclosures, at Maiden Castle and Crickley Hill in Gloucestershire (Dixon 1988), and another may post-date a mortuary enclosure at North Stoke, Oxfordshire (Case 1982). Analyses of snails from the Crickley Hill mound have produced the rather surprising result that they came from quite different micro-environments, such of which would have occurred no nearer than 3 km away (Mercer 1990a). The creation of this monument thus involved the incorporation of turf or soil from a variety of different places in the landscape within this culturally important space.

Cursus monuments are rather better known, with several having been subjected to small-scale examination (Hedges and Buckley 1981; Bradley 1986; Barrett *et al.* 1991: 36–58; Barclay *et al.* 1995). They typically comprise a pair of parallel ditches a few tens of metres apart, closed at both ends by a cross-ditch, with the material quarried from the ditches being piled in low banks along the insides of the ditches. They clearly span the Early and Late Neolithic, with radiocarbon dates of 3800 BC onwards and both Early and Late Neolithic material in the ditches of various sites. A number of examples show episodes of construction rather than a single build. There are occasional hints of mortuary practice, with human skeletal material in the ditches, but this may represent subsequent activity. More general links are undoubtedly made with sites of ancestral importance in a number of cases; the Dorset Cursus (Bradley 1986; Barrett *et al.* 1991: 36–58) incorporated two existing long barrows, while at the Martin Down end it changed course to terminate beside a prominent long barrow. This long barrow was then transformed into a bank barrow by the addition of a tail to the mound (Barrett *et al.* 1991: 51). The Dorchester-on-Thames Cursus incorporated a D-shaped enclosure which cut a pit containing splinters of bone from an adult and an adolescent, direct dated to *c.* 3500 BC (Whittle *et al.* 1992). Similarly, the Stonehenge Cursus ends some 20 metres from a substantial long barrow (Richards 1990: 96–109), although relative dating is not established here. There is little sign so far of structural activity within cursus sites, except for the Springfield Cursus, which appears to be of Late Neolithic date (Hedges and Buckley 1981).

Three different, but potentially intertwined, purposes have been suggested for bank barrows and cursus monuments (Barclay *et al.* 1995). First, they may link or incorporate other monuments such as mortuary enclosures or barrows. Second, they may act to channel and control movement along them and to produce framed views of the landscape at various points along them (as in the case of the Dorset Cursus – Barrett *et al.* 1991: 47). Third, they may act as markers, denoting a transitional zone between significantly different areas of the landscape. Both the first and third views have been taken of the two Stonehenge cursus monuments, based on a different understanding of the major divide in the cultural landscape. Thus Bradley (1993: 53) has a western funerary zone and an eastern domestic zone, with the two linked by the Stonehenge Cursus. For Julian Thomas (1991: 146) the Greater and Lesser Stonehenge Cursus monuments themselves create a division into a southern domestic area and a northern exotic and marginal area. Cleal *et al.* (1995: 473–6) have convincingly argued that these broad divisions are too static, and that a more fluid interpretation would better reflect the archaeological record. However, both bank barrows and cursus monuments do appear to be an attempt to stamp a particular mark on the landscape (the use of turf from various different environments at Crickley Hill being a significant example of this process), an effort perhaps to fix certain patterns of movement and access precisely because these were in reality extremely fluid, and indeed quite possibly an effort which was therefore unsuccessful. Only far tighter chronological resolution will enable us to see which particular stage in a constantly changing landscape was current at the time there was this attempt to freeze the action. Once these monuments were created they were recut, enlarged and presented with offerings to ensure that they remained active (Thomas 1991: 118), so their lives as monuments may have become more important than the fulfilling of their original purpose.

The other major monument form of the Early Neolithic is the enclosure, often the causewayed enclosure. Some sixty of these are known (Mercer 1990b: 5), predominantly from southern England, although with possible cases from northern Britain (Edmonds 1994) and definite examples from the Isle of Man (Denison 1995) and Northern Ireland (Mallory and McNeill 1991: 33–6). Although more enclosures will undoubtedly be found in northern Britain and Ireland, the continuing pace of discoveries in southern England makes it unlikely that the centre of their distribution will shift. The distribution is not continuous, even in southern England, and it is notable that there are still no certain enclosures in Hampshire, although Butser Hill has been cited as a potential candidate (e.g. Gardiner 1984). Enclosures were being constructed by 4000 BC, so they were a significant monumental element from the beginning of the Neolithic.

Two quite different approaches have been taken to the location of enclosures relative to settlements and the settled landscape. Barker and Webley (1978) argued that causewayed enclosures in Wessex were central settlements located at the heart of a territory which they controlled. However, this was largely a theoretically based study, whereas subsequent examination of environmental data from enclosures points to them being located instead in peripheral locations, away from the main areas of contemporary settlement, often in small woodland clearings (K. Thomas 1982; R. W. Smith 1984; Robertson-Mackay 1987; Evans *et al.* 1988; Evans 1988b; Whittle 1991: 93; Lobb 1995). Fieldwalking around the Hambledon Hill enclosure has also failed to locate contemporary settlement (J. Thomas 1991: 33). One suggestion has been that the activities carried out inside enclosures were seen as socially dangerous and therefore had to be separated from the main settlement area (Evans *et al.* 1988; J. Thomas 1991: 165). The siting of enclosures in a liminal situation may therefore be essential to some of the social roles which enclosures came to embody.

One other element in the location of enclosures which has been little considered is pre-existing activities which may have made that particular place in the landscape a significant one. Although there are enclosures which show little or no sign of previous occupation, many have produced remains. At Crickley Hill (Dixon 1988) a small mound surrounded by an interrupted ditch and a series of round huts preceded the construction of the enclosure, although Dixon has concluded from the lack of associated artefacts and hearths that this phase may have been short-lived. At Windmill Hill (Whittle 1993) small clusters of pits (one containing an adult male inhumation), postholes and scatters of bone and artefacts were all found below the outer bank. Similarly, at Robin Hood's Ball (N. Thomas 1964) intensive activity pre-dated the enclosure, which may relate to the group of pits located outside the enclosure (Richards 1990: 61–5).

The layout of enclosures is undoubtedly significant (see Figure 7.5), although it has been little discussed (Evans 1988a is a notable exception). Many enclosures share a concentric spatial arrangement, which has a potential for a hierarchical relationship between the spatially successive zones. The formation of boundaries clearly creates a basic division between that which is inside and that which is outside, and also a liminal or transitional zone represented by the actual boundary itself. This can be both a physical and a mental boundary, with the two often reinforcing each other. The notion of crossing the boundary may therefore have been of crucial significance (Evans 1988a).

The nature of the boundary in the case of Early Neolithic causewayed enclosures is significant, in that it consisted of multiple ditches with gaps between them. These ditches were the primary focus of depositional activity of various kinds (see pp. 174–7), but also see episodes of recutting (although not universally – Edmonds 1994). Mercer (1980: 36) has suggested that the different ditch segments at Hambledon Hill may have been maintained by particular family or clan groups, whose relationship with a specific area of ditches may have been sustained by oral tradition. This would also explain the enormous variability of ditch segments and their later contents, which will have reflected the history of the group responsible for them.

Chris Evans (1988a) also stresses the significance of the provision of multiple concentric boundaries for the formation of a periphery and a centre to the enclosure; the centre could be reached only by passing through a series of

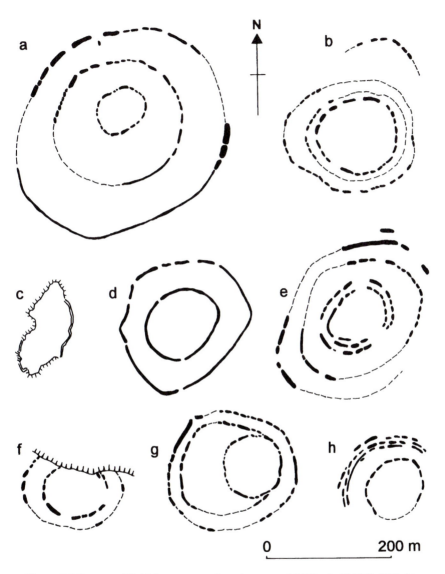

Figure 7.5 Layout of British causewayed enclosures – (a) Windmill Hill, Wiltshire, (b) The Trundle, Sussex, (c) Carn Brea, Cornwall, (d) Robin Hood's Ball, Wiltshire, (e) Whitehawk Camp, Sussex, (f) Coombe Hill, Sussex, (g) Briar Hill, Northamptonshire, (h) Orsett, Essex (after Piggott 1954 and Mercer 1990b)

bounded spaces, the 'deepest' space at the centre of the enclosure being the most difficult to reach. Principles of exclusion thus lie behind the enclosures and their layout. This realisation of the potentially complex spatial arrangements of what may be termed enclosure complexes has led to the reconsideration of a number of earthworks. At Hambledon Hill, Mercer (1988) believes that a third enclosure, in addition to the Main Enclosure and the Stepleton Enclosure, existed, below the Iron Age hillfort, all three being in turn enclosed by a series of outworks. At Maiden Castle (Sharples 1991: 38) there are also potential related earthworks in the form of a cross-ridge dyke outside the western entrance of the Iron Age hill-fort. Pairs of enclosures may have existed at Whitesheet Hill and Robin Hood's Ball in Wiltshire (Thorpe 1989: 121).

One of the clearest cases of emphasising the enclosure boundary through depositional practice occurs at the Main Enclosure at Hambledon Hill (Mercer 1988). Roughly forty-five burials were recovered from the 20 per cent of the ditch excavated, pointing to some two hundred bodies altogether; those excavated were dominated by children, found twice as often as adults. Some 110 inhumation burials were recorded from the site as a whole, with adults slightly outnumbering children elsewhere (Thorpe 1989: 126–7). Within Wessex this is a general pattern (Thorpe 1984), with children being much more common burials at causewayed enclosures than in earthen long barrows (see Figure 7.6). A link between burials at enclosures and in chambered tombs has long been proposed, with Isobel Smith (1965) suggesting that bones had been removed from the Cotswold–Severn tomb at West Kennet and taken to the nearby Windmill Hill enclosure. A general pattern, which suggests a quite close tie, emerges when the available figures for body parts from both enclosures and earthen long barrows in Wessex are plotted (Thorpe 1984). The two patterns are quite clearly complementary, with skulls present in high numbers at enclosures, while under-represented at long barrows (see Figure 7.7). The circulation of bones or a multiple-stage burial rite is strongly implied by this evidence. Mercer (1980: 63) has argued that the exposure of bodies took place on the surface inside the Main Enclosure at Hambledon Hill, but the available evidence suggests an alternative (Thorpe 1989: 127); preliminary analysis of the bones shows that in general they were not weathered, and the ninety-seven pits in the Main Enclosure contained small bone fragments along with stone axes, gabbroic pottery from Cornwall and fossils, which may have been grave goods accompanying bodies while they became at least partly disarticulated. It is important to remember that at several enclosures complete skeletons have been recovered, so not all bodies necessarily went through several stages of mortuary rite.

Elsewhere, enclosures have consistently produced human skeletal remains when on soils conducive to bone survival and if excavated on any scale (Kinnes 1979: 120–1; Evans 1988b; Hodder 1992: 213–40). The Etton enclosure in Cambridgeshire (Pryor 1987; 1988a; 1988b) is unique in containing a cemetery of over fifty cremations in pits, along with stone axes and an axe polisher, pottery, flintwork, a saddle quern and rubbing stone, animal bones and antlers and

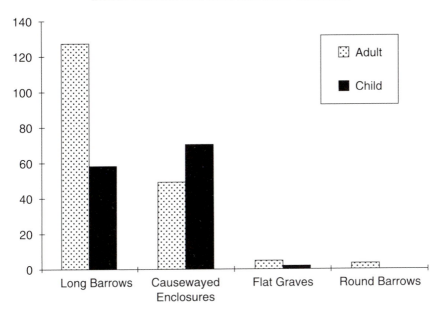

Figure 7.6 Contexts of burial in Early Neolithic Wessex for children and adults

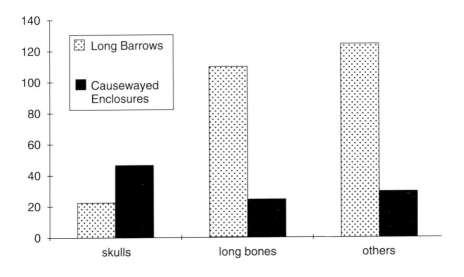

Figure 7.7 Context of deposition of body parts in Early Neolithic Wessex

numerous hazelnuts and acorns. Many of these cremations appear to be token deposits, in some cases of parts of bodies, including skulls. In the ditch were unburnt human skulls and other bones, and two objects which may have symbolised skulls – an upturned pot and a fossil echinoid with a hole pecked in the base.

This skeletal material was accompanied in the ditch at Etton by a variety of objects (Pryor 1987). Special placed deposits included small heaps of butchered animal bones on the ditch base, including a neatly tied bundle of cattle bones next to a partly dispersed group of hazelnuts, the complete upturned vessel on a birch bark mat, a sheet of folded and trimmed birch bark. Similar deposits were discussed by Isobel Smith (1965) at Windmill Hill, who interpreted them in terms of feasts and offerings, a view shared by Whittle (1993) as a result of his recent excavations. At Hambledon Hill (Mercer 1988) long narrow deposits of organic material containing animal bone, pottery, flintwork and human bone were placed along the bottom of the ditch, possibly in leather bags. The animal bones have been identified as feasting debris (Legge 1981). Analysis of pottery from Wessex enclosures (Howard 1981; J. Thomas 1991: 35) has shown an emphasis on cups and open bowls, which would suggest consumption. Most enclosures have produced clear evidence of structured deposits, often of unusual objects, within ditches, and, less often, in pits in the enclosure interior. The ditch deposits may vary significantly between individual segments, as at Etton (Pryor 1987), or between different ditch circuits, as at Maiden Castle (Sharples 1991: 253), where midden layers rich in both artefacts and ecofacts were deposited in the inner ditch at the same time as the outer ditch was backfilled with chalk.

It is also revealing that enclosures often produce exotic materials from such contexts, leading to suggestions that they may have played a major role in exchange practices. Stone axes are quite common finds at enclosures (Edmonds 1993), frequently appearing at long distances from their source. Thus at Windmill Hill (Smith 1965) there were axes from the Lake District, as there were at Hambledon Hill (Mercer 1988), along with Welsh axes and even nephrite and jadeite axes from Continental Europe (see pp. 179–80). Gabbroic pottery (Peacock 1969), presumably from the Lizard in Cornwall, has been found at Windmill Hill, Hambledon Hill, Robin Hood's Ball and Maiden Castle, where it formed 5–9 per cent of the assemblage recovered from the recent excavations (Cleal in Sharples 1991: 171–3). It is important not to take this as evidence for enclosures as markets (e.g Megaw and Simpson 1979: 84), from which material would merely be redistributed, for the exotic items brought to enclosures remained there in the vast majority of cases (Bradley 1982), as part of the acts of consumption.

So far the enclosures are implicated in a variety of essential social acts, particularly consumption, which were enacted in a bounded area set aside from the rest of the cultural landscape. However, there are a number of sites which appear to have become more like the world outside them, in that they were transformed into major settlements (Bradley 1984: 35). The clearest candidates for this process are Hambledon Hill (Mercer 1988), Carn Brea (Mercer 1981b) and Helman Tor (Mercer 1986) in Cornwall, and Crickley Hill (Dixon 1988), although other sites have been proposed. At Hambledon Hill the Stepleton Enclosure is interpreted as a settlement, with a rather different assemblage to the Main Enclosure. Mercer sees it as a high status settlement, which was eventually attacked and destroyed. He has put forward a similar interpretation of events at Carn Brea, arguing that the site was possibly destroyed by the inhabitants of Helman Tor (Mercer 1989). Conflict of this kind between neighbouring centres has also been proposed for Northern Ireland (Mallory and McNeill 1991: 36), where the Donegore Hill enclosure contained several houses which had apparently been burnt down, the occupants of nearby Lyles Hill being favoured as the culprits. Crickley Hill is a more complex case, as the causewayed enclosure ditch containing feasting debris was replaced by a defended enclosure which was then attacked and destroyed, followed by the construction of a bank barrow. This gives the impression of a cycle of ritual to domestic to ritual for the site, but within the settlement was a possible shrine which may have formed the focal point of the site. Similarly, the Main Enclosure at Hambledon Hill continued in use in tandem with the Stepleton Enclosure. The ritual authority residing in such centres may have been crucial to their transformation into defensive settlements, given that they existed on the edge of the settled landscape, rather than at its centre, where one would expect the pressure on resources to be at its greatest. The other major factor may have been the potential control over exchange processes which permanent occupation of an enclosure could bring, were exotic items to become a source of social power. Such developments involved only a minority of sites, but these changes potentially involved important attempts at political centralisation, although they did not succeed.

EXCHANGE, REGIONAL PATTERNS AND WARFARE

The question of exchange practices needs to be set in a wider framework than simply the role of exotic artefacts in enclosures, for this was perhaps merely a single stage in their history. Initial and final stages of production, exchange and consumption all need to be considered if a reading of the significance of artefacts in the Early Neolithic is to be attempted. The production of flintwork is inevitably dominated by consideration of polished flint axes, given their numbers. It has long been noted that flint axes were often produced from different flint to those of the other artefacts with which they were found, leading to the development of the view that polished flint axes came from, and were the principal product of, flint mines (Piggott 1954). It is important to remember, however, that many areas lack seams of flint buried in chalk and that here there may be exploitation of surface material, as in Yorkshire where flint eroding from the boulder clay was collected on beaches (Henson 1985), and in Hampshire with quarrying on clay-with-flints soils (Gardiner 1984).

The mines of Sussex were in production by 3800 BC, making mostly axes, but also, at least at Cissbury, backed knives, laurel leaves, fine chisels, sickles and miniature axes (Gardiner 1984). A degree of specialisation between different mine sites is possible, but given the small sample of known shafts excavated, this is difficult to assess. The absence of settlement evidence in the vicinity of mine sites at least points to the absence of communities of specialist miners (Edmonds 1993). Some final preparation may have been carried out at enclosures themselves: at Maiden Castle, for example, there was a significant production of axes, which do not seem to have been produced at contemporary sites elsewhere in the vicinity, even though flint was readily available (Edmonds 1994).

This provides a pointer to the wider significance of axes beyond the fulfilling of economic tasks, such as tree felling and woodworking. Plentiful evidence exists for the movement of flint between communities, for which the motive was almost certainly not purely economic. Preliminary results from analyses of flint raw material composition led to the conclusion that many axes were made from carefully selected non-local flint (Craddock *et al.* 1983). Tracking the exchange of flint through visual examination of artefacts alone is extremely difficult, although some distinct varieties can be traced, such as the Antrim flint from Northern Ireland which reached Scotland (Mallory and McNeill 1991: 49).

With the production of stone axes the focus is clearly on quarry sites, a number of which have now been investigated, with exploitation by 4000 BC, and a move to larger-scale production at a later date (Smith 1979). The most significant investigation of a stone axe quarry has been that of the massive Langdale group of sites in the Lake District (Bradley and Edmonds 1993). Its most unexpected finding was that people chose to quarry rock on remote ledges on the mountainside although equally good sources were available in more accessible locations. It seems as though this was determined by a desire to control access to the raw material, with specific quarry sites possibly being exploited by groups coming from different areas (Bradley and Edmonds 1993: 142–3). The final polishing of stone axes may have taken place at some distance from the source, thus the Balleygalley site (Simpson 1993) produced a number of unfinished axes from the Tievebulliagh source some 30 km away.

There is little doubt that stone axes travelled widely across Britain and Ireland, and indeed between the two (Sheridan 1986). Suggestions of direct coastal transport (e.g. Cummins 1979) are situated within an inappropriate trading model, and a model of 'down the line exchange' in which stone axes were passed on from group to group seems to fit the evidence far better (Hodder and Lane 1982; Bradley 1990: 65). The widespread distribution of the products of particular quarries need not, therefore, imply direct contacts between widely separated areas, and instead it may be more useful to envisage a situation in which particular axes were passed on between communities, acquiring a history and added significance as they went. The sites at which they were eventually deposited, such as Balleygalley in Ireland (see pp. 152–4), or numerous enclosures, would thus take on some of this significance.

The very act of polishing axes itself was significant, for although it would improve the performance of the cutting edge during use, make it less liable to flake and make it easier to haft, the extent of the polished surface goes beyond what was necessary on functional grounds (Bradley 1990: 44). Interestingly, this was not the case in Ireland (Woodman 1992b), where polished flint axes are quite rare, and the most common form only has the edge polished. In Ireland, too, the hoarding of flint axes does not occur, a clear contrast to Britain; scrapers are by far the most frequent type in Irish hoards (Woodman 1992b). Indeed, few stone axe hoards are known from Ireland, although one is the Malone Road, Belfast, hoard of eighteen porcellanite axes and a chisel from the Tievebulliagh source, which are much larger than the average, more highly polished and show no signs of having been used (Sheridan *et al.* 1992). The significance of axes as a symbol of the Neolithic is clearly relevant here.

In Britain large numbers of stone axe hoards occur, but they cannot be positively dated to the Early Neolithic in the absence of other evidence, although it is highly likely that the majority of instances do belong here. The argument that hoards represent merchants' stock (Cummins 1979) is also derived from an anachronistic trading model, and an alternative view in which they represent offerings offers more possibilities (Bradley 1990: 65). They would still be significant in maintaining the social fabric, so the possession of a degree of control over their production and distribution would be a powerful mechanism for raising the status of certain social groups (Edmonds 1987). It is noteworthy that in Yorkshire, for example, axes from the Lake District were nearly always completely polished, while axes from local rock sources were more often than not unpolished (Thorpe 1989: 190–2).

Other items were also exchanged, particularly gabbroic pottery (see p. 176). In contrast, only small amounts of jet (Pryor 1974) and shale (Darvill 1982: 25) moved any distance from their sources, so the networks established through the exchange of axes and pottery were not applied to ornaments. The same applies to continental contacts, as there is no sign of the importation of amber into Britain and Ireland during the Early Neolithic, as occurred during the Early Bronze Age. Only two finds of amber have been made in Early Neolithic contexts (Beck and Shennan 1991: 66–9), both in Yorkshire barrows (the Kilham long barrow and the Burythorpe round barrow). They are both simple pieces: a bead and a pendant. They probably represent the local exploitation of naturally occurring coastal amber. Far more bulky items were, however, brought across the English Channel, most notably jadeite and nephrite axes (Woolley *et al.* 1979), probably derived from the Alpine region (Ricq-de Bouard 1993). Well over a hundred of these are now known, although very few have been found other than as surface finds. Notable exceptions are the complete example found next to the Sweet Track in the Somerset Levels (Coles *et al.* 1974), the two ploughed up from the Hambledon Hill Main Enclosure (Mercer 1980: 23), and fragments from the High Peak enclosure ditch in Devon and the Cairnholy chambered tomb. A few axes from the Seledin axe source in Brittany also found their way to Britain (Le Roux 1979). Given the lack of Danish amber in Britain, the presence of a thick-butted Scandinavian axe in a pit cut into the mound of the long barrow at Julieberrie's Grave in Kent (Jessup 1939) is intriguing.

At the same time as this evidence for wide-reaching exchange networks, the existence of apparent barriers to the movement of artefacts should be recognised. From an initial situation of widespread fine carinated bowls, which may have acted as a highly visible symbol of the Neolithic (Herne 1988) in a similar way to polished axes, a situation of regional pottery styles developed. These do appear to be real regional differences, although Cleal (1992) has questioned the application of too rigid a framework and instead points to the movement of pottery across style zones. It should be noted here that Cleal's analysis was based largely on enclosures, which in their liminal situation may be argued to lie outside such expressions of regional difference. Even here, however, the regional styles could be quite tightly maintained, as at Maiden Castle (Cleal in Sharples 1991: 184), where only very slight influences of Windmill Hill decorated style could be observed, despite the site being on the edge of the southwestern plain style. The major breaks in pottery style can also be matched by regional traditions in enclosure building (Bradley 1984: 34). Particular groups of burial monument such as the U-ditched earthen long barrows of Cranborne Chase may also be relevant here, as is the emergence of cursus monuments and bank barrows, with their supposed role of demarcating areas of the landscape.

This evidence for regional traditions and the division of the cultural landscape could potentially relate to the increasing body of evidence suggesting that conflict between groups in the early Neolithic boiled over into open warfare. The clearest signs of this come from Hambledon Hill (Mercer 1988), where a young adult male killed by an arrowhead was buried in the ditch at the time that the timber palisade was burnt down. A similar defensive work may have been present at the Hembury enclosure in Devon (Liddell 1935), where the ditch contains extensive traces of burning and over 120 arrowheads, many of them burnt. The Crickley Hill enclosure (Dixon 1988) suffered an identical fate, with the burning of the palisade, accompanied by large numbers of arrow-heads, preceding the abandonment of the site for settlement. Concentrations of arrowheads have also been held to denote an attack at Carn Brea (Mercer 1981b) and the newly discovered enclosure on the Isle of Man (Denison 1995). Destruction within the enclosure at Donegore Hill (Mallory and McNeill 1991: 36) is thought to represent an attack there.

There are also clear individual examples of death through arrowhead injury at the chambered tombs of Ascott-under-Wychwood and Tulloch of Assery in Scotland, with the arrowhead being embedded in a vertebra (Corcoran 1964–6; Selkirk 1971). This was also the preferred interpretation of the complete leaf-shaped arrowhead found in the throat region of a burial at West Kennet (Piggott 1962a: 25). A similar explanation may be appropriate in the case of the tip of a leaf-shaped arrowhead found in the entrance to the northern passage at Hazleton, as Saville (1990: 264) has argued, given that the rest of the piece was not present. The articulated and disarticulated skeletons from this area of the passage were all male, although it might have entered with one of the bodies which were located in the chamber to which the passage had originally led. Less well recorded examples have come from the burial deposits in several other chambered tombs (Saville 1990: 264). Outside chambered tombs, the Fengate mutiple burial (Pryor 1984: 19) included an adult male with an arrowhead lodged between his ribs. The individual examples of death through arrowhead injury are all adult males, where the sex has been identified.

The motives for this warfare are unclear, with population growth, over-exploitation of land and control of axe exchange all proposed. It is more likely, however, that this evidence forms part of a general trend towards struggles for prestige by individuals within communities. Leading a successful war band is one way in which individual status could have been built up in a relatively short time. This may well match other indicators of a move towards the greater demonstration of individual status at this time, within long barrows in the South (Thorpe 1984) and with the emergence of round barrows in the North (Kinnes 1979; Thorpe 1989: 188–9). This takes the form of single burials, most often of adult males, and the systematic use of grave goods, although not in the same quantities as in the Late Neolithic. Although this may not be a universally applicable pattern, and much of the evidence is difficult to place chronologically, new sites continue to flesh out this broad pattern and distinct regional developments may start to become apparent. It does, however, represent a clear contrast to the situation in southern Scandinavia, where communal rituals became increasingly stressed through the Early Neolithic.

What is not yet clear is how far this trend towards an acknowledgement of individual status may have its roots in Mesolithic society. There may yet prove to be distinct regional traditions within the Early Neolithic, presently hinted at by the discontinuous distribution of monument types, and regional differences within those broad types and by the pottery style zones. The difference in the treatment of axes between Britain and Ireland may also reflect a real divide, given the probable symbolic significance of the axe, and may well relate in some way to the use of flint and ground stone axes in the Irish Late Mesolithic. These could in turn quite conceivably be present, although masked, from the beginning of the Neolithic, and owe their origin to pre-existing structures within the Mesolithic. At present there is still a strong tendency to see the Early Neolithic in terms of a checklist of attributes which ought to be present, and thus a tendency to overlook local variation in favour of producing a fit with a more general pattern. Until the Late Mesolithic in Britain and Ireland is better understood in social terms it will be difficult to assess the question, but the indications from southern Scandinavia are that it would be a fruitful avenue of future research. This is not to say, however, that the local should be emphasised wholly at the expense of the general, for communities were not completely isolated, and it is likely that a number of the major actions which they took were with other communities in mind. A comparative approach was no doubt adopted during the Neolithic as it has been here.

BIBLIOGRAPHY

Affleck, T., Edwards, K. J. and Clarke, A. (1988) 'Archaeological and Palynological Studies at the Mesolithic Pitchstone and Flint Site at Auchareoch, Isle of Arran', *Proceedings of the Society of Antiquaries of Scotland* 118: 37–59.

Ahlgren, C. E. (1966) 'Small Mammals and Reforestation Following Burning', *Journal of Forestry* 64: 614–18.

Albrethsen, S. E. and Brinch Petersen, E. (1976) 'Excavation of a Mesolithic Cemetery at Vedbæk, Denmark', *Acta Archaeologica* 47: 1–28.

Alcock, L. (1969) 'Excavations at South Cadbury Castle, 1968', *Antiquaries Journal* 49: 30–40.

Ammerman, A. J. (1989) 'On the Neolithic Transition in Europe: A Comment on Zvelebil and Zvelebil', *Antiquity* 63: 162–5.

Ammerman, A. J. and Cavalli-Sforza, L. L. (1971) 'Measuring the Rate of Spread of Early Farming in Europe', *Man* 6: 674–88.

—— (1973) 'A Population Model for the Diffusion of Early Farming in Europe', in C. Renfrew (ed.) *The Explanation of Culture Change*, London: Duckworth, 343–57.

—— (1984) *The Neolithic Transition and the Genetics of Populations in Europe*, Princeton: Princeton University Press.

Andersen, N. H. (1988a) 'The Neolithic Causewayed Enclosures at Sarup, on South-West Funen, Denmark', in C. Burgess, P. Topping, C. Mordant and M. Maddison (eds) *Enclosures and Defences in the Neolithic of Western Europe*, Oxford: British Archaeological Reports International Series 403, 337–63.

—— (1988b) 'Sarup: Two Neolithic Enclosures in South-West Funen', *Journal of Danish Archaeology* 7: 93–144.

—— (1988c) *Sarup. Befæstede kultpladser fra bondestenalderen*, Århus: Jysk arkæologisk Selskab.

—— (1988d) 'Hygind', *Journal of Danish Archaeology* 7: 248.

—— (1993) 'Causewayed Camps of the Funnel Beaker Culture', in S. Hvass and B. Storgaard (eds) *Digging into the Past*, Århus: Jutland Archaeological Society, 100–3.

Andersen, N. H. and Madsen, T. (1977) 'Skåle og bægre med storvinkelbånd fra yngre stenalder', *Kuml*: 131–60.

Andersen, S. H. (1973–4) 'Ringkloster, en jysk inlandsboplads med Ertebøllekultur', *Kuml*: 11–108.

—— (1978) 'Aggersund. En Ertebølleboplads ved Limfjorden', *Kuml*: 7–56.

—— (1980) Ertebøllekunst. Nye østjyske fund af mønstrede Ertebølle oldsager', *Kuml*: 7–59.

—— (1985) 'Tybrind Vig. A Preliminary Report on a Sumerged Ertebølle Settlement on the West Coast of Fyn', *Journal of Danish Archaeology* 4: 52–69.

—— (1986a) 'Mesolithic Dug-outs and Paddles from Tybrind Vig, Denmark', *Acta Archaeologia* 57: 87–106.

—— (1986b) 'Ringkloster', *Journal of Danish Archaeology* 5: 258.

—— (1987a) 'Køkkenmøddinger – en truet fundgruppe', *Arkæologiske udgravninger i Danmark*: 28–43.

—— (1987b) 'Tybrind Vig: A Submerged Ertebølle Settlement in Denmark', in J. M. Coles and A. J. Lawson (eds) *European Wetlands in Prehistory*, Oxford: Clarendon Press, 253–80.

—— (1989) 'Norsminde. A Køkkenmødding with Late Mesolithic and Early Neolithic Occupation', *Journal of Danish Archaeology* 8: 13–40.

—— (1991) 'Bjørnsholm. A Stratified Køkkenmødding on the Central Limfjord, North Jutland', *Journal of Danish Archaeology* 10: 59–96.

Andersen, S. H. and Johansen, E. (1986) 'Ertebølle Revisited', *Journal of Danish Archaeology* 5: 31–61.

—— (1988) 'Åle', *Journal of Danish Archaeology* 7: 246.

—— (1990) 'An Early Neolithic Grave at Bjørnsholm, North Jutland', *Journal of Danish Archaeology* 9: 38–58.

Andersen, S. H. and Malmros, C. (1984) 'Madskorpe på Ertebøllekar fra Tybrind Vig', *Aarbøger for Nordisk Oldkyndighed og Historie*: 78–95.

Andersen, S. T. (1978) 'Identification of Wild Grass and Cereal Pollen', *Danmarks Geologiske Undersøgelse, Årbog*: 69–92.

—— (1987) 'The Bog Find from Sigersdal: Comment by the Excavator', *Journal of Danish Archaeology* 6: 220–2.

—— (1988) 'Pollen Spectra from the Double Passage-Grave Klekkendehøj, on Møn', *Journal of Danish Archaeology* 7: 77–92.

—— (1990) 'Pollen Spectra from two Early Neolithic Lugged Jars in the Long Barrow at Bjørnsholm, Denmark', *Journal of Danish Archaeology* 9: 59–63.

—— (1992–3) 'History of Vegetation and Agriculture at Hassing Huse Mose, Thy, Northwest Denmark, Since the Ice Age', *Journal of Danish Archaeology* 11: 57–79.

—— (1993) 'Early- and Middle-Neolithic Agriculture in Denmark: Pollen Spectra from Soils in Burial Mounds of the Funnel Beaker Culture', *Journal of European Archaeology* 1: 153–80.

Andersen, S. T., Aaby, B. and Odgaard, B. V. (1983) 'Environment and Man: Current Studies in Vegetational History at the Geological Survey of Denmark', *Journal of Danish Archaeology* 2: 184–96.

Anderson, P. C. (1991) 'Harvesting of Wild Cereals During the Natufian as seen from Experimental Cultivation and Harvest of Wild Einkorn Wheat and Microwear Analysis of Stone Tools', in O. Bar-Yosef and F. R. Valla (eds) *The Natufian Culture in the Levant*, Ann Arbor: International Monographs in Prehistory Archaeological Series 1, 521–56.

Angel, J. L. (1984) 'Health as a Crucial Factor in the Changes from Hunting to Developed Farming in the Eastern Mediterranean', in M. H. Cohen and G. J. Armelagos (eds) *Palaeopathology at the Origins of Agriculture*, New York: Academic Press, 51–73.

ApSimon, A. M. (1976) 'Ballynagilly and the Beginning and End of the Irish Neolithic', in S. J. de Laet (ed.) *Acculturation and Continuity in Atlantic Europe*, Bruges: Dissertationes Archaeologicae Gandenses 16, 15–30.

Armit, I. and Finlayson, B. (1992) 'Hunter-gatherers Transformed: The Transition to Agriculture in Northern and Western Europe', *Antiquity* 66: 664–76.

Arrhenius, B. and Lidén, K. (1988) 'Fisksoppa eller vegetabilisk gröt? Diskussion kring matresterna från Tybrind Vig', *Laborativ Arkeologi* 3: 7–15.

Arts, N. (1989) 'Archaeology, Environment and the Social Evolution of Later Band Societies in a Lowland Area', in C. Bonsall (ed.) *The Mesolithic in Europe*, Edinburgh: John Donald, 291–312.

Ashbee, P. (1966) 'The Fussell's Lodge Long Barrow Excavations', *Archaeologia* 100: 1–80.

—— (1970) *The Earthen Long Barrow in Britain*, London: Dent.

Ashbee, P., Smith, I. F. and Evans, J. G. (1979) 'Excavation of Three Long Barrows near Avebury, Wiltshire', *Proceedings of the Prehistoric Society* 45: 207–300.

Ashton, N. (1988) 'Tranchet Axe Manufacture from Cliffe, Kent', *Proceedings of the Prehistoric Society* 54: 315–33.

Atkinson, R. J. C. (1965) 'Wayland's Smithy', *Antiquity* 39: 126–33.

Bahn, P. G. (1991) 'Pleistocene Images Outside Europe', *Proceedings of the Prehistoric Society* 57, Part 1: 91–102.

Bailey, G. N. (1978) 'Shell Middens as Indicators of Postglacial Economies: A Territorial Perspective', in P. Mellars (ed.) *The Early Postglacial Settlement of Northern Europe*, London: Duckworth, 37–63.

Bamford, H. M. (1985) *Briar Hill: Excavation 1974–1978*, Northampton: Northamptonshire Development Corporation Archaeological Monograph 3.

Barclay, G. J. (1983) 'Sites of the Third Millennium BC to the First Millennium BC at North Mains, Strathallan, Perthshire', *Proceedings of the Society of Antiquaries of Scotland* 113: 122–281.

Barclay, G. J., Maxwell, G. S., Simpson, I. A. and Davidson, D. A. (1995) 'The Cleaven Dyke: A Neolithic Cursus Monument/Bank Barrow in Tayside Region, Scotland', *Antiquity* 69: 317–26.

Barker, G. (1985) *Prehistoric Farming in Europe*, Cambridge: Cambridge University Press.

Barker, G. and Webley, D. P. (1978) 'Causewayed Camps and Early Neolithic Economies in Central Southern England', *Proceedings of the Prehistoric Society* 44: 161–86.

Barrett, J. C. (1994) *Fragments from Antiquity*, Oxford: Blackwell.

Barrett, J. C., Bradley, R. and Green, M. (1991) *Landscape, Monuments and Society: The Prehistory of Cranborne Chase*, Cambridge: Cambridge University Press.

Barton, R. N. E. (1994) 'Second Interim Report on the Survey and Excavations in the Wye Valley, 1994', *Proceedings of the University of Bristol Spelaeological Society* 20: 63–73.

Baruch, U. and Bottema, S. (1991) 'Palynological Evidence for Climatic Changes in the Levant ca. 17,000–9000 B.P.', in O. Bar-Yosef and F. R. Valla (eds) *The Natufian Culture in the Levant*, Ann Arbor: International Monographs in Prehistory Archaeological Series 1, 11–20.

Bar-Yosef, O. (1991) 'The Archaeology of the Natufian Layer at Hayonim Cave', in O. Bar-Yosef and F. R. Valla (eds) *The Natufian Culture in the Levant*, Ann Arbor: International Monographs in Prehistory Archaeological Series 1, 81–92.

Bar-Yosef, O. and Belfer-Cohen, A. (1989) 'The Origins of Sedentism and Farming Communities in the Levant', *Journal of World Prehistory* 3: 447–98.

—— (1992) 'From Foraging to Farming in the Mediterranean Levant', in A. B. Gebauer and T. D. Price (eds) *Transitions to Agriculture in Prehistory*, Madison: Prehistory Press, Monographs in World Archaeology 4, 21–48.

Bar-Yosef, O. and Kislev, M. E. (1989) 'Early Farming Communities in the Jordan Valley', in D. R. Harris and G. C. Hillman (eds) *Foraging and Farming*, London: Unwin Hyman, 632–42.

Bar-Yosef, O. and Sillen, A. (1993) 'Implications of the New Accelerator Date of the Charred Skeletons from Kebara Cave (Mount Carmel)' *Paléorient* 19: 205–8.

Bech, J.-H. (1985) 'Morup Mølle', *Journal of Danish Archaeology* 4: 215–16.

Bech, J.-H. and Olsen, A. L. H. (1984) 'Morup Mølle' *Journal of Danish Archaeology* 3: 229.

Beck, C. and Shennan, S. (1991) *Amber in Prehistoric Britain*, Oxford: Oxbow Monograph 8.

Becker, C. J. (1947) 'Mosefundne lerkar fra yngre stenalder. Studier over tragtbægerkulturen i Danmark', *Aarbøger for Nordisk Oldkyndighed og Historie*: 1–318.

—— (1949) 'Hafted Neolithic Celts II. With Observations on a New Funnel-Beaker Type from Zealand', *Acta Archaeologica* 20: 231–48.

—— (1958) '4000 årig flintminedrift i Thy', *Nationalmuseets Arbejdsmark*: 77–82.

—— (1959) 'Flint Mining in Neolithic Denmark', *Antiquity* 33: 87–93.

—— (1966) 'Vor ældste industri', *Skalk*: 3–7.

—— (1973) 'Problemer omkring overgangen fra fangstkulturer til bondekulturer i Sydskandinavien', in P. Simonsen and G. S. Munch (eds) *Bonde–Veidemann, Bofast–ikke Bofast i Nordisk Forhistorie*, Tromsø: Tromsø Museums Skrifter XIV, 6–21.

—— (1980) 'DK Dänemark: Hov-Bjerre-Aalborg-Hillerslev-Fornaes-Stevns Klint', in G. Weisgerber (ed.) *5000 Jahre Feuersteinbergbau*, Bohum: Deutsches Bergbau Museum, 456–73.

Belfer-Cohen, A. (1991) 'The Natufian in the Levant', *Annual Review of Anthropology* 20: 167–86.

Belfer-Cohen, A. and Hovers E. (1992), 'In the Eye of the Beholder: Mousterian and Natufian Burials in the Levant', *Current Anthropology* 33: 463–71.

Belfer-Cohen, A., Schepartz, L. A. and Arensburg, B. (1991) 'New Biological Data for the Natufian Populations in Israel', in O. Bar-Yosef and F. R. Valla (eds) *The Natufian Culture in the Levant*, Ann Arbor: International Monographs in Prehistory Archaeological Series 1, 411–24.

Bender, B. (1978) 'Gatherer-hunter to Farmer: A Social Perspective', *World Archaeology* 10: 204–22.

—— (1985) 'Prehistoric Developments in the American Midcontinent and in Brittany, Northwest France', in T. D. Price and J. A. Brown (eds) *Prehistoric Hunter-Gatherers: The Emergence of Complexity*, London: Academic Press, 21–58.

—— (1989). 'The Roots of Inequality', in D. Miller, M. Rowlands and C. Tilley (eds) *Domination and Resistance*, London: Unwin Hyman, One World Archaeology 3, 83–95.

—— (1992) 'The Neolithic Rethought', *Cambridge Archaeological Journal* 2: 270–3.

Bennett, K. D., Simonson, W. D. and Pegler, S. M. (1990) 'Fire and Man in Post-Glacial Woodlands of Eastern England', *Journal of Archaeological Science* 17: 635–42.

Bennicke, P. (1985) *Palaeopathology of Danish Skeletons*, København: Akademisk Forlag.

—— (1988) 'Human Remains from the Grøfte Dolmen', *Journal of Danish Archaeology* 7: 70–6.

Bennicke, P. and Ebbesen, K. (1986) 'The Bog Find from Sigersdal', *Journal of Danish Archaeology* 5: 85–115.

Bennicke, P., Ebbesen, K. and Bender Jørgensen, L. (1986) 'Early Neolithic Skeletons from Bolkilde Bog, Denmark', *Antiquity* 60: 199–209.

Benson, D. and Clegg, I. (1978) 'Cotswold Burial Rites', *Man* (N.S.) 13: 134–7.

Berglund, B. E. and Kolstrup, E. (1991) 'The Romele Area: Vegetation and Landscape Through Time', in B. E. Berglund (ed.) *The Cultural Landscape During 6000 Years in Southern Sweden – The Ystad Project*, Lund: Ecological Bulletin 41, 247–9.

Berglund, B. E. and Larsson, L. (1991) 'The Late Mesolithic Landscape', in B. E. Berglund (ed.) *The Cultural Landscape During 6000 Years in Southern Sweden – The Ystad Project*, Lund: Ecological Bulletin 41, 65–8.

Berglund, B. E., Hjelmros, M. and Kolstrup, E. (1991) 'The Köpinge Area: Vegetation and Landscape Through Time', in B. E. Berglund (ed.) *The Cultural Landscape During 6000 Years in Southern Sweden – The Ystad Project*, Lund: Ecological Bulletin 41, 109–12.

Bewley, R. (1994) *English Heritage Book of Prehistoric Settlements*, London: Batsford.

Binford, L. R. (1968) 'Post-Pleistocene Adaptations', in S. R. Binford and L. R. Binford (eds) *New Perspectives in Archeology*, Chicago: Aldine, 313–41.

—— (1983) *In Pursuit of the Past*, London: Thames and Hudson.

Birks, H. J. B., Deacon, J. and Pegler, S. (1975) 'Pollen Maps for the British Isles some 5000 years ago', *Philosophical Transactions of the Royal Society of London* B 189: 87–105.

Blankholm, H. P. (1987) 'Late Mesolithic Hunter-Gatherers and the Transition to Farming in Southern Scandinavia', in P. Rowley-Conwy, M. Zvelebil and H. P. Blankholm (eds) *Mesolithic Northwest Europe: Recent Trends*, Sheffield: University of Sheffield Department of Archaeology and Prehistory, 155–62.

Bloch, M. and Parry, J. (1982) 'Introduction', in M. Bloch and J. Parry (eds) *Death and the Regeneration of Life*, Cambridge: Cambridge University Press, 1–44.

Bogucki, P. (1984) 'Linear Pottery Ceramic Sieves and their Economic Implications', *Oxford Journal of Archaeology* 3: 15–30.

—— (1987) 'The Establishment of Agrarian Communities on the North European Plain', *Current Anthropology* 28: 1–24.

—— (1988) *Forest Farmers and Stockherders: Early Agriculture and Its Consequences in North-Central Europe*, Cambridge: Cambridge University Press.

Bogucki, P. and Grygiel, R. (1993) 'The First Farmers of Europe: A Survey Article', *Journal of Field Archaeology* 20: 399–425.

Boismier, W. A. (1991) 'The Role of Research Design in Surface Collection: An Example from Broom Hill, Braishfield, Hampshire', in A. J. Schofield (ed.) *Interpreting Artefact Scatters: Contributions to Ploughzone Archaeology*, Oxford: Oxbow, 13–25.

Bolomey, A. (1973) 'An Outline of the Late Epipalaeolithic Economy at the "Iron Gates": The Evidence on Bones', *Dacia* 17: 41–52.

Bonsall, C. and Smith, C. (1990) 'Bone and Antler Technology in the British Late Upper Palaeolithic and Mesolithic: The Impact of Accelerator Dating', in P. Vermeersch and P. van Peer (eds) *Contributions to the Mesolithic in Europe*, Leuven: Leuven University Press, 359–68.

Bonsall, C., Sutherland, D., Tipping, R. and Cherry, J. (1989) 'The Esmeals Project: Late Mesolithic Settlement and Environment in North-west England', in C. Bonsall (ed.) *The Mesolithic in Europe*, Edinburgh: John Donald, 175–205.

Boroneanţ, V. (1989) 'Thoughts on the Chronological Relations Between the Epi-Paleolithic and the Neolithic of the Low Danube', in C. Bonsall (ed.) *The Mesolithic in Europe*, Edinburgh: John Donald, 475–80.

—— (1990) 'Les enterrements de Schela Cladovei: nouvelles données', in P. Vermeersch and P. van Peer (eds) *Contributions to the Mesolithic in Europe*, Leuven: Leuven University Press, 121–5.

Boujet, C. and Cassen, S. (1993) 'A Pattern of Evolution for the Neolithic Funerary Structures of the West of France', *Antiquity* 67: 477–91.

Boyd, B. (1992) 'The Transformation of Knowledge: Natufian Mortuary Practices at Hayonim, Western Galilee', *Archaeological Review from Cambridge* 11: 19–38.

Bradley, J. (1991) 'Excavations at Moynagh Lough, County Meath', *Journal of the Royal Society of Antiquaries of Scotland* 121: 5–26.

Bradley, R. (1978) *The Prehistoric Settlement of Britain*, London: Routledge and Kegan Paul.

—— (1982) 'Position and Possession: Assemblage Variation in the British Neolithic', *Oxford Journal of Archaeology* 1: 27–38.

—— (1984) *The Social Foundations of Prehistoric Britain*, London: Longman.

—— (1986) *The Dorset Cursus: The Archaeology of the Enigmatic*, Salisbury: Council for British Archaeology Group 12, Wessex Lecture 3.

—— (1987) 'Flint Technology and the Character of Neolithic Settlement', in A. G. Brown and M. Edmonds (eds) *Lithic Analysis and Later British Prehistory*, Oxford: British Archaeological Reports, British Series 162, 181–5.

—— (1990) *The Passage of Arms*, Cambridge: Cambridge University Press.

—— (1992) 'The Excavation of an Oval Barrow beside the Abingdon Causewayed Enclosure, Oxfordshire', *Proceedings of the Prehistoric Society* 58: 127–42.

—— (1993) *Altering the Earth*, Edinburgh: Society of Antiquaries of Scotland Monograph Series 8.

Bradley, R. and Edmonds, M. (1993) *Interpreting the Axe Trade*, Cambridge: Cambridge University Press.

Bradley, R. and Gordon, K. (1988) 'Human Skulls from the River Thames, their Dating and Significance', *Antiquity* 62: 503–9.

Bradley, R. and Lewis, E. (1974) 'A Mesolithic Site at Wakeford's Copse, Havant', *Rescue Archaeology in Hampshire* 2: 5–18.

Braidwood, R. J. and Willey, G. R. (eds) (1962) *Courses Towards Urban Life*, Chicago: Viking Fund Publications in Anthropology 32.

Bratlund, B. (1991) 'The Bone Remains of Mammals and Birds from the Bjørnsholm Shell-Mound', *Journal of Danish Archaeology* 10: 97–104.

Brewster, T. C. M. (1968) 'Kemp Howe', *Ministry of Public Buildings and Works Excavations Annual Report*: 13.

—— (1984) *The Excavation of Whitegrounds Barrow, Burythorpe*, Wintringham: John Gett.

Brinch Petersen, E. (1970) 'Ølby Lyng. En østsjællands kystboplads med Ertebøllekultur', *Aarbøger for Nordisk Oldkyndighed og Historie*. 5–42.

—— (1974) 'Graverne ved Dragsholm. Fra jægere til bonder for 6000 år siden', *Nationalmuseets Arbejdsmark*: 112–20.

—— (1987) 'Late Palaeolithic and Mesolithic', *Arkæologiske udgravninger i Danmark*: 79–81.

—— (1988) 'Late Palaeolithic and Mesolithic', *Arkæologiske udgravninger i Danmark*: 73–5.

—— (1989a) 'Late Palaeolithic and Mesolithic', *Arkæologiske udgravninger i Danmark*: 93–5.

—— (1989b) 'Vænget Nord: Excavation, Documentation and Interpretation of a Mesolithic Site at Vedbæk, Denmark', in C. Bonsall (ed.) *The Mesolithic in Europe*, Edinburgh: John Donald, 325–30.

—— (1990a) 'Late Palaeolithic and Mesolithic', *Arkæologiske udgravninger i Danmark*: 79–82.

—— (1990b) 'Nye grave fra Jægerstenalderen', *Nationalmuseets Arbejdsmark*: 19–33.

Brinch Petersen, E., Alexandersen, V. and Meiklejohn, C. (1993) 'Vedbæk, graven midt i byen', *Nationalmuseets Arbejdsmark*: 61–9.

Brindley, A. L. and Lanting, J. N. (1995) 'Irish Bog Bodies: The Radiocarbon Dates', in R. C. Turner and R. G. Scaife (eds) *Bog Bodies: New Discoveries and New Perspectives*, London: British Museum Press, 133–6.

Brindley, A. L., Lanting, J. N. and Mook, W. G. (1983) 'Radiocarbon Dates from the Neolithic Burials at Ballintruer More, Co. Wicklow, and Ardcrony, Co. Tipperary', *Journal of Irish Archaeology* 1: 1–9.

Britnell, W. J. and Savory, H. N. (1984) *Gwernvale and Penywyrlod*, Bangor: Cambrian Archaeological Monographs 2.

Brock, V. and Bourget, E. (1989) 'Analyses of Shell Increment and Migrogrowth Band Formation to Establish Seasonality of Mesolithic Shellfish Collection', *Journal of Danish Archaeology* 8: 7–12.

Brøndsted, J. (1957) *Danmarks Oldtid. I, Stenalderen*, København: Glydendal.

Broodbank, C. and Strasser, T. F. (1991) 'Migrant Farmers and the Neolithic Colonization of Crete', *Antiquity* 65: 233–45.

Brothwell, D. R. (1973) 'The Human Biology of the Neolithic Population of Britain', *Fundamenta* 3: 280–99.

Burenhult, G. (1980) *The Archaeological Excavation at Carrowmore, Co. Sligo, Ireland, Excavation Seasons 1977–79*, Stockholm: Theses and Papers in North-European Archaeology 9.

—— (1984) *The Archaeology of Carrowmore*, Stockholm: Theses and Papers in North-European Archaeology 14.

Bush, M. R. and Flenley, J. R. (1987) 'The Age of the British Chalk Grassland', *Nature* 329: 434–6.

Byrd, B. F. (1989) 'The Natufian: Settlement Variability and Economic Adaptations in the Levant at the End of the Pleistocene', *Journal of World Prehistory* 3: 159–97.

Campana, D. V. and Crabtree, P. J. (1990) 'Communal Hunting in the Natufian of the Southern Levant: The Social and Economic Implications', *Journal of Mediterranean Archaeology* 3: 223–43.

Care, V. (1979) 'The Production and Distribution of Mesolithic Axes in Southern England', *Proceedings of the Prehistoric Society* 45: 93–102.

—— (1982) 'The Collection and Distribution of Lithic Materials During the Mesolithic and Neolithic Periods in Southern England', *Oxford Journal of Archaeology* 1: 269–85.

Case, H. J. (1969) 'Neolithic Explanations', *Antiquity* 43: 176–86.

—— (1976) 'Acculturation and the Earlier Neolithic in Western Europe', in S. J. de Laet (ed.) *Acculturation and Continuity in Atlantic Europe*, Bruges: Dissertationes Archaeologicae Gandenses 16, 45–58.

—— (1982) 'The Linear Ditches and Southern Enclosure', in H. J. Case and A. W. R. Whittle (eds) *Settlement Patterns in the Oxford Region*, London: Council for British Archaeology Research Report 44, 60–75.

Caseldine, C. and Hatton, J. (1993) 'The Development of High Moorland on Dartmoor: Fire and the Influence of Mesolithic Activity on Vegetational Change', in F. M. Chambers (ed.) *Climatic Change and Human Impact on the Landscape*, London: Chapman and Hall, 119–31.

Cassen, S. (1993) 'Material Culture and Chronology of the Middle Neolithic of Western France', *Oxford Journal of Archaeology* 12: 197–208.

Caulfield, S. (1983) 'The Neolithic Settlement of North Connaught', in T. Reeves-Smyth and F. Hamond (eds) *Landscape Archaeology in Ireland*, Oxford: British Archaeological Reports, British Series 116, 195–215.

Cauvin, J. (1978) *Les Premiers villages de Syrie-Palestine du IXème au VIIème Millénaire avant J.C.*, Lyon: Maison de l'Orient.

—— (1989) 'La néolithisation au Levant et sa première diffusion', in O. Aurenche and J. Cauvin (eds) *Néolithisations*, Oxford: British Archaeological Reports, International Series 516, 3–36.

Chapman, J. (1989) 'Demographic Trends in Neothermal South-east Europe', in C. Bonsall (ed.) *The Mesolithic in Europe*, Edinburgh: John Donald, 500–15.

—— (1992) 'Social Power in the Iron Gates Mesolithic', in J. Chapman and P. Dolukhanov (eds) *Cultural Transformations and Interactions in Eastern Europe*, Aldershot: Avebury Worldwide Archaeology 6, 71–121.

Chapman, R. (1981) 'The Emergence of Formal Disposal Areas and the "Problem" of Megalithic Tombs in Prehistoric Europe', in R. Chapman, I. Kinnes and K.

Randsborg (eds) *The Archaeology of Death*, Cambridge: Cambridge University Press, 71–81.

Cherry, J. F. (1990) 'The First Colonization of the Mediterranean Islands: A Review of Recent Research', *Journal of Mediterranean Archaeology* 3: 145–221.

Chesterman, J. T. (1977) 'Burial Rites in a Cotswold Long Barrow', *Man* (N.S.) 12: 22–32.

Childe, V. G. (1928) *The Most Ancient East*, London: Routledge and Kegan Paul.

—— (1929) *The Danube in Prehistory*, London: Oxford University Press.

—— (1934) *New Light on the Most Ancient East*, London: Kegan Paul, Trench, Trubner.

Clark, J. G. D. (1938) 'A Neolithic House at Haldon, Devon', *Proceedings of the Prehistoric Society* 4: 222–3.

—— (1952) *Prehistoric Europe – The Economic Basis*, London: Methuen.

—— (1966) 'The Invasion Hypothesis in British Archaeology', *Antiquity* 40: 172–89.

—— (1975) *The Earlier Stone Age Settlement of Scandinavia*, Cambridge: Cambridge University Press.

—— (1979) *World Prehistory: A New Outline* (3rd edition), Cambridge: Cambridge University Press.

—— (1980) *Mesolithic Prelude*, Edinburgh: Edinburgh University Press.

Clarke, D. V. (1976) *The Neolithic Village at Skara Brae, Excavations 1972–73, an Interim Report*, Edinburgh: HMSO.

Clason, A. (1980) 'Padina and Starčevo: Game, Fish and Cattle', *Palaeohistoria* 22: 141–73.

Cleal, R. M. J. (1992) 'Significant Form: Ceramic Styles in the Earlier Neolithic of Southern England', in N. Sharples and A. Sheridan (eds) *Vessels for the Ancestors*, Edinburgh: John Donald, 286–304.

Cleal, R. M. J., Walker, K. E. and Montague, R. (1995) *Stonehenge in its Landscape*, London: English Heritage Archaeological Report 10.

Cloutman, E. W. (1988) 'Palaeoenvironments in the Vale of Pickering. Part 2: Environmental History of Seamer Carr', *Proceedings of the Prehistoric Society* 54: 21–36.

Coggins, D., Laurie, T. and Young, R. (1989) 'The Late Upper Palaeolithic and Mesolithic of the Northern Pennine Dales in the Light of Recent Fieldwork', in C. Bonsall (ed.) *The Mesolithic in Europe*, Edinburgh: John Donald, 164–74.

Cohen, M. H. (1977) *The Food Crisis in Prehistory*, New Haven: Yale University Press.

—— (1989) *Health and the Rise of Civilization*, New Haven: Yale University Press.

Cohen, M. H. and Armelagos, G. J. (1984) 'Palaeopathology at the Origins of Agriculture: Editors' Summation', in M. H. Cohen and G. J. Armelagos (eds) *Palaeopathology at the Origins of Agriculture*, New York: Academic Press, 51–73.

—— (eds) (1984) *Palaeopathology at the Origins of Agriculture*, New York: Academic Press.

Coles, J. M. (1971) 'The Early Settlement of Scotland: Excavations at Morton, Fife', *Proceedings of the Prehistoric Society* 37: 284–366.

—— (1989) 'Prehistoric Settlement in the Somerset Levels', *Somerset Levels Papers* 15: 14–33.

Coles, J. M., Orme, B., Bishop, A. C. and Woolley, A. R. (1974) 'A Jade Axe from the Somerset Levels', *Antiquity* 48: 216–20.

Collins, A. E. P. (1954) 'Excavation of a Double-horned Cairn at Audleystown', *Ulster Journal of Archaeology* 17: 7–56.

—— (1959) 'Further Work at Audleystown Long Cairn', *Ulster Journal of Archaeology* 22: 47–70.

Connock, K. D., Finlayson, B. and Mills, C. M. (1991–2) 'Excavation of a Shell Midden Site at Carding Mill Bay, near Oban, Scotland', *Glasgow Archaeological Journal* 17: 25–38.

Coombs, D. G. (1976) 'Callis Wold Round Barrow, Humberside', *Antiquity* 50: 130–1.

Cooney, G. (1987–8) 'Irish Neolithic Settlement and its European Context', *Journal of Irish Archaeology* 4: 7–11.

Corcoran, J. W. X. P. (1964–6) 'The Excavation of Three Chambered Cairns at Loch Calder, Caithness', *Proceedings of the Society of Antiquaries of Scotland* 98: 1–75.

Craddock, P. T., Cowell, M. R., Leese, M. N. and Hughes, M. J. (1983) 'The Trace Element Composition of Polished Flint Axes as One Indicator of Source', *Archaeometry* 25: 135–63.

Cullen, T. (1995) 'Mesolithic Mortuary Ritual at Franchthi Cave, Greece', *Antiquity* 69: 270–89.

Cummins, W. A. (1979) 'Neolithic Stone Axes: Distribution and Trade in England and Wales', in T. H. McK. Clough and W. A. Cummins (eds) *Stone Axe Studies*, London: Council for British Archaeology Research Report 23, 5–12.

Cunliffe, B. (1993) *Wessex to A.D. 1000*, London: Longman.

Damm, C. B. (1991) 'Burying the Past: An Example of Social Transformation in the Danish Neolithic', in P. Garwood, P. Jennings, R. Skeates and J. Toms (eds) *Sacred and Profane*, Oxford: Oxford University Committee for Archaeology Monograph 32, 43–9.

Daniel, G. E. (1958) *The Megalith Builders of Western Europe*, London: Hutchinson.

Darvill, T. C. (1982) *The Megalithic Chambered Tombs of the Cotswold–Severn Region*, Highworth: Vorda Research Series 5.

Darwin, C. R. (1875) *The Variation of Animals and Plants under Domestication* (2nd edition), London: Murray.

Davis, J. B. and Thurnam, J. (1865) *Crania Britannica* (2 volumes), London.

Davis, J. L. (1992) 'Review of Aegean Prehistory I: The Islands of the Aegean', *American Journal of Archaeology* 96, 699–756.

Davis, S. J. M. (1987) *The Archaeology of Animals*, London: Batsford.

Degerbøhl, M. (1942) 'Et Knoglemateriale fra Dyrholmen-Bopladsen, en ældre Stenalder-Køkkenmødding. Med særlight henblik paa Uroksens Køns-Dimorphisme og paa Kannibalismen i Danmark', in T. Mathiassen, M. Degerbøhl and J. Troels-Smith (eds) *Dyrholmen. En Stenalderboplads paa Djursland*, København: Det Kongelige Danske Videnskabernes Selskab, Arkæologisk-Kunsthistoriske Skrifter, Bind 1, Nr. 1, 77–135.

—— (1963) 'Prehistoric Cattle in Denmark and Adjacent Areas', in A. E. Mourant and F. E. Zeuner (eds) *Man and Cattle*, London: Occasional Paper of the Royal Anthropological Institute 18, 68–79.

Demoule, J.-P. and Perlès, C. (1993) 'The Greek Neolithic: A New Review', *Journal of World Prehistory* 7: 355–416.

Denison, S. (1995) 'Manx Discoveries', *British Archaeology* 8: 4.

Dennell, R. W. (1976) 'Prehistoric Crop Cultivation in Southern England: A Reconsideration', *Antiquaries Journal* 56: 11–23.

—— (1983) *European Economic Prehistory: A New Approach*, London: Academic Press.

—— (1985) 'The Hunter-Gatherer/Agricultural Frontier in Prehistoric Temperate Europe', in S. W. Green and S. M. Perlman (eds) *The Archaeology of Frontiers and Boundaries*, London: Academic Press, 113–39.

—— (1992) 'The Origins of Crop Agriculture in Europe', in C. W. Cowan and P. J. Watson (eds) *The Origins of Agriculture*, Washington, DC: Smithsonian Institution Press, 71–100.

Dixon, P. (1988) 'The Neolithic Settlements on Crickley Hill', in C. Burgess, P. Topping, C. Mordant and M. Maddison (eds) *Enclosures and Defences in the Neolithic of Western Europe*, Oxford: British Archaeological Reports, International Series 403, 75–87.

Dohrn-Ihmig, M. (1983) 'Das bandkeramische Gräberfeld von Aldenhoven-Niedermerz, Kreis Düren', *Rheinische Ausgrabungen* 24: 47–189.

Domanska, L. (1991) 'Is there a 'Preceramic Event' in Poland?', *Mesolithic Miscellany* 12: 1–9.

Donahue, R. E. (1992) 'Desperately seeking Ceres: A Critical Examination of Current Models for the Transition to Agriculture in Mediterranean Europe', in A. B. Gebauer and T. D. Price (eds) *Transitions to Agriculture in Prehistory*, Madison: Prehistory Press, Monographs in World Archaeology 4, 73–80.

Duhamal, P. and Presteau, M. (1987) 'Les populations néolithiques du bassin Parisien', *Archéologia* 230: 54–65.

Earnshaw, J. R. (1973) 'The Site of a Medieval Post Mill and Prehistoric Site at Bridlington', *Yorkshire Archaeological Journal* 45: 19–40.

Ebbesen, K. (1984) 'Tragtbægerkulturens Grønstenøkser', *Kuml*: 113–53.

—— (1988) 'The Long Dolmen at Grøfte, South-west Zealand', *Journal of Danish Archaeology* 7: 53–69.

Ebbesen, K. and Brinch Petersen, E. (1973) 'Fuglebæksbanken', *Aarbøger for Nordisk Oldkyndighed og Historie*: 73–106.

Edmonds, M. (1987) 'Rocks and Risk: Problems with Lithic Procurement Strategies', in A. G. Brown and M. Edmonds (eds) *Lithic Analysis and Later British Prehistory*, Oxford: British Archaeological Reports, British Series 162, 155–79.

—— (1993) 'Towards a Context for Production and Exchange: The Polished Axe in Earlier Neolithic Britain', in C. Scarre and F. Healy (eds) *Trade and Exchange in Prehistoric Europe*, Oxford: Oxbow Archaeological Monographs 33, 69–86.

—— (1994) 'Interpreting Causewayed Enclosures in the Past and the Present', in C. Tilley (ed.) *Interpretative Archaeology*, London: Berg, 99–142.

Edwards, K. J. (1982) 'Man, Space and the Woodland Edge: Speculations on the Detection and Interpretation of Human Impact in Pollen Profiles', in M. Bell and S. Limbrey (eds) *Archaeological Aspects of Woodland Ecology*, Oxford: British Archaeological Reports, International Series 146, 5–22.

—— (1989a) 'Meso-Neolithic Vegetational Impacts in Scotland and Beyond: Palynological Considerations', in C. Bonsall (ed.) *The Mesolithic in Europe*, Edinburgh: John Donald, 143–55.

—— (1989b) 'The Cereal Pollen Record and Early Agriculture', in A. Milles, D. Williams and N. Gardner (eds) *The Beginnings of Agriculture*, Oxford: British Archaeological Reports, International Series 496, 113–35.

—— (1993) 'Models of Mid-Holocene Forest Farming for North-west Europe', in F. M. Chambers (ed.) *Climatic Change and Human Impact on the Landscape*, London: Chapman and Hall, 132–45.

Edwards, K. J. and Hirons, K. R. (1984) 'Cereal Pollen Grains in Pre-elm Decline Deposits: Implications for the Earliest Agriculture in Britain and Ireland', *Journal of Archaeological Science* 11, 71–80.

Edwards, P. C. (1989) 'Revising the Broad Spectrum Revolution and its Rôle in the Origins of Southwest Asian Food Production', *Antiquity* 63: 225–46.

Enghoff, I. B. (1986) 'Freshwater Fishing from a Sea-coast Settlement – the Ertebølle *Locus Classicus* Revisited', *Journal of Danish Archaeology* 5: 62–76.

—— (1989) 'Fishing from the Stone Age Settleement Norsminde', *Journal of Danish Archaeology* 8: 41–50.

—— (1991) 'Mesolithic Eel-fishing at Bjørnsholm, Denmark, Spiced with Exotic Species', *Journal of Danish Archaeology* 10: 105–18.

Entwistle, R. and Grant, A. (1989) 'The Evidence for Cereal Cultivation and Animal Husbandry in the Southern British Neolithic and Bronze Age', in A. Milles, D. Williams and N. Gardner (eds) *The Beginnings of Agriculture*, Oxford: British Archaeological Reports, International Series 496, 243–61.

Eogan, G. (1983) 'A Flint Macehead at Knowth, Co. Meath, Ireland', *Antiquity* 57: 45–6.

—— (1984) *Excavations at Knowth 1: Smaller Passage Tombs, Neolithic Occupation and Beaker Activity*, Dublin: Royal Irish Academy Monographs in Archaeology 1.

—— (1991) 'Prehistoric and Early Historic Culture Change at Brugh na Bóinne', *Proceedings of the Royal Irish Academy* 91C: 105–32.

Eriksen, L. B. (1991) 'Orenehus på Stevns – en tidligneolitisk hustomt', *Aarbøger for Nordisk Oldkyndighed og Historie*: 7–19.

Eriksen, P. and Madsen, T. (1984) 'Hanstedgård. A Settlement Site from the Funnel Beaker Culture', *Journal of Danish Archaeology* 3: 63–82.

Evans, C. (1988a) 'Acts of Enclosure: A Consideration of Concentrically-organised Causewayed Enclosures', in C. Burgess, P. Topping, C. Mordant and M. Maddison (eds) *Enclosures and Defences in the Neolithic of Western Europe*, Oxford: British Archaeological Reports, International Series 403, 85–96.

—— (1988b) 'Excavations at Haddenham, Cambridgeshire: A "Planned" Enclosure and its Regional Affinities', in C. Burgess, P. Topping, C. Mordant and M. Maddison (eds) *Enclosures and Defences in the Neolithic of Western Europe*, Oxford: British Archaeological Reports, International Series 403, 127–48.

Evans, E. E. (1940) 'Sherds from a Gravel-pit, Killaghy, Co. Armagh', *Ulster Journal of Archaeology* 3: 139–41.

Evans, J. G. (1975) *The Environment of Early Man in the British Isles*, London: Elek.

Evans, J. G. and Simpson, D. D. A. (1991) 'Giants' Hills 2 Long Barrow, Skendleby, Lincolnshire', *Archaeologia* 109: 1–45.

Evans, J. G., Rouse, A. J. and Sharples, N. M. (1988) 'The Landscape Setting of Causewayed Camps: Recent Work on the Maiden Castle Enclosure' in J. C. Barrett and I. A. Kinnes (eds) *The Archaeology of Context in the Neolithic and Bronze Age: Recent Trends*, Sheffield: University of Sheffield Department of Archaeology and Prehistory, 73–84.

Fairweather, A. D. and Ralston, I. B. M. (1993) 'The Neolithic Timber Hall at Balbridie, Grampian Region, Scotland', *Antiquity* 67: 313–23.

Fansa, M. and Kampffmeyer, U. (1985) 'Vom Jäger und Sammler zum Ackerbauern', in K. Wilhelmi (ed.) *Ausgrabungen in Niedersachsen, Archäologische Denkmalpflege 1979–1984*, Stuttgart: Konrad Theiss, 108–11.

Finlayson, W. (1993) 'Post-glacial Hunter/gatherers in Europe and their Adaptation to Change', *Proceedings of the Society of Antiquaries of Scotland* 123: 461–2.

Fischer, A. (1981) 'Handel med skoloestøkser og landbrugets indførelse i Danmark', *Aarbøger for Nordisk Oldkyndighed og Historie*: 5–16.

—— (1982) 'Trade in Danubian Shaft-Hole Axes and the Introduction of Neolithic economy in Denmark', *Journal of Danish Archaeology* 1: 7–12.

—— (1986) 'Kongemose A and L', *Journal of Danish Archaeology* 5: 258–9.

—— (1993) 'Mesolithic Inland Settlement', in S. Hvass and B. Storgaard (eds) *Digging into the Past*, Århus: Jutland Archaeological Society, 58–63.

Fischer, A. and Asmussen, E. (1988) 'Spangkonge', *Journal of Danish Archaeology* 7: 245.

Fowler, P. J. (1983) *The Farming of Prehistoric Britain*, Cambridge: Cambridge University Press.

Fowler, P. J. and Evans, J. G. (1967) 'Plough-marks, Lynchets, and Early Fields', *Antiquity* 41: 289–301.

Gardiner, J. (1984) 'Lithic Distributions and Neolithic Settlement Patterns in Central Southern England', in R. Bradley and J. Gardiner (eds) *Neolithic Studies: A Review of Some Current Research*, Oxford: British Archaeological Reports, British Series 133, 15–40.

Garton, D. (1987) 'Buxton', *Current Archaeology* 103: 250–3.

Gebauer, A. B. (1988) 'The Long Dolmen at Asnæs Forskov, West Zealand', *Journal of Danish Archaeology* 7: 40–52.

Gebauer, A. B. and Price, T. D. (1990) 'The End of the Mesolithic in Eastern Denmark: A Preliminary Report on the Saltbæk Vig Project', in P. Vermeersch and P. van Peer (eds) *Contributions to the Mesolithic in Europe*, Leuven: Leuven University Press, 259–80.

Gebhardt, A. (1993) 'Micromorphological Evidence of Soil Deterioration since the Mid-Holocene at Archaeological Sites in Brittany, France', *The Holocene* 3: 333–41.

Geddes, D. S. (1981) 'Les mouton mésolithiques dans le Midi de la France: implications pour les origines de l'élevage en Méditerranée occidentale', *Bulletin de la Société Préhistorique Française* 78: 227.

Gilks, J. A. and Lord, T. C. (1985) 'A Late Neolithic Crevice Burial from Selside, Ribblesdale, North Yorkshire', *Yorkshire Archaeological Journal* 57: 1–5.

Girling, M. and Greig, J. (1985) 'A First Fossil Record for Scolytus scolytus (F.) (Elm Bark Beetle): Its Occurrence in Elm-decline Deposits from London and the Implications for Neolithic Elm Disease', *Journal of Archaeological Science* 12: 347–51.

Glass, M. (1991) *Animal Production Systems in Neolithic Central Europe*, Oxford: British Archaeological Reports, International Series 572.

Glob, P. V. (1949) 'Barkær. Danmarks ældste landsby', *Nationalmuseets Arbejdsmark*: 1–12.

—— (1975) 'De dødes lange huse', *Skalk* No. 6: 10–14.

Godwin, H. (1940) 'Pollen Analysis and the Forest History of England and Wales', *New Phytologist* 39: 370–400.

—— (1975) *The History of the British Flora* (2nd edition), Cambridge: Cambridge University Press.

Göransson, H. (1988) 'Pollen Analytical Investigations at Skateholm, Southern Sweden', in L. Larsson (ed.) *The Skateholm Project. I. Man and Environment*, Lund: Acta Regiae Societatis Humaniorum Litterarum Lundensis LXXXIX, 8–19.

Gowen, M. (1988) *Three Irish Gas Pipelines: New Archaeological Evidence in Munster*, Dublin: Wordwell.

Gowen, M. and Halpin, E. (1992) 'A Neolithic House at Newtown', *Archaeology Ireland* 6: 25–7.

Gowen, M. and Tarbett, C. (1988) 'A Third Season at Tankardstown', *Archaeology Ireland* 2: 156.

Gramsch, B. (1987) 'Ausgrabungen auf dem mesolithischen Moorfundplatz bei Freisack, Bezirk Potsdam', *Veröffentlichungen des Museums für Ur- und Frühgeschichte Potsdam* 21: 75–100.

Green, H. S. (1980) *The Flint Arrowheads of the British Isles*, Oxford: British Archaeological Reports, British Series 75.

Green, S. W. and Zvelebil, M. (1990) 'The Mesolithic Colonization and Agricultural Transition of South-east Ireland', *Proceedings of the Prehistoric Society* 56: 57–88.

Gregg, A. S. (1988) *Foragers and Farmers*, Chicago: University of Chicago Press.

Greig, J. (1989) 'From Lime Forest to Heathland – Five Thousand Years of Change at West Heath Spa, Hampstead, as Shown by the Plant Remains', in D. Collins and D. Lorimer (eds) *Excavations at the Mesolithic Site on West Heath, Hampstead*, Oxford: British Archaeological Reports, British Series 217, 89–99.

Grigson (1981) 'Porridge and Pannage: Pig Husbandry in Neolithic England', in M. Bell and S. Limbrey (eds) *Archaeological Aspects of Woodland Ecology*, Oxford: British Archaeological Reports, International Series 146, 297–314.

—— (1982) 'Sexing Neolithic Domestic Cattle Skulls and Horncores', in B. Wilson,

C. Grigson and S. Payne (eds) *Ageing and Sexing Animal Bones from Archaeological Sites*, Oxford: British Archaeological Reports, British Series 109, 25–35.

—— (1989a) 'Size and Sex: Evidence for the Domestication of Cattle in the Near East', in A. Milles, D. Williams and N. Gardner (eds) *The Beginnings of Agriculture*, Oxford: British Archaeological Reports, International Series 496, 77–109.

—— (1989b) 'Bird-foraging Patterns in the Mesolithic', in C. Bonsall (ed.) *The Mesolithic in Europe*, Edinburgh: John Donald, 60–72.

Grimes, W. F. (1960) *Excavations on Defence Sites*, London: HMSO.

Grinsell, L. V. (1958) *The Archaeology of Wessex*, London: Methuen.

Grogan, E. (1988) 'The Pipeline Sites and the Prehistory of the Limerick Area', in M. Gowen, *Three Irish Gas Pipelines: New Archaeological Evidence in Munster*, Dublin: Wordwell, 148–57.

Grøn, O. and Skaarup, J. (1991) 'Møllegabet II – A Submerged Mesolithic Site and a "Boat Burial" from Ærø', *Journal of Danish Archaeology* 10: 38–50.

Gronenborn, D. (1990) 'Mesolithic–Neolithic Interactions – The Lithic Industry of the Earliest Bandkeramik Culture Site at Friedburg-Bruchenbrücken, Wetteraukreis (West Germany)', in P. Vermeersch and P. van Peer (eds) *Contributions to the Mesolithic in Europe*, Leuven: Leuven University Press, 173–82.

Halstead, P. (1989) 'Like Rising Damp? An Ecological Approach to the Spread of Farming in South East and Central Europe', in A. Milles, D. Williams and N. Gardner (eds) *The Beginnings of Agriculture*, Oxford: British Archaeological Reports, International Series 496, 23–53.

Hansen, J. M. (1991) *The Palaeoethnobotany of Franchthi Cave*, Bloomington: Indiana University Press.

Hansen, J. M. and Renfrew, J. (1978) 'Palaeolithic–Neolithic Seed Remains at Franchthi Cave, Greece', *Nature* 271: 349–52.

Harris, D. R. (1986) 'Plant and Animal Domestication and the Origins of Agriculture: The Contribution of Radiocarbon Accelerator Dating', in J. A. J. Gowlett and R. E. M. Hedges (eds) *Archaeological Results from Accelerator Dating*, Oxford: Oxford University Committee for Archaeology, 5–12.

—— (1990) *Settling Down and Breaking Ground: The Neolithic Revolution*, Amsterdam: Twaalfde Kroon-Voordracht.

Hassan, F. A. (1981) *Demographic Archaeology*, London: Academic Press.

Hayden, B. (1990) 'Nimrods, Piscators, Pluckers, and Planters: The Emergence of Food Production', *Journal of Anthropological Archaeology* 9: 31–69.

—— (1993) *Archaeology: The Science of Once and Future Things*, New York: W. H. Freeman.

Hedges, J. D. and Buckley, D. G. (1981) *Springfield Cursus and the Cursus Problem*, Chelmsford: Essex County Council Occasional Paper 1.

Hedges, R. E., Housley, R. A., Law, J. A. and Bronk, C. R. (1989) 'Radiocarbon Dates from the Oxford AMS System: *Archaeometry* Datelist 9', *Archaeometry* 31: 207–34.

Hedges, R. E., Housley, R. A., Bronk, C. R. and van Klinken, G. J. (1991) 'Radiocarbon Dates from the Oxford AMS System: *Archaeometry* Datelist 13', *Archaeometry* 33: 279–96.

Hedges, R. E., Housley, R. A., Bronk Ramsay, C. and van Klinken, G. J. (1993) 'Radiocarbon Dates from the Oxford AMS System: *Archaeometry* Datelist 17', *Archaeometry* 35: 305–26.

—— (1994) 'Radiocarbon Dates from the Oxford AMS System: *Archaeometry* Datelist 18', *Archaeometry* 36: 337–74.

—— (1995) 'Radiocarbon Dates from the Oxford AMS System: *Archaeometry* Datelist 19', *Archaeometry* 37: 195–214.

Helbaek, H. (1952) 'Early Crops in Southern England', *Proceedings of the Prehistoric Society* 18: 194–233.

Hemp, W. J. (1930) 'The Chambered Cairn of Bryn Celli Ddu', *Archaeologia* 80: 179–214.

Henry, D. O. (1989) *From Foraging to Agriculture: The Levant at the End of the Ice Age*, Philadelphia: University of Pennsylvania Press.

Henson, D. (1985) 'The Flint Resources of Yorkshire and the East Midlands', *Lithics* 6: 2–9.

Herne, A. (1988) 'A Time and a Place for the Grimston Bowl', in J. C. Barrett and I. A. Kinnes (eds) *The Archaeology of Context in the Neolithic and Bronze Age: Recent Trends*, Sheffield: University of Sheffield Department of Archaeology and Prehistory, 9–29.

Hertz, R. [1909] (1960) *Death and the Right Hand*, Aberdeen: Cohen and West.

Hillam, J., Groves, C. M., Brown, D. M., Baillie, M. G. L., Coles, J. M. and Coles, B. J. (1990) 'Dendrochronology of the English Neolithic', *Antiquity* 64: 210–20.

Hillier, W. (1854) 'Discovery of an Ancient Tumulus at Winterbourne Monkton', *Wiltshire Archaeological Magazine* 1: 303–4.

Hillman, G. C. and Davies, M. S. (1990) 'Measured Domestication Rates in Wild Wheats and Barley under Primitive Cultivation, and their Archaeological Implications', *Journal of World Prehistory* 4: 157–222.

Hillman, G. C., Colledge, S. M. and Harris, D. R. (1989) 'Plant-food Economy during the Epipalaeolithic Period at Tell Abu Hureyra, Syria: Dietary Diversity, Seasonality, and Modes of Exploitation', in D. R. Harris and G. C. Hillman (eds) *Foraging and Farming*, London: Unwin Hyman, 240–68.

Hingst, H. (1970) 'Eine jungsteinzeitliche Siedlung in Büdelsdorf', *Heimatkundliches Jahrbuch für den Kreis Rendsburg* 20: 55–69.

Hodder, I. (1984) 'Burials, Houses, Women and Men in the European Neolithic', in D. Miller and C. Tilley (eds) *Ideology, Power and Prehistory*, Cambridge: Cambridge University Press, 51–68.

—— (1990) *The Domestication of Europe*, Oxford: Basil Blackwell.

—— (1992) *Theory and Practice in Archaeology*, London: Routledge.

Hodder, I. and Lane, P. (1982) 'A Contextual Examination of Neolithic Axe Distribution in Britain', in J. E. Ericson and T. K. Earle (eds) *Contexts for Prehistoric Exchange*, London: Academic Press, 213–35.

Hodder, I. and Shand, P. (1988) 'The Haddenham Long Barrow: An Interim Statement', *Antiquity* 62: 349–53.

Hogestun, J. W. (1990) 'From Swifterbant to TRB in the Ijssel–Vecht Basin – Some Suggestions', in D. Jankowska (ed.) *Die Trichterbecherkultur: Neue Forschungen und Hypothesen*, Poznán: Institut Prahistorii Uniwersyteta im. Adam Mickiewicza, 163–80.

Hole, F. (1989) 'A Two-part, Two-stage Model of Domestication', in J. Clutton-Brock (ed.) *The Walking Larder*, London: Unwin Hyman, 97–104.

Holgate, R. (1988) *Neolithic Settlement of the Thames Basin*, Oxford: British Archaeological Reports, British Series 194.

Howard, H. (1981) 'In the Wake of Distribution: Towards an Integrated Approach to Cramic Studies in Prehistoric Britain', in H. Howard and E. Morris (eds) *Production and Distribution: A Ceramic Viewpoint*, Oxford: British Archaeological Reports, International Series 120, 1–30.

Hunt, D. (1987) *Early Farming Communities in Scotland*, Oxford: British Archaeological Reports, British Series 159.

Hunt, J. (1967) 'Prehistoric Burials at Cahirguillarmore, Co. Limerick', in E. Rynne (ed.) *North Munster Studies*, Limerick, 20–42.

Iregren, E. (1988) 'Finds of Brown Bear (Ursus arctos) in Southern Scandinavia –

Indications of Local Hunting or Trade?', in B. Hårdh, L. Larsson, D. Olausson and R. Petré (eds) *Trade & Exchange in Prehistory*, Lund: Acta Archaeologica Lundensis Series in 8°, 16, 295–308.

Iversen, J. (1941) 'Landnam i Danmarks stenalder', *Danmarks Geologiske Undersøgelse II, Række Nr. 66*: 1–68.

Jacobi, R. M. (1981) 'The Last Hunters in Hampshire' in S. J. Shennan and R. T. Schadla-Hall (eds) *The Archaeology of Hampshire*, Winchester: Hampshire Field Club and Archaeological Society Monograph 1, 10–25.

—— (1982) 'Later Hunters in Kent: Tasmania and the Earliest Neolithic', in P. E. Leach (ed.) *Archaeology in Kent to AD 1500*, London: Council for British Archaeology Research Report 48, 12–24.

—— (1987) 'Misanthropic Miscellany: Musings on British Early Flandrian Archaeology and other Flights of Fancy', in P. Rowley-Conwy, M. Zvelebil and H. P. Blankholm (eds) *Mesolithic Northwest Europe: Recent Trends*, Sheffield: University of Sheffield Department of Archaeology and Prehistory, 163–8.

Jacobi, R. M., Tallis, J. H. and Mellars, P. A. (1976) 'The Southern Pennine Mesolithic and the Ecological Record', *Journal of Archaeological Science* 3: 307–20.

Jacobsen, T. W. (1976). '17,000 Years of Greek Prehistory', *Science* 234: 76–87.

Jennbert, K. (1984) *Den Productiva Gåvan: Tradition och innovation i Sydskandiavien för omkring 5300 år sedan*, Lund: Acta Archaeologia Lundensia Series in 4°, 16.

—— (1985) 'Neolithisation – a Scanian Perspective', *Journal of Danish Archaeology* 4: 196–7.

—— (1988) 'Der Neolithisierungsprozeß in Südskandinavien', *Praehistorische Zeitschrift* 63: 1–22.

Jensen, J. (1982) *The Prehistory of Denmark*, London: Methuen.

Jessup, R. (1939) 'Excavations at Julieberrie's Grave, Chilham, Kent', *Antiquaries Journal* 19: 260–81.

Johansen, E. (1992) 'Late Palaeolithic and Mesolithic', *Arkæologiske udgravninger i Danmark*: 109–13.

—— (1993) 'Late Palaeolithic and Mesolithic', *Arkæologiske udgravninger i Danmark*: 86–9.

Jones, G. and Legge, A. (1987) 'The Grape (Vitis Vinafora) in the Neolithic of Britain', *Antiquity* 61: 452–5.

Jonsson, L. (1988) 'The Vertebrate Faunal Remains from the Late Atlantic Settlement Skateholm in Scania, South Sweden', in L. Larsson (ed.) *The Skateholm Project. I. Man and Environment*, Lund: Acta Regiae Societatis Humaniorum Litterarum Lundensis LXXXIX, 56–88.

Jørgensen, E. (1977) 'Braendende langdysser', *Skalk* No. 5: 7–13.

Jørgensen, G. (1976) 'Et kornfund fra Sarup. Bidrag til belysning af tragtbægerkulturens agerbrug', *Kuml*: 47–64.

—— (1981) 'Korn frå Sarup. Med nogle bemærkningen om agerbruget i yngre stenalder i Danmark', *Kuml*: 221–331.

Juel Jensen, H. (1986) 'Unretouched Blades in the Late Mesolithic of South Scandinavia. A Functional Study', *Oxford Journal of Archaeology* 5: 19–33.

—— (1988a) 'Functional Analysis of Prehistoric Flint Tools by High-Power Microscopy: A Review of West European Research', *Journal of World Prehistory* 2: 53–88.

—— (1988b) 'Plant Harvesting and Processing with Flint Implements in the Danish Stone Age. A View from the Microscope', *Acta Archaeologica* 59: 131–42.

—— (1994) *Flint Tools and Plant Working: Hidden Traces of Stone Age Technology*, Århus: Åarhus University Press.

Kaelas, L. (1981) 'Megaliths of the Funnel Beaker Culture in Germany and

Scandinavia', in C. Renfrew (ed.) *The Megalithic Monuments of Western Europe*, London: Thames and Hudson, 77–91.

Kalis, A. J. and Zimmerman, A. (1988) 'An Interactive Model for the Use of Different Landscapes in Linearbandkeramik Times', in J. L. Bintliff, J. A. Davidson and E. C. Grant (eds) *Conceptual Issues in Environmental Archaeology*, Edinburgh: Edinburgh University Press, 145–52.

Kampffmeyer, U. (1983) 'Die neolithische Siedlungsplatz Hüde I am Dümmer', in G. Wegner (ed.) *Frühe Bauernkulturen in Niedersachsen*, Oldenburg: Staatliches Museum für Naturkunde und Vorgeschichte, 119–34.

Katz, S. and Voigt, M. (1986) 'Bread and Beer: The Early Use of Cereals in Human Diet', *Expedition* 28: 23–34.

Kaufman, D. (1986) 'A Reconsideration of Adaptive Changes in the Levantine Epipalaeolithic', in L. G. Straus (ed.) *The End of the Paleolithic in the Old World*, Oxford: British Archaeological Reports, International Series 284, 117–28.

Kaul, F. (1987) 'Neolitiske gravanlæg på Onsved Mark, Horns Herred, Sjælland', *Aarbøger for Nordisk Oldkyndighed og Historie*: 27–83.

—— (1988) 'Skræppekærgård', *Journal of Danish Archaeology* 7: 247–8.

Keeley, L. H. (1992) 'The Introduction of Agriculture to the Western North European Plain', in A. B. Gebauer and T. D. Price (eds) *Transitions to Agriculture in Prehistory*, Madison: Prehistory Press, Monographs in World Archaeology 4, 81–95.

Keeley, L. H. and Cahen, D. (1989) 'Early Neolithic Forts and Villages in NE Belgium: A Preliminary Report', *Journal of Field Archaeology* 16: 157–76.

Kinnes, I. A. (1979) *Round Barrows and Ring-ditches in the British Neolithic*, London: British Museum Occasional Paper 7.

—— (1982) 'Les Fouillages and Megalithic Origins', *Antiquity* 61: 24–30.

—— (1985) "Circumstance not Context: The Neolithic of Scotland as seen from the Outside', *Proceedings of the Society of Antiquaries of Scotland* 108: 80–93.

—— (1988) 'The Cattleship Potemkin: Reflections on the First Neolithic in Britain', in J. C. Barrett and I. A. Kinnes (eds) *The Archaeology of Context in the Neolithic and Bronze Age: Recent Trends*, Sheffield: University of Sheffield Department of Archaeology and Prehistory, 2–8.

—— (1992a) *Non-Megalithic Long Barrows and Allied Structures in the British Neolithic*, London: British Museum Occasional Paper 52.

—— (1992b) 'Balnagowan and After: The Context of Non-Megalithic Mortuary Sites in Scotland', in N. Sharples and A. Sheridan (eds) *Vessels for the Ancestors*, Edinburgh: John Donald, 83–103.

Kinnes, I. A. and Hibbs, J. (1989) 'Le Gardien du Tombeau: Further Reflections on the Initial Neolithic', *Oxford Journal of Archaeology* 8: 159–66.

Kinnes, I. A. and Thorpe, I. J. (1986) 'Radiocarbon Dating: Use and Abuse', *Antiquity* 60: 221–3.

Kinnes, I. A., Schadla-Hall, T., Chadwick, P. and Dean, P. (1983) 'Duggleby Howe Reconsidered', *Archaeological Journal* 140: 83–108.

Kjærum, P. (1977) 'En langhøjs tilblivelse', *Antikvariske Studier* 1: 19–26.

Koch, E. (1990) 'Aspekte der Feuchtbodenfunde mit Keramik der Trichterbecherkultur aus Seeland', in D. Jankowska (ed.) *Die Trichterbecherkultur: Neue Forschungen und Hypothesen*, Poznán: Institut Prahistorii Uniwersyteta im. Adam Mickiewicza, 43–53.

Kolstrup, E. (1988) 'Late Atlantic and Early Subboreal Vegetational Development at Trundholm, Denmark', *Journal of Archaeological Science* 15: 503–13.

Kouchi, M. (1986) 'Geographic Variations in Modern Japanese Somatometric Data: A Secular Change Hypothesis', in T. Akazawa and C. M. Aikens (eds) *Prehistoric Hunter-Gatherers in Japan*, Tokyo: University of Tokyo Bulletin 27, 93–106.

Kristensen, I. K. (1989) 'Storgard IV. An Early Neolithic Long Barrow near Fjelsø, North Jutland', *Journal of Danish Archaeology* 8: 72–87.

Kristiansen, K. (1982) 'The Formation of Tribal Systems in Later European Prehistory. Northern Europe 4000–500 BC', in C. Renfrew, M. Rowlands and B. S. Segraves (eds) *Theory and Explanation in Archaeology*, New York: Academic Press, 271–80.

Lamplough, W. H. and Lidster, J. R. (1959) 'The Excavation of King Alfrid's Cave, Ebberston', *Transactions of the Scarborough and District Archaeological Society* 1: 22–31.

Larsen, K. (1957) 'Stenalderhuse på Knardrup Galgebakke', *Kuml*: 24–43.

Larsson, L. (1984) 'The Skateholm Project', *Meddelanden från Lunds Universitets Historiska Museum* 5: 5–38.

—— (1987–8) 'A Construction for Ceremonial Activities from the Late Mesolithic', *Meddelanden från Lunds universitets historiska museum* 7: 5–18.

—— (1988a) 'Aspects of Exchange in Mesolithic Societies', in B. Hårdh, L. Larsson, D. Olausson and R. Petré (eds) *Trade & Exchange in Prehistory*, Lund: Acta Archaeologica Lundensis Series in 8°, 16, 25–32.

—— (1988b) 'The Skateholm Project: Late Mesolithic Settlement at a South Swedish Lagoon', in L. Larsson (ed.) *The Skateholm Project. I. Man and Environment*, Lund: Acta Regiae Societatis Humaniorum Litterarum Lundensis LXXXIX, 9–19.

—— (1989a) 'Late Mesolithic Settlements and Cemeteries at Skateholm, Southern Sweden', in C. Bonsall (ed.) *The Mesolithic in Europe*, Edinburgh: John Donald, 367–78.

—— (1989b) 'Big Dog and Poor Man', in T. B. Larsson and H. Lundmark (eds) *Approaches to Swedish Prehistory*, Oxford: British Archaeological Reports, International Series 500, 211–23.

—— (1990a) 'The Mesolithic of Southern Scandinavia', *Journal of World Prehistory* 4: 257–309.

—— (1990b) 'Dogs in Fraction – Symbols in Action', in P. Vermeersch and P. van Peer (eds) *Contributions to the Mesolithic in Europe*, Leuven: Leuven University Press, 153–60.

Larsson, M. (1985) *The Early Neolithic Funnel-Beaker Culture in South-west Scania, Sweden*, Oxford: British Archaeological Reports, International Series 264.

—— (1985–6) 'Bredasten – an Early Ertebølle Site with a Dwelling Structure in South Scania', *Meddelanden från Lunds universitets historiska museum* 6: 52–83.

—— (1986) 'Neolithization in Scania – a Funnel Beaker Perspective', *Journal of Danish Archaeology* 5: 244–7.

—— (1988) 'Exchange and Society in Scania, Sweden', in B. Hårdh, L. Larsson, D. Olausson and R. Petré (eds) *Trade & Exchange in Prehistory*, Lund: Acta Archaeologica Lundensis Series in 8°, 16, 83–98.

—— (1990) 'Settlement Sites from the Early- and Middle Neolithic at Kabusa, Southern Scania, Sweden', in D. Jankowska (ed.) *Die Trichterbecherkultur: Neue Forschungen und Hypothesen*, Poznán: Institut Prahistorii Uniwersyteta im. Adam Mickiewicza, 117–34.

—— (1991) 'The Moving Family: Aspects of the Early Neolithic in Southern Sweden', in B. E. Berglund (ed.) *The Cultural Landscape During 6000 Years in Southern Sweden – the Ystad Project*, Lund: Ecological Bulletin 41, 315–21.

Legge, A. J. (1981) 'Aspects of Cattle Husbandry', in R. Mercer (ed.) *Farming Practice in British Prehistory*, Edinburgh: Edinburgh University Press, 169–81.

—— (1986) 'Seeds of Discontent: Accelerator Dates on some Charred Plant Remains from the Kebaran and Natufian Cultures', in J. A. J. Gowlett and R. E. M. Hedges (eds) *Archaeological Results from Accelerator Dating*, Oxford: Oxford University Committee for Archaeology, 13–21.

—— (1989) 'Milking the Evidence: A Reply to Entwistle and Grant', in A. Milles, D. Williams and N. Gardner (eds) *The Beginnings of Agriculture*, Oxford: British Archaeological Reports, International Series 496, 217–42.

Legge, A. J. and Rowley-Conwy, P. (1986) 'New Radiocarbon Dates for Early Sheep at Tell Abu Hureyra, Syria', in J. A. J. Gowlett and R. E. M. Hedges (eds) *Archaeological Results from Accelerator Dating*, Oxford: Oxford University Committee for Archaeology, 23–35.

—— (1987) 'Gazelle Killing in Stone Age Syria', *Scientific American* 257: 88–95.

—— (1985) 'New Excavations at Gavrinis', *Antiquity* 59: 183–7.

L'Helgouach, J. (1971) 'Les débuts du néolithique en Armorique au quatrième millénaire et son développement au troisième millénaire', in J. Lüning (ed.) *Die Anfänge des Neolithikums vom Orient bis Nordeuropa*, Köln: Bohlau, Teil VI, 178–200.

—— (1976) 'Les civilisations néolithiques en Armorique', in J. Guilaine (ed.) *La Préhistoire Française 2. Civilisations Néolithiques et Protohistoriques*, Paris: CRNS, 365–74.

Le Roux, C.-T. (1979) 'Stone Axes of Brittany and the Marches', in T. H. McK. Clough and W. A. Cummins (eds) *Stone Axe Studies*, London: Council for British Archaeology Research Report 23, 49–56.

Liddell, D. (1935) 'Report on the Excavations at Hembury Fort', *Proceedings of the Devon Archaeological and Exploration Society* 2: 134–75.

Lieberman, D. E. (1991) 'Seasonality and Gazelle Hunting at Hayonim Cave: New Evidence for "Sedentism" During the Natufian', *Paléorient* 19: 205–8.

Liversage, D. (1968) 'Excavations at Dalkey Island, Co. Dublin, 1956–59', *Proceedings of the Royal Irish Academy* 66C: 53–233.

—— (1983) 'Træbyggede grave fra den ældste bondestenalder', *Nationalmuseets Arbejdsmark*: 5–16.

—— (1992) *Barkær: Long Barrows and Settlements*, København: Arkæologiske Studier IX.

Lobb, S. (1995) 'Excavations at Crofton Causewayed Enclosure', *Wiltshire Archaeological Magazine* 88: 18–25.

Louwe Kooijmans, L. P. (1976) 'Local Developments in a Borderland. A Survey of the Neolithic at the Lower Rhine', *Oudheidkundige Mededelingen* 57: 227–97.

—— (1987) 'Neolithic Settlement and Subsistence in the Wetlands of the Rhine/Meuse Delta of the Netherlands', in J. M. Coles and A. J. Lawson (eds) *European Wetlands in Prehistory*, Oxford: Clarendon Press, 227–56.

—— (1993) 'The Mesolithic/Neolithic Transformation in the Lower Rhine Basin', in P. Bogucki (ed.) *Case Studies in European Prehistory*, Boca Raton: CRC Press, 95–145.

Lüning, J. (1982) 'Research into the Bandkeramik Settlement of the Aldenhovener Platte in the Rhineland', *Analecta Praehistorica Leidensia* 15: 1–29.

Lüning, J. and Stehli, P. (1989) 'Die Bandkeramik in Mitteleuropa: von der Natur-zur Kulturlandschaft', *Spektrum der Wissenschaft*: 78–88.

McCorriston, J. (1994) 'Acorn Eating and Agricultural Origins: California Ethnographies as Analogies for the Ancient Near East', *Antiquity* 68: 97–107.

McCorriston, J. and Hole, F. (1991) 'The Ecology of Seasonal Stress and the Origins of Agriculture in the Near East', *American Anthropologist* 93: 46–69.

MacNeish, R. S. (1992) *The Origins of Agriculture and Settled Life*, Norman: University of Oklahoma Press.

Madsen, A. P., Müller, S., Neergaard, C., Petersen, C. G. J., Rostrup, E., Steenstrup, K. J. T. V., and Winge, H. (1900) *Affaldsdynger fra Stenalderen i Danmark. Undersøgte for Nationalmuseet*, København: C. A. Reitzel.

Madsen, B. and Fiedel, R. (1987) 'Pottery Manufacture at a Neolithic Causewayed Enclosure near Hevringholm, East Jutland', *Journal of Danish Archaeology* 6: 78–86.

Madsen, T. (1977) 'Toftum ved Horsens. Et "befæstet" anlæg tilhørende tragt-bægerkulture', *Kuml* 161–84.

—— (1978) 'Bebyggelsesarkæologisk forskningsstrategi: Overvejelser i forbindelse med et projekt over Tragtbægerkulturen i Østjylland', *Skrifter fra Historisk Institut, Odense Universitet* 23: 64–76.

—— (1979) 'Earthen Long Barrows and Timber Structures: Aspects of the Early Neolithic Mortuary Practice in Denmark', *Proceedings of the Prehistoric Society* 45: 301–20.

—— (1982) 'Settlement Systems of Early Agricultural Societies in East Jutland, Denmark: A Regional Study of Change', *Journal of Anthropological Archaeology* 1: 197–236.

—— (1986) 'Where did all the Hunters go? – An Assessment of an Epoch-making Episode in Danish Prehistory', *Journal of Danish Archaeology* 5: 229–39.

—— (1988) 'Causewayed Enclosures in South Scandinavia', in C. Burgess, P. Topping, C. Mordant and M. Maddison (eds) *Enclosures and Defences in the Neolithic of Western Europe*, Oxford: British Archaeological Reports, International Series 403, 301–36.

—— (1991) 'The Social Structure of Early Neolithic Society in South Scandinavia', in J. Lichardus (ed.) *Die Kupferzeit als Historische Epoche*, Bonn: Saarbrücker Beitrage zur Altertumskunde 55, 489–96.

—— (1993) 'Barrows with Timber-built Structures', in S. Hvass and B. Storgaard (eds) *Digging into the Past*, Århus: Jutland Archaeological Society, 96–9.

Madsen, T. and Juel Jensen, H. (1982) 'Settlement and Land Use in Early Neolithic Denmark', *Analecta Praehistorica Leidensia* 15: 63–86.

Madsen, T. and Petersen, J. E. (1982–3) 'Tidligneolitiske Anlæg ved Mosegården. Regionale og kronologiske forskelle i tidligneolitikum', *Kuml*: 61–120.

Makkay, J. (1987) 'The Linear Pottery and the Early Indo-Europeans', in S. N. Skomal and E. C. Polomé (eds) *Proto-Indo-European: The Archaeology of a Linguistic Problem*, Washington, DC: Institute for the Study of Man, 165–84.

Mallory, J. P. (1989) *In Search of the Indo-Europeans*, London: Thames and Hudson.

Mallory, J. P. and McNeill, T. E. (1991) *The Archaeology of Ulster*, Belfast: Institute of Irish Studies.

Manby, T. G. (1970) 'Long Barrows of Northern England: Structural and Dating Evidence', *Scottish Archaeological Forum* 2: 2–27.

—— (1976) 'The Excavation of the Kilham Long Barrow, East Riding of Yorkshire', *Proceedings of the Prehistoric Society* 42: 111–60.

—— (1988) 'The Neolithic Period in Eastern Yorkshire', in T. G. Manby (ed.) *Archaeology in Eastern Yorkshire*, Sheffield: University of Sheffield Department of Archaeology and Prehistory, 35–88.

Marshall, A. (1981) 'Environmental Adaptation and Structural Design in Axially-pitched Longhouses from Neolithic Europe', *World Archaeology* 13: 101–21.

Mathiassen, T. (1935) 'Blubber lamps in the Ertebølle Culture?', *Acta Archaeologica* 6: 139–52.

—— (1940) 'Havnelev – Strandegaard', *Aarbøger for Nordisk Oldkyndighed og Historie*: 1–55.

—— (1959) 'Ravsmykker fra ældre Stenalder', *Aarbøger for Nordisk Oldkyndighed og Historie*: 184–200.

Megaw, J. V. S. and Simpson, D. D. A. (1979) *Introduction to British Prehistory*, Leicester: Leicester University Press.

Meiklejohn, C. and Zvelebil, M. (1991) 'Health Status of European Populations at the Agricultural Transition and the Implications for the Adoption of Farming', in H. Bush and M. Zvelebil (eds) *Health in Past Societies*, Oxford: British Archaeological Reports, International Series 567, 129–45.

Mellars, P. A. (1975) 'Ungulate Populations, Economic Patterns and the Mesolithic Landscape', in J. G. Evans, S. Limbrey and H. Cleere (eds) *The Effect of Man on the Landscape: The Highland Zone*, London: Council for British Archaeology Research Report 11, 49–57.

—— (1976) 'Fire Ecology, Animal Populations and Man: A Study of Some Ecological Relationships in Prehistory', *Proceedings of the Prehistoric Society* 42: 15–45.

—— (1987) *Excavations on Oronsay*, Edinburgh: Edinburgh University Press.

Mellars, P. A. and Wilkinson, M. (1980) 'Fish Otoliths as Evidence for Seasonality in Prehistoric Shell Middens: The Evidence from Oronsay (Inner Hebrides)', *Proceedings of the Prehistoric Society* 46: 19–44.

Mercer, R. (1980) *Hambledon Hill – a Neolithic Landscape*, Edinburgh: Edinburgh University Press.

—— (1981a) 'Introduction', in R. J. Mercer (ed.) *Farming Practice in British Prehistory*, Edinburgh: Edinburgh University Press, ix–xxvi.

—— (1981b) 'Excavations at Carn Brea, Illogan, Cornwall, 1970–73', *Cornish Archaeology* 20: 1–204.

—— (1986) *Excavation of a Neolithic Enclosure at Helman Tor, Lanlivery, Cornwall. 1986. Interim Report*, Edinburgh, University of Edinburgh Department of Archaeology Project Paper 4.

—— (1988) 'Hambledon Hill, Dorset, England', in C. Burgess, P. Topping, C. Mordant and M. Maddison (eds) *Enclosures and Defences in the Neolithic of Western Europe*, Oxford: British Archaeological Reports, International Series 403, 89–106.

—— (1989) 'Helman Tor', *Past* 6: 6–7.

—— (1990a) 'The Inception of Farming in the British Isles and the Emergence of Indo-European Languages in NW Europe', in T. L. Markey and J. A. C. Greppin (eds) *When Worlds Collide: Indo-Europeans and Pre-Indo-Europeans*, Ann Arbor: Karoma, 101–14.

—— (1990b) *Causewayed Enclosures*, Princes Risborough: Shire.

Midgley, M. (1985) *The Origin and Function of the Earthen Long Barrows of Northern Europe*, Oxford: British Archaeological Reports, International Series 259.

—— (1992) *TRB Culture*, Edinburgh: Edinburgh University Press.

Midgley, M., Pavlů, I., Rulf, J. and Zápotocká, M. (1993) 'Fortified Settlements or Ceremonial Sites: New Evidence from Bylany, Czechoslovakia', *Antiquity* 67: 91–6.

Milisauskas, S. (1978) *European Prehistory*, London: Academic Press.

—— (1986) *Early Neolithic Settlement and Society at Olszanica*, Ann Arbor: University of Michigan Memoirs in Anthropology 19.

Milisauskas, S. and Kruk, J. (1989) 'Neolithic Economy in Central Europe', *Journal of World Prehistory* 3: 403–46.

Miller, N. F. (1992) 'The Origins of Plant Cultivation in the Near East', in C. W. Cowan and P. J. Watson (eds) *The Origins of Agriculture*, Washington, DC: Smithsonian Institution Press, 39–58.

Mithen, S., Finlayson, B., Finlay, N. and Lake, M. (1992) 'Excavations at Bolsay Farm, a Mesolithic Settlement on Islay', *Cambridge Archaeological Journal* 2: 242–53.

Moffett, L., Robinson, M. A. and Straker, V. (1989) 'Cereals, Fruits and Nuts: Charred Plant Remains from Neolithic Sites in England and Wales and the Neolithic Economy', in A. Milles, D. Williams and N. Gardner (eds) *The Beginnings of Agriculture*, Oxford: British Archaeological Reports, International Series 496, 243–61.

Møhl, U. (1978) 'Aggersund-bopladsen zoologiskt belyst. Svanejagt som årsag til bosæt-telse?', *Kuml*: 57–75.

Monk, M. A. (1993) 'People and Environment: In Search of the Farmers', in E. Shee Twohig and M. Ronayne (eds) *Past Perspectives*, Cork: Cork University Press, 35–52.

Moore, A. M. T. (1989) 'The Transition from Foraging to Farming in Southwest Asia; Present Problems and Future Directions', in D. R. Harris and G. C. Hillman (eds) *Foraging and Farming*, London: Unwin Hyman, 620–31.

—— (1991) 'Abu Hureyra 1 and the Antecedents of Agriculture on the Middle Euphrates', in O. Bar-Yosef and F. R. Valla (eds) *The Natufian Culture in the Levant*, Ann Arbor: International Monographs in Prehistory Archaeological Series 1, 11–20.

Morrison, A. (1980) *Early Man in Britain and Ireland*, London: Croom Helm.

—— (1982) 'The Mesolithic Period in South-west Scotland: A Review of the Evidence', *Glasgow Archaeological Journal* 9: 1–14.

Mortimer, J. R. (1905) *Forty Years' Researches into British and Saxon Burial Mounds of East Yorkshire*, London: Brown.

Nandris, J. (1970) 'The Development and Relationships of the Earlier Greek Neolithic', *Man* 5: 191–213.

Newell, R. R. and Constandse-Westermann, T. S. (1988) 'The Significance of Skateholm I and Skateholm II to the Mesolithic of Western Europe', in L. Larsson (ed.) *The Skateholm Project. I. Man and Environment*, Lund: Acta Regiae Societatis Humaniorum Litterarum Lundensis LXXXIX, 164–74.

Newell, R. R., Kielman, D., Constandse-Westermann, T. S., van der Sanden, W. A. B. and van Gijn, A. (1990) *An Inquiry Into the Ethnic Resolution of Mesolithic Regional Groups*, Leiden: E. J. Brill.

Nielsen, E. K. (1986) 'Ertebølle and Funnel Beaker Pots as Tools: On Traces of Production Techniques and Use', *Acta Archaeologica* 57: 107–20.

Nielsen, E. K. and Brinch Petersen, E. (1993) 'Burials, People and Dogs', in S. Hvass and B. Storgaard (eds) *Digging into the Past*, Århus: Jutland Archaeological Society, 76–81.

Nielsen, J. N. (1982) 'Sejlflod, North Jutland', *Journal of Danish Archaeology* 1: 169.

Nielsen, P. O. (1977) 'Die Flintbeile der frühen Trichterbecherkultur in Dänemark', *Acta Archaeologica* 48: 61–138.

—— (1984a) 'De første bønder', *Aarbøger for Nordisk Oldkyndighed og Historie*: 96–126.

—— (1984b) 'Flint Axes and Megaliths – The Time and Context of the Early Dolmens in Denmark', in G. Burenhult *The Archaeology of Carrowmore*, Stockholm: Theses and Papers in North-European Archaeology 14, 376–87.

—— (1986) 'The Beginning of the Neolithic – Assimilation or Complex Change?', *Journal of Danish Archaeology* 5: 240–3.

—— (1991) 'Neolithic', *Arkæologiske udgravninger i Danmark*: 97–100.

—— (1993) 'Settlement', in S. Hvass and B. Storgaard (eds) *Digging into the Past*, Århus: Jutland Archaeological Society, 92–5.

Noe-Nygaard, N. (1967) 'Recent "kokkenmøddinger" in Ghana', *Geografisk Tidsskrift* 66: 179–97.

—— (1987) 'Taphonomy in Archaeology with Special Emphasis on Man as a Biassing Factor', *Journal of Danish Archaeology* 6: 7–52.

Norling-Christensen, H. and Bröste, K. (1945) 'Skeletgraven fra Korsør Nor', *Nationalmuseets Arbejdsmark*: 19–33.

Noy, T. (1991) 'Art and Decoration of the Natufian at Nahel Oren', in O. Bar-Yosef and F. R. Valla (eds) *The Natufian Culture in the Levant*, Ann Arbor: International Monographs in Prehistory Archaeological Series 1, 557–68.

Nygaard, S. E. (1989) 'The Stone Age of Northern Scandinavia: A Review', *Journal of World Prehistory* 3: 71–116.

O'Connell, M. (1987) 'Early Cereal-type Pollen Records from Connemara, Western Ireland and their Possible Significance', *Pollen et Spores* 29: 207–24.

Odgaard, B. (1989) 'Cultural Landscape Development through 5500 Years at Lake Skånso, Northwestern Jutland as Reflected in a Regional Pollen Diagram', *Journal of Danish Archaeology* 8: 200–10.

Ó Floinn, R. (1992) 'A Neolithic Cave Burial in Limerick', *Archaeology Ireland* 6: 19–21.

—— (1995) 'Recent Research into Irish Bog Bodies', in R. C. Turner and R. G. Scaife (eds) *Bog Bodies: New Discoveries and New Perspectives*, London: British Museum Press, 137–45.

O'Kelly, M. J. (1989) *Early Ireland*, Cambridge: Cambridge University Press.

Olausson, D. S., Rudebeck, E. and Säfvestad, U. (1980) 'Die südschwedischen Feueresteingruben – Ergebnisse und Probleme', in G. Weisgerber (ed.) *5000 Jahre Feuersteinbergbau*, Bohum: Deutsches Bergbau Museum, 183–204.

O'Malley, M. (1978) 'Broom Hill, Braishfield: Mesolithic Dwelling', *Current Archaeology* 63: 117–20.

O'Malley, M. and Jacobi, R. M. (1978) 'The Excavation of a Mesolithic Occupation Site at Broom Hill, Braishfield, Hampshire', *Rescue Archaeology in Hampshire* 4: 16–38.

O'Nuallain, S. (1972) 'A Neolithic House at Ballyglass, Co. Mayo', *Journal of the Royal Society of Antiquaries of Ireland* 102: 49–57.

Ó Riordáin, S. P. (1954) 'Lough Gur Excavations: Neolithic and Bronze Age Houses on Knockadoon', *Proceedings of the Royal Irish Academy* 56C: 297–459.

Ørsnes, M. (1956) 'Om jættestues konstruktion og brug', *Aarbøger for Nordisk Oldkyndighed og Historie*: 221–32.

Österholm, I. and Österholm, S. (1984) 'The Kitchen Middens Along the Coast of Ballysadare Bay', in G. Burenhult *The Archaeology of Carrowmore*, Stockholm: Theses and Papers in North-European Archaeology 14, 326–45.

Ottaway, B. (1973) 'Earliest Copper Ornaments in Northern Europe', *Proceedings of the Prehistoric Society* 39: 294–331.

Palmer, S. (1970) 'The Stone Age Industries of Portland, Dorset, and the Utilisation of Portland Chert as an Artefact Material in Southern England', *Proceedings of the Prehistoric Society* 36: 82–115.

—— (1989) 'Mesolithic Sites of Portland and their Significance', in C. Bonsall (ed.) *The Mesolithic in Europe*, Edinburgh: John Donald, 254–7.

—— (1990) 'Culverwell – Unique Opportunities for Studying the Intra-site Structure of a Mesolithic Habitation Site in Dorset, England', in P. Vermeersch and P. van Peer (eds) *Contributions to the Mesolithic in Europe*, Leuven: Leuven University Press, 87–91.

Paludan-Müller, C. (1978) 'High Atlantic Food Gathering in Northwestern Zealand: Ecological Conditions and Spatial Representation', in K. Kristiansen and C. Paludan-Müller (eds) *New Directions in Scandinavian Archaeology*, Odense: National Museum of Denmark, 120–57.

Parker Pearson, M. (1993) *English Heritage Book of Bronze Age Britain*, London: Batsford.

Patton, M. (1991) 'Axes, Men and Women: Symbolic Dimensions of Neolithic Exchange in Armorica (North-west France)', in P. Garwood, P. Jennings, R. Skeates and J. Toms (eds) *Sacred and Profane*, Oxford: Oxford University Committee for Archaeology Monograph 32, 65–79.

—— (1993) *Statements in Stone*, London: Routledge.

—— (1994) 'Neolithisation and Megalithic Origins in North-western France: A Regional Interaction Model', *Oxford Journal of Archaeology* 13: 279–93.

Peacock, D. P. S. (1969) 'Neolithic Pottery Production in Cornwall', *Antiquity* 43: 145–9.

Péquart, M. and Péquart, S. J. (1954) *Hoèdic, deuxieme station-nécropole du mésolithique côtier armoricain*, Anvers: de Sikkel.

Péquart, M., Péquart, S. J., Boule, M. and Vallois, H. V. (1937) *Téviec, station-nécropole mésolithique du Morbihan*, Paris: Archives de l'Institut de Paléontologie Humaine XVIII.

Perry, I. and Moore, P. D. (1987) 'Dutch Elm Disease as an Analogue of Neolithic Elm Decline', *Nature* 326: 72–3.

Persson, O. and Persson, E. (1988) 'Anthropological Report Concerning the Interred Mesolithic Populations from Skateholm, Southern Sweden: Excavation Seasons 1983–1984', in L. Larsson (ed.) *The Skateholm Project. I. Man and Environment*, Lund: Acta Regiae Societatis Humaniorum Litterarum Lundensis LXXXIX, 89–105.

Pierpoint, S. J. (1979) 'Three Radiocarbon Dates for Yorkshire Prehistory', *Antiquity* 53: 224–5.

Piggott, S. (1929) 'Neolithic Pottery and Other Remains from Pangbourne, Berkshire, and Caversham, Oxfordshire', *Proceedings of the Prehistoric Society of East Anglia* 6: 30–9.

—— (1954) *The Neolithic Cultures of the British Isles*, Cambridge: Cambridge University Press.

—— (1955) 'Windmill Hill – East or West?', *Proceedings of the Prehistoric Society* 21: 96–101.

—— (1962a) *The West Kennet Long Barrow*, London: HMSO.

—— (1962b) 'Heads and Hoofs', *Antiquity* 36: 110–18.

—— (1967) '"Unchambered" Long Barrows in Neolithic Britain', *Palaeohistoria* 12: 381–93.

—— (1972) 'The Beginning of the Neolithic in the British Isles', in *Die Anfänge des Neolithikums vom Orient bis Nordeuropa, Teil VII*, Koln: Fundamenta Reihe A Band 3, 217–32.

Pollard, A. (1990) 'Down Through the Ages: A Review of the Oban Cave Deposits', *Scottish Archaeological Review* 7: 58–74.

Price, T. D. (1981) 'Swifterbant, Oost Flevoland, Netherlands: Excavations at the River Dune Sites S21–S24, 1976', *Palaeohistoria* 23: 75–104.

—— (1989a) 'Multi-element Studies of Diagenesis in Prehistoric Bone', in T. D. Price (ed.) *The Chemistry of Prehistoric Human Bone*, Cambridge: Cambridge University Press, 126–54.

—— (1989b) 'The Reconstruction of Mesolithic Diets' in C. Bonsall (ed.) *The Mesolithic in Europe*, Edinburgh: John Donald, 48–59.

—— (1991) 'The Mesolithic of Northern Europe', *Annual Review of Anthropology* 20: 211–33.

Proudfoot, E. (1965) 'Bishops Cannings, Roughridge Hill', *Wiltshire Archaeological Magazine* 60: 133.

Pryor, F. (1974) *Excavation at Fengate, Peterborough, England: The First Report*, Toronto: Royal Ontario Museum Archaeology Monograph 3.

—— (1976) 'A Neolithic Multiple Burial from Fengate, Peterborough', *Antiquity* 50: 232–3.

—— (1984) *Excavation at Fengate, Peterborough, England: the Fourth Report*, Northampton: Northamptonshire Archaeological Society Monograph 2.

—— (1987) 'Etton 1986: Neolithic Metamorphoses', *Antiquity* 61: 78–80.

—— (1988a) 'Earlier Neolithic Organised Landscapes and Ceremonial in Lowland Britain', in J. C. Barrett and I. A. Kinnes (eds) *The Archaeology of Context in the Neolithic and Bronze Age: Recent Trends*, Sheffield: University of Sheffield Department of Archaeology and Prehistory.

—— (1988b) 'Etton, Near Maxey, Cambridgeshire: A Causewayed Enclosure on the Fen-Edge', in C. Burgess, P. Topping, C. Mordant and M. Maddison (eds) *Enclosures and Defences in the Neolithic of Western Europe*, Oxford: British Archaeological Reports, International Series 403, 107–26.

Rackham, O. (1980) *Ancient Woodland: Its History, Vegetation and Uses in England*, London: Arnold.

Randsborg, K. (1978) 'Resource Distribution and the Function of Copper in Early Neolithic Denmark', in M. Ryan (ed.) *The Origins of Metallurgy in Atlantic Europe*, Dublin: Proceedings of the Fifth Atlantic Colloquium, 303–18.

Rankine, W. F., Rankine, W. M. and Dimbleby, G. W. (1960) 'Further Excavations at a Mesolithic Site at Oakhanger, Selborne, Hants', *Proceedings of the Prehistoric Society* 26: 246–62.

Redding, R. W. (1988) 'A General Explanation of Subsistence Change: From Hunting and Gathering to Food Production', *Journal of Anthropological Archaeology* 7: 56–97.

Reed, R. C. (1974) 'Earthen Long Barrows: A New Perspective', *Archaeological Journal* 131: 33–57.

Renfrew, A. C. (1973) *Before Civilisation*, London: Jonathan Cape.

—— (1976) 'Megaliths, Territories and Populations', in S. J. de Laet (ed.) *Acculturation and Continuity in Atlantic Europe*, Bruges: Dissertationes Archaeologicae Gandenses 16, 198–220.

—— (1987) *Archaeology and Language*, London: Jonathan Cape.

Renfrew, A. C. and Aspinall, A. (1990) 'Aegean Obsidian and Franchthi Cave', in C. Perlès, *Les industries lithiques taillée de Franchthi (Argolide, Grèce). Tome II: Les Industries du Mésolithique et du Néolithique initial*, Bloomington: Indiana University Press, 257–70.

Reynolds, P. (1981) 'Deadstock and Livestock', in R. J. M. Mercer (ed.) *Farming Practice in British Prehistory*, Edinburgh: Edinburgh University Press, 97–122.

Richards, J. (1986–90) 'Death and the Past Environment', *Berkshire Archaeological Journal* 73: 1–42.

—— (1990) *The Stonehenge Environs Project*, London: English Heritage Archaeological Report 16.

Ricq-de Bouard, M. (1993) 'Trade in Neolithic Jadeite Axes from the Alps: New Data', in C. Scarre and F. Healy (eds) *Trade and Exchange in Prehistoric Europe*, Oxford: Oxbow Archaeological Monographs 33, 61–7.

Robb, J. (1993) 'A Social Prehistory of European Languages', *Antiquity* 67: 747–60.

Robertson-Mackay, R. (1987) 'Excavations at Staines, Middlesex', *Proceedings of the Prehistoric Society* 63: 1–147.

Roche, H. (1989) 'Pre-Tomb Habitation Found at Knowth, Co. Meath, Spring 1989', *Archaeology Ireland* 3: 101–3.

Rønne, P. (1979) 'Høj over høj', *Skalk* No. 5: 3–8.

Roosevelt, A. C. (1984) 'Population, Health, and the Evolution of Subsistence: Conclusions from the Conference', in M. H. Cohen and G. J. Armelagos (eds) *Palaeopathology at the Origins of Agriculture*, New York: Academic Press, 559–83.

Rosenberg, M. (1990) 'The Mother of Invention: Evolutionary Theory, Territoriality, and the Origins of Agriculture', *American Anthropologist* 92: 399–415.

Rowley-Conwy, P. (1981) 'Slash and Burn in the Temperate European Neolithic', in R. Mercer (ed.) *Farming Practice in British Prehistory*, Edinburgh: Edinburgh University Press, 85–96.

—— (1982) 'Forest Grazing and Clearance in Temperate Europe with Special Reference to Denmark: An Archaeological View', in M. Bell and S. Limbrey (eds) *Archaeological Aspects of Woodland Ecology*, Oxford: British Archaeological Reports, International series 146: 199–215.

—— (1983) 'Sedentary Hunters: The Ertebølle Example', in G. Bailey (ed.) *Hunter-Gatherer Economy in Prehistory*, Cambridge: Cambridge University Press, 111–26.

—— (1984) 'The Laziness of the Short Distance Hunter: The Origins of Agriculture in Western Denmark', *Journal of Anthropological Archaeology* 3: 300–24.

—— (1985) 'The Origin of Agriculture in Denmark: a Review of Some Theories', *Journal of Danish Archaeology* 4: 196–7.

Rowley-Connwy, P. (1987) 'The Interpretation of Ard Marks', *Antiquity* 61: 263–6.

Rowley-Conwy, P. and Zvelebil, M. (1989) 'Saving it for Later: Storage by Prehistoric Hunter-gatherers in Europe', in P. Halstead and J. O'Shea (eds) *Bad Year Economics*, Cambridge: Cambridge University Press, 40–56.

Rudebeck, E. (1987) 'Flintmining in Sweden during the Neolithic Period: New Evidence from the Kvarnby–S. Sallerup Area', in G. de G. Sieveking and M. H. Newcomer (eds) *The Human Uses of Flint and Chert*, Cambridge: Cambridge University Press, 151–7.

Runnels, C. (1989) 'Trade Models in the Study of Agricultural Origins and Dispersals', *Journal of Mediterranean Archaeology* 2: 149–56.

Runnels, C. and Van Andel, T. H. (1988) 'Trade and the Origins of Agriculture in the Eastern Mediterranean', *Journal of Mediterranean Archaeology* 1: 83–109.

Ryan, M. (1981) 'Poulawack, Co. Clare: The Affinities of the Central Burial Structure', in D. O'Corrain (ed.) *Irish Antiquities*, Cork: Tower Books, 134–46.

Sauer, C. O. (1952) *Agricultural Origins and Dispersals*, New York: American Geographical Society.

—— (1969) *Seeds, Spades, Hearths and Herds*, Cambridge, Mass.: MIT Press.

Saville, A. (1989) 'A Mesolithic Flint Assemblage from Hazleton, Gloucestershire, England, and its Implications', in C. Bonsall (ed.) *The Mesolithic in Europe*, Edinburgh: John Donald, 258–63.

—— (1990) *Hazleton North, Gloucestershire, 1979–1982: The Excavation of a Neolithic Long Cairn of the Cotswold–Severn Group*, London: English Heritage Archaeological Report 13.

Saville, A. and Hallén, Y. (1994) 'The "Obanian Iron Age"; Human Remains from the Oban Cave Sites, Argyll, Scotland', *Antiquity* 68: 715–23.

Saville, A. and Miket, R. (1994) 'An Corran Rock-shelter, Skye: A Major New Mesolithic Site', *Past* 18: 9–10.

Scarre, C. (1992) 'The Early Neolithic of Western France and Megalithic Origins in Atlantic Europe', *Oxford Journal of Archaeology* 11: 121–54.

Scarre, C., Switsur, R. and Mohen, J.-P. (1993) 'New Radiocarbon Dates from Bougon and the Chronology of French Passage-graves', *Antiquity* 67: 856–9.

Schmidt, O. A. and Sterum, N. T. (1986), 'Kongenshøjvej', *Journal of Danish Archaeology* 5: 261.

Schwabedissen, H. (1967) 'Ein horizontierter "Breitkeil" aus Satrup und die mannigfachen Kulturbindungen der beginnenden Neolithikums im Norden und Nordwesten', *Palaeohistoria* 12: 409–68.

—— (1972) 'Rosenhof (Ostholstein): ein Ellerbek-Wohnplatz am einstigen Ostseeufer', *Archäologisches Korrespondenzblatt* 2: 1–8.

—— (1981) 'Ertebølle/Ellerbeck – Mesolithikum oder Neolithikum?', in B. Gramsch (ed.) *Mesolithikum in Europa*, Potsdam: Veröffentlichung des Museums für Ur- und Frühgeschichte 14/15, 129–42.

Scott, J. G. (1969) 'The Clyde Cairns of Scotland', in T. G. E. Powell (ed.) *Megalithic Enquiries in the West of Britain*, Liverpool: Liverpool University Press, 175–222.

Selkirk, A. (1971) 'Ascott-under-Wychwood', *Current Archaeology* 24: 7–10.

Shand, P. and Hodder, I. (1990) 'Haddenham', *Current Archaeology* 113: 339–42.

Sharples, N. (1991) *Maiden Castle: Excavations and Field Survey 1985–6*, London: English Heritage Archaeological Report 19.

Sheridan, A. (1985–6) 'Megaliths and Megalomania: An Account, and Interpretation, of the Development of Passage Tombs in Ireland', *Journal of Irish Archaeology* 3: 17–30.

—— (1986) 'Porcellanite Artefacts: A New Survey', *Ulster Journal of Archaeology* 49: 19–32.

Sheridan, A., Cooney, G. and Grogan, E. (1992) 'Stone Axe Studies in Ireland', *Proceedings of the Prehistoric Society* 58: 389–416.

Sherratt, A. (1990) 'The Genesis of Megaliths: Monumentality, Ethnicity and Social Complexity in Neolithic North-west Europe', *World Archaeology* 22: 147–67.

Sillen, A. and Lee-Thorp, J. A. (1991) 'Dietary Change in the Late Natufian', in O. Bar-Yosef and F. R. Valla (eds) *The Natufian Culture in the Levant*, Ann Arbor: International Monographs in Prehistory Archaeological Series 1, 399–410.

Simmons, I. G. and Innes, J. B. (1987) 'Mid-Holocene Adaptations and Later Mesolithic Forest Disturbance in Northern England', *Journal of Archaeological Science* 14: 385–403.

Simmons, I. G., Atherden, M., Cundill, P. R., Innes, J. B. and Jones, R. T. (1982) 'Prehistoric Environments', in D. A. Spratt, *Prehistoric and Roman Archaeology of North-East Yorkshire*, Oxford: British Archaeological Reports, British Series 104.

Simpson, D. D. A. (1968) 'Timber Mortuary Houses and Earthen Long Barrows', *Antiquity* 42: 142–4.

—— (1990) 'Neolithic Settlement Site at Balleygalley, Co. Antrim', *Archaeology Ireland* 4: 43–4.

—— (1993) 'Balleygalley', *Current Archaeology* 134: 60–2.

Skaarup, J. (1973) *Hesselø–Sølager. Jagdstation der südskandinavischen Trichterbecher-kultur*, København: Arkæologiske Studier 1.

—— (1975) *Stengade. Ein langeländischer Wohnpltaz mit Hausresten aus der frühne-olithischen Zeit*, Rudkøbing: Meddelelser fra Langelands Museum.

—— (1990) 'Burials, Votive Offerings and Social Structure in Early Neolithic Farmer Society of Denmark', in D. Jankowska (ed.) *Die Trichterbecherkultur: Neue Forschungen und Hypothesen*, Poznán: Institut Prahistorii Uniwersyteta im. Adam Mickiewicza, 73–91.

—— (1993) 'Megalithic graves', in S. Hvass and B. Storgaard (eds) *Digging into the Past*, Århus: Jutland Archaeological Society, 104–9.

Sloan, D. (1984) 'Shell Middens and Chronology in Scotland', *Scottish Archaeological Review* 3: 73–9.

Smith, A. G. (1981) 'The Neolithic', in I. G. Simmons and M. J. Tooley (eds) *The Environment in British Prehistory*, London: Duckworth, 210–49.

Smith, C. (1989) 'British Antler Mattocks', in C. Bonsall (ed.) *The Mesolithic in Europe*, Edinburgh: John Donald, 272–83.

—— (1992) *Late Stone Age Hunters of the British Isles*, London: Routledge.

Smith, I. F. (1965) *Windmill Hill and Avebury*, Oxford: Clarendon Press.

—— (1974) 'The Neolithic', in C. Renfrew (ed.) *British Prehistory: A New Outline*, London: Duckworth, 100–36.

—— (1979) 'The Chronology of British Stone Implements', in T. H. McK. Clough and W. A. Cummins (eds) *Stone Axe Studies*, London: Council for British Archaeology Research Report 23, 13–22.

Smith, P. (1989) 'Paleonutrition and Subsistence Patterns in the Natufians', in I. Hershkovitz (ed.) *People and Culture in Change*, Oxford: British Archaeological Reports, International Series 508, 375–84.

—— (1991) 'The Dental Evidence for Human Sedentism in Southwest Asia during the Natufian', in O. Bar-Yosef and F. R. Valla (eds) *The Natufian Culture in the Levant*, Ann Arbor: International Monographs in Prehistory Archaeological Series 1, 425–32.

Smith, P., Bar-Yosef, O. and Sillen, A. (1984) 'Archaeological and Skeletal Evidence for Dietary Change During the Late Pleistocene/Early Holocene in the Levant', in M. H. Cohen and G. J. Armelagos (eds) *Palaeopathology at the Origins of Agriculture*, New York: Academic Press, 101–36.

Smith, R. W. (1984) 'The Ecology of Neolithic Farming Systems as Exemplified by the Avebury Region of Wiltshire', *Proceedings of the Prehistoric Society* 50: 99–120.

Sokal, R. R., Oden, N. L. and Wilson, C. (1991) 'Genetic Evidence for the Spread of Agriculture in Europe', *Nature* 351: 143–5.

Solberg, B. (1989) 'The Neolithic Transition in Southern Scandinavia: Internal Development or Migration?', *Oxford Journal of Archaeology* 8: 261–96.

Soudský, B. and Pavlů, I. (1972) 'The Linear Pottery Culture Settlement Patterns of Central Europe', in P. J. Ucko, R. Tringham and G. W. Dimbleby (eds) *Man, Settlement and Urbanism*, London: Duckworth, 317–28.

Srejović, D. (1972) *Lepenski Vir*, London: Thames and Hudson.

—— (1989) 'The Mesolithic of Serbia and Montenegro', in C. Bonsall (ed.) *The Mesolithic in Europe*, Edinburgh: John Donald, 481–91.

Stainton, B. (1989) 'Excavation of an Early Prehistoric Site at Stratford's Yard, Chesham', *Records of Buckinghamshire* 31: 49–74.

Steensberg, A. (1957) 'Some Recent Danish Experiments in Neolithic Agriculture', *Agricultural History Review* 5: 66–73.

Stenberger, M. (1967) *Sweden*, London: Thames and Hudson.

Stonehouse, W. P. B. (1990) 'Some Mesolithic Sites in the Central Pennines', *The Manchester Archaeological Bulletin* 5: 58–64.

Stringer, C. B. (1986) 'Direct Dates for the Fossil Record', in J. A. J. Gowlett and R. E. M. Hedges (eds) *Archaeological Results from Accelerator Dating*, Oxford: Oxford University Committee for Archaeology, 45–50.

Strömberg, M. (1977–8) 'Three Neolithic Sites. A Local Seriation?', *Meddelanden från Lunds universitets historiska museum* 2: 68–97.

—— (1987–8) 'A Complex Hunting and Production Area', *Meddelanden från Lunds universitets historiska museum* 7: 53–80.

Stürup, B. (1965) 'En jordgrave fra tidlig-neolitisk tid', *Kuml*: 13–22.

Taborin, Y. (1974) 'La parure en coquillage', *Gallia Préhistoire* 17: 101–79.

Tangri, D. (1989) 'On Trade and Assimilation in European Agricultural Origins', *Journal of Mediterranean Archaeology* 2: 139–48.

Tauber, H. (1965) 'Differential Pollen Dispersion and the Interpretation of Pollen Diagrams', *Danmarks Geologiske Undersøgelse II, Række Nr. 89*: 7–69.

—— (1981) '¹³C Evidence for Dietary Habits of Prehistoric Man in Denmark', *Nature* 292: 332–3.

—— (1982) 'Carbon-13 Evidence for the Diet of Prehistoric Humans in Denmark', *Journal of the European Study Group on Physical, Chemical and Mathematical Techniques Applied to Archaeology* 7: 235–7.

Tchernov, E. (1991) 'Biological Evidence for Human Sedentism in Southwest Asia during the Natufian', in O. Bar-Yosef and F. R. Valla (eds) *The Natufian Culture in the Levant*, Ann Arbor: International Monographs in Prehistory Archaeological Series 1, 315–40.

Testart, A. (1982) *Les Chasseurs-Cueilleurs ou L'Origine des Inégalités*, Paris: Sociéte d'Ethnographie.

Thomas, D. (1992) 'Nant Hall Road, Prestatyn', *Archaeology in Wales* 32: 59.

Thomas, J. (1988a) 'Neolithic Explanations Revisited: The Mesolithic–Neolithic Transition in Britain and South Scandinavia', *Proceedings of the Prehistoric Society* 54: 59–66.

—— (1988b) 'The Social Significance of Cotswold–Severn Burial Practice', *Man* (N.S.) 23: 540–59.

—— (1991) *Rethinking the Neolithic*, Cambridge: Cambridge University Press.

—— (1994) 'Discourse, Totalization and "The Neolithic"', in C. Tilley (ed.) *Interpretative Archaeology*, London: Berg, 357–94.

Thomas, J. and Tilley, C. (1994) 'The Axe and the Torso: Symbolic Structures in the Neolithic of Brittany', in C. Tilley (ed.) *Interpretative Archaeology*, London: Berg, 225–324.

Thomas, J. and Whittle, A. W. R. (1986) 'Anatomy of a tomb – West Kennet Revisited', *Oxford Journal of Archaeology* 5: 129–56.

Thomas, K. D. (1982) 'Neolithic Enclosures and Woodland Habitats on the South Downs in Sussex, England', in M. Bell and S. Limbrey (eds) *Archaeological Aspects of Woodland Ecology*, Oxford: British Archaeological Reports, International Series 146, 147–70.

Thomas, N. (1964) 'The Neolithic Causewayed Camp at Robin Hood's Ball, Shrewton', *Wiltshire Archaeological and Natural History Society Magazine* 59: 1–27.

Thomson, P. O. (1984) 'Toftlundgård', *Journal of Danish Archaeology* 3: 228.

Thorpe, I. J. (1984) 'Ritual, Power and Ideology: A Reconstruction of Earlier Neolithic Rituals in Wessex', in R. Bradley and J. Gardiner (eds) *Neolithic Studies: A Review of Some Current Research*, Oxford: British Archaeological Reports, British Series 133, 41–60.

—— (1989) 'Neolithic and Earlier Bronze Age Wessex and Yorkshire: A Comparative Study', University of London Ph.D. thesis.

Thorvildsen, K. (1941) 'Dyssetidens Gravfund i Danmark', *Aarbøger for Nordisk Oldkyndighed og Historie*: 22–87.

Thrane, H. (1989) 'Danish Plough-Marks from the Neolithic and Bronze Age', *Journal of Danish Archaeology* 8: 111–25.

Thurnam, J. (1856) 'On a Cromlech-tumulus called Lugbury, near Littleton Drew', *Wiltshire Archaeological and Natural History Magazine* 3: 164–73.

—— (1869) 'On Ancient British Barrows: Part 1, Long Barrows', *Archaeologia* 42: 161–244.

Tooley, M. J. (1975) 'A Prehistoric Skeleton from Hartlepool', *Bulletin of the Durham Conservation Trust*: 31–5.

Troels-Smith, J. (1953) 'Ertebøllekultur – Bondekultur. Resultater af de sidste 10 Aars Undersøgelsen i Aamosen, Vestsjælland', *Aarbøger for Nordisk Oldkyndighed og Historie*: 5–62.

—— (1959) 'The Muldbjerg Dwelling Place: An Early Neolithic Archaeological Site in the Aamosen Bog, West-Zealand, Denmark', *Annual Report of the Smithsonian Institution*: 577–601.

—— (1960) 'Ivy, Mistletoe and Elm. Climate Indicators – Fodder Plants', *Danmarks Geologiske Undersogelse* Series IV, 4: 1–32.

—— (1967) 'The Ertebølle Culture and its Background', *Palaeohistoria* 12: 505–28.

—— (1982) 'Vegetationshistoriske vidnesbyrd om skovrydninger, planteavl og husdyrhold i Europa, specielt Skandinavien', in T. Sjøvold (ed.) *Introduksjon av jord-bruk i Norden*, Oslo: Universitetsforlaget, 39–62.

Turner, R. C. (1995) 'Recent Research into British Bog Bodies', in R. C. Turner and R. G. Scaife (eds) *Bog Bodies: New Discoveries and New Perspectives*, London: British Museum Press, 108–22.

Unger-Hamilton, R. (1989) 'The Epi-Palaeolithic Southern Levant and the Origins of Cultivation', *Current Anthropology* 30: 88–103.

—— (1991) 'Natufian Plant Husbandry in the Southern Levant and Comparison with that of the Neolithic Periods: The Lithic Perspective', in O. Bar-Yosef and F. R. Valla (eds) *The Natufian Culture in the Levant*, Ann Arbor: International Monographs in Prehistory Archaeological Series 1, 483–520.

Valla, F. R. (1991) 'Les Natoufiens de Mallaha et l'espace', in O. Bar-Yosef and F. R. Valla (eds) *The Natufian Culture in the Levant*, Ann Arbor: International Monographs in Prehistory Archaeological Series 1, 111–22.

Van Gennep, A. [1909] (1960) *The Rites of Passage*, London: Routledge and Kegan Paul.

Van Zeist, W. and Palfenier-Vegter, R. M. (1981) 'Seeds and Fruits from the Swifterbant S3 Site', *Palaeohistoria* 23: 105–68.

Vang Petersen, P. (1984) 'Chronological and Regional Variation in the Late Mesolithic of Eastern Denmark', *Journal of Danish Archaeology* 3: 7–18.

—— (1987) 'Grisby', *Journal of Danish Archaeology* 6: 244.

Vatcher, F. de M. (1961) 'The Excavation of the Long Mortuary Enclosure on Normanton Down, Wilts', *Proceedings of the Prehistoric Society* 27: 160–73.

Veit, U. (1993) 'Burials Within Settlements of the Linienbandkeramik and Stichbandkeramik Cultures of Central Europe', *Journal of European Archaeology* 1: 107–40.

Vencl, S. (1986) 'The Role of Hunting-gathering Populations in the Transition to Farming: A Central-European perspective', in M. Zvelebil (ed.) *Hunters in Transition*, Cambridge: Cambridge University Press, 43–51.

Voytek, B. A. and Tringham, R. (1989) 'Rethinking the Mesolithic: The Case of Southeast Europe', in C. Bonsall (ed.) *The Mesolithic in Europe*, Edinburgh: John Donald, 492–9.

Vyner, B. (1984) 'The Excavation of a Neolithic Cairn at Street House, Loftus, Cleveland', *Proceedings of the Prehistoric Society* 50: 151–95.

Waddell, J. (1978) 'The Invasion Hypothesis in Irish Prehistory', *Antiquity* 52: 121–8.

Wahl, J. and König, H. G. (1987) 'Anthropologisch-traumatologische Untersuchung der menschlichen Skelettreste aus dem Bandkeramischen Massengrab bei Talheim, Kreis Heilbronn, *Fundberichte aus Baden-Württemberg* 12: 65–193.

Walker, D. (1966) 'The Late Quaternary History of the Cumberland Lowland', *Philosophical Transactions of the Royal Society of London* B 251: 1–211.

Wansleeben, M. and Verhart, L. B. M. (1990) 'Meuse Valley Project: The Transition from the Mesolithic to the Neolithic in the Dutch Meuse Valley', in P. Vermeersch and P. van Peer (eds) *Contributions to the Mesolithic in Europe*, Leuven: Leuven University Press, 389–402.

Watkins, T. (1992) 'The Beginnings of the Neolithic: Searching for Meaning in Material Culture Change', *Paléorient* 18: 63–75.

Watt, M. (1983) 'Grisby, Bornholm', *Journal of Danish Archaeology* 2: 213.

Weiner, J. (1994) 'Well On My Back – An Update on the Bandkeramik Wooden Well of Erkelenz-Kückhoven, *Newswarp* 16: 5–17.

Welinder, S. (1989) 'Mesolithic Forest Clearance in Scandinavia', in C. Bonsall (ed.) *The Mesolithic in Europe*, Edinburgh: John Donald, 362–6.

Wheeler, R. E. M. (1943) *Maiden Castle*, London: Reports of the Research Committee of the Society of Antiquaries of London 12.

Whittle, A. W. R. (1977) *The Earlier Neolithic of Southern England and its Continental Background*, Oxford: British Archaeological Reports, International Series 35.

—— (1985) *Neolithic Europe: A Survey*, Cambridge: Cambridge University Press.

—— (1987) 'Neolithic Settlement Patterns in Temperate Europe: Progress and Problems', *Journal of World Prehistory* 1: 5–52.

—— (1988a) 'Contexts, Activities, Events – Aspects of Neolithic and Copper Age Enclosures in Central and Western Europe', in C. Burgess, P. Topping, C. Mordant and M. Maddison (eds) *Enclosures and Defences in the Neolithic of Western Europe*, Oxford: British Archaeological Reports, International Series 403, 1–19.

—— (1988b) *Problems in Neolithic Archaeology*, Cambridge: Cambridge University Press.

—— (1990a) 'Radiocarbon Dating of the Linear Pottery Culture: The Contribution of Cereal and Bone Samples', *Antiquity* 64: 297–302.

—— (1990b) 'A Model for the Mesolithic–Neolithic Transition in the Upper Kennet Valley, North Wiltshire', *Proceedings of the Prehistoric Society* 56: 101–10.

—— (1991) 'Wayland's Smithy, Oxfordshire: Excavations at the Neolithic Tomb in 1962–63 by R. J. C. Atkinson and S. Piggott', *Proceedings of the Prehistoric Society* 57, Part 2: 61–101.

—— (1993) 'The Neolithic of the Avebury Area: Sequence, Environment, Settlement and Monuments', *Oxford Journal of Archaeology* 12: 29–53.

Whittle, A. W. R., Atkinson, R. J. C., Chambers, R. and Thomas, N. (1992) 'Excavations on the Neolithic and Bronze Age Complex at Dorchester-on-Thames, Oxfordshire, 1947–1952 and 1981', *Proceedings of the Prehistoric Society* 58: 143–201.

Willerding, U. (1980) 'Zum Ackerbau der Bandkeramiker', *Materialhefte Ur- und Fruhgeschichte Niedersachsens* 16: 421–56.

Williams, C. T. (1985) *Mesolithic Exploitation Patterns in the Central Pennines*, Oxford: British Archaeological Reports, British Series 139.

Williams, E. (1989) 'Dating the Introduction of Food Production into Britain and Ireland', *Antiquity* 63: 510–21.

Winther, J. (1935) *Troldebjerg, en bymæssig bebyggelse fra Danmarks yngre stenalder*, Rudkøbing.

Woodman, P. C. (1978) *The Mesolithic in Ireland*, Oxford: British Archaeological Reports British Series 58.

—— (1989) 'A Review of the Scottish Mesolithic: A Plea for Normality', *Proceedings of the Society of Antiquaries of Scotland* 119: 1–32.

—— (1992a) 'Filling in the Spaces in Irish Prehistory', *Antiquity* 66: 295–314.

—— (1992b) 'Excavations at Mad Man's Window, Glenarm, Co. Antrim: Problems of Flint Exploitation in East Antrim', *Proceedings of the Prehistoric Society* 58: 77–106.

Woodman, P. C. and Anderson, E. (1990) 'The Irish Later Mesolithic: A Partial Picture', in P. Vermeersch and P. van Peer (eds) *Contributions to the Mesolithic in Europe*, Leuven: Leuven University Press, 377–87.

Woodman, P. C. and O'Brien, M. (1993) 'Excavations at Ferriter's Cove, Co. Kerry: An Interim Statement', in E. Shee Twohig and M. Ronayne (eds) *Past Perspectives*, Cork: Cork University Press, 25–34.

Woodward, P. J. (1991) *The South Dorset Ridgeway: Survey and Excavations 1977–84*, Dorchester: Dorset Natural History and Archaeological Society Monograph 8.

Woolley, A. R., Bishop, A. C., Bishop, R. J. and Kinnes, I. A. (1979) 'European Neolithic Jade Implements: A Preliminary Mineralogical and Typological Study', in T. H. McK. Clough and W. A. Cummins (eds) *Stone Axe Studies*, London: Council for British Archaeology Research Report 23, 90–6.

Wright, H. E. (1993) 'Environmental Determinism in Near Eastern Prehistory', *Current Anthropology* 34: 458–69.

Wymer, J. (1991) *Mesolithic Britain*, Princes Risborough: Shire.

Wyszomirska, B. (1988) *Ekonomisk Stabilitet vid Kusten: Nymölla III*, Lund: Acta Archaeologica Lundensis Series in 8°, 17.

Y'Edynak, G. (1978) 'Culture, Diet and Dental Reduction in Mesolithic Forager-fishers of Yugoslavia', *Current Anthropology* 19: 616–18.

Zeiler, J. T. (1991) 'Hunting and Animal Husbandry at Neolithic Sites in the Western and Central Netherlands: Interaction Between Man and the Environment', *Helinium* 31: 60–125.

Zohary, D. and Hopf, M. (1993) *Domestication of Plants in the Old World* (2nd edition), Oxford: Clarendon Press.

Zvelebil, M. (1986) 'Mesolithic Prelude and Neolithic Revolution', in M. Zvelebil (ed.) *Hunters in Transition*, Cambridge: Cambridge University Press, 5–15.

—— (1989) 'On the Transition to Farming, or What was Spreading with the Neolithic: A Reply to Ammerman (1989)', *Antiquity* 63: 379–83.

Zvelebil, M. (1994) 'Plant Use in the Mesolithic and its Role in the Transition to Farming', *Proceedings of the Prehistoric Society* 60: 35–74.

Zvelebil, M. and Dolukhanov, P. (1991) 'The Transition to Farming in Eastern and Northern Europe', *Journal of World Prehistory* 5: 233–78.

Zvelebil, M. and Rowley-Conwy, P. (1984) 'Transition to Farming in Northern Europe: a Hunter-Gatherer Perspective', in *Norwegian Archaeological Review* 17: 104–28.

—— (1986) 'Foragers and Farmers in Atlantic Europe', in M. Zvelebil (ed.) *Hunters in Transition*, Cambridge: Cambridge University Press, 67–93.

Zvelebil, M. and Zvelebil, K. V. (1988) 'Agricultural Transition and Indo-European Dispersals', *Antiquity* 62: 574–83.

—— (1990) 'Agricultural Transition, "Indo-European Origins" and the Spread of Farming', in T. L. Markey and J. A. C. Greppin (eds) *When Worlds Collide: Indo-Europeans and Pre-Indo-Europeans*, Ann Arbor: Karoma, 237–66.

Zvelebil, M., Green, S. W. and Macklin, M. G. (1992) 'Archaeological Landscapes, Lithic Scatters, and Human Behaviour', in J. Rossignol and L. Wandsnider (eds) *Space, Time and Archaeological Landscapes*, London: Plenum Press, 193–226.

INDEX